GENERATIONS
APART

Contemporary Issues

Series Editors: Robert M. Baird
Stuart E. Rosenbaum
All volumes have been edited by the series editors, except where otherwise noted.

Other titles in this series:

GENERATIONS APART

XERS vs BOOMERS vs THE ELDERLY

EDITED BY
RICHARD D. THAU & JAY S. HEFLIN

Prometheus Books

59 John Glenn Drive
Amherst, New York 14228-2197

Published 1997 by Prometheus Books

Inquiries should be addressed to
Prometheus Books, 59 John Glenn Drive, Amherst, New York 14228–2197.
VOICE: 716–691–0133, ext. 207. FAX: 716–564–2711.
WWW.PROMETHEUSBOOKS.COM

03 02 01 00 99   7 6 5 4 3 2

Library of Congress Cataloging-in-Publication Data

Generations apart : Xers vs. boomers vs. the elderly / edited by Richard D.
        Thau& Jay S. Heflin.
                p.   cm. — (Contemporary issues)
        ISBN 1–57392–174-2 (paper : alk. paper)
        1. Conflict of generations—United States. 2. Generation X—United
States. 3. Baby boom generation—United States. 4. Aged—United States. 5.
Generations—Economic aspects—United States. 6. Generations—Political aspects—United States. I. Thau, Richard D. II. Heflin, Jay S. III. Series: Contemporary issues (Buffalo, N.Y.)
HN90.I58G45   1997
305.2—dc21   97-34296
                                                                   CIP

Printed in the United States of America on acid-free paper

To our children and grandchildren, yet to be born,
who will someday judge us prophets or fools.

Contents

Introduction

There has been a lot of talk about generational warfare over the past few years. Some politicians have claimed that young adults, members of so-called Generation X, will soon recognize the onerous financial burdens being placed on them by older Americans and launch a rebellion.

This scenario is doubtful—for now. Members of this younger generation have it pretty good, and they know it. While their payroll taxes may be the highest in history, and the national debt may exceed $5 trillion, they haven't been drafted into a war they didn't want to fight, nor are they being systematically denied their civil rights. They can vote if they so choose, yet they take that right for granted and avoid the polls on election day.

While Generation X may be complacent here at the turn of the century, there are warning signs that suggest Xers themselves, their Baby Boomer parents, and their own children (many yet to be born) may find themselves embroiled in a difficult struggle for America's financial resources in the early twenty-first century.

A wealth of information published within the 1990s predicts a fundamental shift in American demographics over the next 30 or so years. In brief, the federal government and other sources project the number of Americans over age 70 will double to 48 million between now and 2030, while the rest of the population will grow far less quickly. This will lead all of America to look much the way Florida does today—with consequences that could be catastrophic if not recognized and anticipated now.

As this anthology demonstrates, there have long been differences of opinion, and indeed struggles, between generations. These persist today. Consider the press coverage of the 1996 presidential campaign, where, in a *Newsweek* story by Joe Klein, the nominees were reduced in the headline to single-word descriptions of their generations: "Saxophone" (i.e., Bill Clinton as the jazzy, hip Baby Boomer who likes to hang out) vs. "Sacrifice" (i.e., Bob Dole as the injured World War II hero who didn't dodge the draft).

The question for the reader is this: do these differences, particularly between Xers and Boomers who will be around in 30 years, set the stage for a true generational war in the future? What will happen in 2030, when a large, vocal, and likely well-organized senior population attempts to draw the Social Security and Medicare benefits to which it believes it is entitled, while the rest of the population must endure crippling tax hikes to pay the bills?

Barring an unforeseen disaster, such as a war that would wipe out a sizable portion of the U.S. population, or a massive wave of legal immigration that would support the Baby Boomers in retirement, there is a strong likelihood that tomorrow's seniors will be an extremely costly demographic group to pass through retirement. Whether that cost is borne smoothly or disruptively is, in large part, for us to determine now.

Currently, senior citizens are the dominant demographic group politically in the United States. Represented by the 30 million-plus strong American Association of Retired Persons (AARP) and other seniors organizations, the elderly have been extremely effective at using their clout to successfully demand the protection of benefits for themselves—without much regard to the cost to others—and without opposition from the Baby Boomers and Generation Xers who are footing the bill.

These two younger generations, busy building their families and their careers, with little free time to get involved in mind-numbing discussions about the entitlement programs that are of great interest to seniors, are unable and unwilling to challenge the seniors lobby.

One great question facing America is whether AARP and other pro status quo seniors groups will be able to attract Baby Boomers in the same way they attracted members of the World War II generation. If they can, what happens when the largest demographic group also becomes the most politically powerful? Is there any way that Generation Xers will be able to organize themselves into a cohesive political voice by the time they hit middle age and be effective in protecting their own interests?

Only time will tell. Meanwhile, it is critical for Americans to judge whether the current tensions between generations, as presented in Part One of this book, are genuine expressions of a larger generational hostility, or simply intellectual rantings from isolated thinkers. If they are the former, does the act of preparing intelligently for the future common good become impossible when generations are already at odds?

Part Two shows that it is essential for readers to consider the skew toward seniors in today's generational politics and the fractured nature of Generation X's political voice. In Part Three, the cyclical nature of generations and how they tend to repeat in American history is described by historians William Strauss and Neil Howe. As readers will find in that section, tensions between generations are nothing new.

Part Four centers on demographics and money: who pays what to whom, and what dynamics of population drive the finances of America, both today and in the future. Finally, Part Five offers myriad perspectives on the programs most likely endangered by the Baby Boom's imminent elderhood: Social Security and Medicare. How these massive and growing programs are or are not reformed could well determine America's economic position in the world for the next 50 years.

For the first time, the leading thinkers on both (or multiple) sides of these vital issues are together in one volume. While the editors of this anthology hold a personal opinion about generational tensions and how best to prepare for the future, we have attempted to present all sides in this discussion.

—Richard Thau and Jay Heflin

Part One

TENSIONS BETWEEN THE GENERATIONS

Young men have a passion for regarding their elders as senile.
—Henry Adams

Age in a virtuous person, of either sex, carries in it an authority
which makes it preferable to all the pleasures of youth.
—Sir Richard Steele

What follows is a sampling of writings from members of one generation taking exception to the opinions of other generations. The first piece, a Generation X-bashing article by Baby Boomer Michael Kinsley that initially appeared in the *New Republic* and the *Washington Post,* prompted Xer Heather Lamm to offer a defense of her contemporaries.

In the piece that follows, Xer Robert A. George taps into the late-90s culture and finds his generation "stuck in the shadows" of the Baby Boom. Watch TV, listen to music, and you will find a society that remains dominated by the youth culture—the youth of the 1960s. The Boomers' cultural hegemony leaves little room for Xers to be taken seriously by their elders, but that doesn't mean there aren't serious messages for Boomers in the music that Xers produce.

Middle-aged economist Lester C. Thurow, in "The Birth of a Revolutionary Class," warns that seniors could wreak havoc on the rest of society. His contemporaries, William Strauss and Neil Howe, complain that the elderly are beneficiaries of "special tax favors" that are unfair to the young.

Finally, *New York Times* columnist Russell Baker tweaks the unthinking young with his "Herky-Jerky Bang-Bang."

1

Back from the Future

Michael Kinsley

The topic of the Younger Generation spread through the company like a yawn.

—Evelyn Waugh, *Vile Bodies*

It's often said that the federal budget deficit or the Social Security system or other fiscally irresponsible arrangements are "borrowing from the future" or "burdening the next generation." (I may even have said it myself, come to think of it.) This is the political dimension of the lament of Generation X, the despairing twentysomethings portrayed in the movie *Reality Bites*. The federal deficit doesn't actually enter into the plot of *Reality Bites* (which, as summarized by Terrence Rafferty in *The New Yorker,* is about "kids born after the baby boom, who now, as they enter adulthood, feel cheated by history"). But a few earnest, politically minded X-ers have tried to make it their generational cri de coeur—an analogy to the war in Vietnam, if you can imagine the effrontery.

Harrumph. This column bows to no one in its alarm about the federal deficit. But if the entire politics of the post-boomer generation is going to rest on the premise that American society is "borrowing from the future," it gives us pleasure to point out that it's not really true. It is very difficult for whole societies, unlike indi-

From *The New Republic* (March 21, 1994): 6. Reprinted by permission of *The New Republic,* © 1994 The New Republic, Inc.

viduals, to "borrow from the future." The assets consumed today must be produced today. They can't be consumed today and produced tomorrow.

Now, society can use its productive capacity in two ways: to produce consumption goods and services, or to produce things (like new factories) that increase society's future productive capacity. We are definitely producing too much of the former and too little of the latter, and we will be poorer than otherwise as a result. Federal government borrowing contributes to this tendency, but future generations have no inherent claim on any particular share of today's productive capacity.

The fact is that future Americans are almost surely going to be richer than current Americans. Among the living generations, Generation X will have a higher standard of living over the course of its life than the baby boomers, just as the boomers will do better than the postwar generation.

From 1970 until today—roughly the lifetime of Generation X—America's Gross Domestic Product has grown by 82 percent in real terms. This is considered to have been a period of alarmingly slow growth, and even so the X-er entering the work force today joins an economy almost twice the size of the one boomers were joining a generation ago.

In the *Washington Post* a few months back, a twentysomething writer named Christopher Georges published a flood of statistics debunking the notion that X-ers are suffering compared with their generational predecessors. My favorite: 30 percent of teenagers today own cars, up from 7 percent in 1968.

When I learned economics a generation ago, we were taught that the national debt didn't matter because "we owe it to ourselves." These days we owe a large chunk of it to foreigners. Because that will have to be paid back, it does amount to "borrowing from the future." But even if this costs future generations a point or two of their GDP, what's left will still be greater than what we've got now.

Likewise with Social Security. Even if it amounts to a large transfer from today's workers to today's retirees, and an even larger transfer from future workers to future retirees, so what? In both cases the younger generation will still be richer than the older one, even after the transfer takes place.

The choice America faces in issues like the federal deficit is how much present consumption we should sacrifice in order to increase our future consumption. But putting the issue in generational terms raises an interesting philosophical puzzle: Why should one group—the current generation—sacrifice anything at all so that a different group—the next generation—can be better off, when the second group will be better off than the first group in any event?

The answer to this puzzle lies less in logic than in emotions: the admirable desire of parents to see their children prosper, and of patriots to see their country thrive. This is, as I say, admirable. Less admirable is future generations demanding this as their due, and accusing the older folks of "borrowing" if they refuse to fork out sufficiently. (Douglas Coupland's clever novel *Generation X*, which coined the term, opens with an X-er vandalizing an Oldsmobile because it has a bumper sticker that says "We're spending our children's inheritance." Why not spend it?)

X-ers are right to suspect that boomer complaints about them are based largely on resentment. No one was ever supposed to be younger than we are. Every generation feels that way; but probably none ever milked The Young Idea as successfully as the boomers did in our time.

Nevertheless, some criticism is fair. Start with originality. C'mon you guys. Generational self-pity and existential despair, which the X-ers are marketing as their own, are hardly new. Read *Vile Bodies*, Evelyn Waugh's great comic sendup of the "Bright Young Things" of London in the 1920s.

Indeed, to preen just a bit, the particular note of self-pity was relatively absent from the self-indulgent generational brooding of the boomers in their youth. The famous Port Huron Statement of 1962, founding document of SDS (Students for a Democratic Society), the premier youth activist group of the 1960s, began: "We are people of this generation, bred in at least modest comfort, housed in universities, looking uncomfortably to the world we inherit." Compare and contrast something called the *Third Millennium Declaration*, a conscious update of the Port Huron Statement issued last year [1993] from a twentysomething activist group: "Like Wile E. Coyote waiting for a twenty-ton Acme anvil to fall on his head, our generation labors in the expanding shadow of a monstrous national debt." Whine, whine, whine.

These kids today. They're soft. They don't know how good they have it. Not only did they never have to fight a war, like their grandparents, they never even had to dodge one.

To be sure, complaints about the Younger Generation are as unoriginal as the self-righteous sniveling of the Younger Generation itself. A piece last October in the *Washington Post* should have killed off this particular genre. It was a rant by a 20-year-old college junior bemoaning the decadent values of kids today in their early and midteens. "Beavis and Butthead" was his text. He noted what a huge fall this represents from "The Simpsons" cult of his day, two to three years ago. He's right, of course. Complaints about the Younger Generation are always right.

2

Respect Your Juniors

Heather Lamm

For Michael Kinsley to equate an entire generation of people in their twenties to the characters in the movie *Reality Bites* is as foolish as if someone were to equate the generation of people in their sixties to the characters in *Cocoon*.

On the one hand, the generation that I am a part of—"Generation X," or the "twentysomethings"—is widely accused of being lazy and apathetic toward politics. Yet when we voice a legitimate concern about a burgeoning national debt that will undoubtedly hurt our future productivity, we're accused by people like Mr. Kinsley of being ungrateful and whiny.

Mr. Kinsley's arguments don't add up. The federal deficit is an enormous problem, he admits. He notes that future generations will have to pay back the debts of today and that perhaps this might cost them a few points of their gross national product.

Mr. Kinsley even admits that federal government's borrowing and our present lack of productive growth will make us a poorer nation one day. But suck it up, lectures Mr. Kinsley. Don't be ungrateful. Respect your elders. They owe you nothing.

The fact is that my generation is asking for nothing that hasn't been given to other generations—that our tax money be spent on our needs, not on servicing our parents' debts. We ask for a healthy environment, a competitive economy and a Social Security and Medicare system that make actuarial sense. This is not unreasonable.

Mr. Kinsley notes that in the past, parents have sacrificed to see their kids succeed and that patriots have sacrificed to see their country thrive. True enough. But when that individual ethic fails to work on a national level, someone needs to speak up.

America cannot expect an entire generation to sit idly by, on the premise of "respect your elders," as its future is auctioned off. The purpose of a group such as Third Millennium is not to lament lazily about being cheated. Rather, it is a thoughtful voicing of legitimate problems facing our generation.

3

Stuck in the Shadows with You: Observations on Post-Boomer Culture

Robert A. George

The music a given generation selects as its "own" is perhaps the best barometer of that group's style, attitudes, and values. After all, it's a lot easier to record a song, even a full-length CD, than it is to produce a movie or write the Great American Novel. Additionally, musicians, at least initially, tend to be younger and closer to the age of their most likely audience. The slogan for Motown Records in its 1960s heyday, recall, was "The Sound of Young America." What, then, are we to say of the landscape now ruled by the allegedly "grown-up" children?

The Baby Boomers, after fomenting revolution in the '60s, have continued to be revolting into the '70s, the '80s, and now, of course, the '90s. "Hope I die before I get old" they declared in 1965. In the early 1980s, Mick Jagger was saying that he didn't want to be singing "(I Can't Get No) Satisfaction" when he was fifty. Of course, he's now well past that and he, Keith, and the other moss-covered Stones are embarking on yet another world tour. Ah, yes, "Satisfaction"—the official anthem of the AARP.

Sex. Drugs. Rock 'n' Roll. The Boomers "invented" them all. They absorbed (in more ways) these cultural arcana, personalized them (as a group experience), and made them their own. But what has been the legacy of their revolution? Well, like most revolutions, it didn't turn out the way the architects drew it up. And when they didn't like the building they helped build, they tore it down.

The Post-boomers have been called many names, "Generation X" being the most prominent, but perhaps "Shadow" is best. We grew up somewhat in darkness—overwhelmed and obscured by a group who rewrote all the rules of life and living as they grew up. In the '60s and '70s, they put an imprint on the culture. In the '90s they make their mark on the political process. How do we impart value to our own tastes and creations in the face of this cultural domination?

As youthful Boomers, recreational sex was a fad. Unfortunately, in the middle of the Shadow's years, we found ourselves combating herpes and AIDS. Sex = Death. As youngsters, the Boomers got high and "experienced." Their experimentation turned into the inner-city experience of crack which turned out not to be quite what it was cracked up to be. Today, the Boomers fight over various substances to ban—illegal drugs, tobacco, alcohol, Kool-Aid, the list goes on. And rock 'n' roll? Well now, there lies a story. Actually, this is the perfect allegory for the war between the Monster Generation and its Shadow and the larger values struggle it represents.

"WHY *DON'T* YOU ALL JUST FADE AWAY?"

Music remains the most significant generational artifact of the Boomers. And as they have gotten older, they have held onto "their" music to a tyrannical degree (just as their public service side tends to do politically). In the 1960s and 1970s, there once was a thing called Top 40 radio, which played a mixture of musical styles: rhythm & blues, rock 'n' roll, country. The rock 'n' roll era included everybody from the Beatles to Aretha Franklin to Johnny Cash. There was something of a common musical culture, in which different styles all had a chance of being played on the same station.

Then a funny thing happened: Boomers grew up and they suddenly decided they didn't like certain kinds of "young people's music" (i.e., music made by people slightly younger than they). So they went about and made sure everything was categorized so *their* music would remain a dominant force. Thus, we got "Classic" Rock, we got Adult Contemporary, we got music divided and further subdivided. When young people in the mid to late '70s (the early Generation X wave) moved toward disco and punk, the music was derided or ignored (and in the case of disco, ultimately banished from the Top 40 airwaves and sent to the ghettos of "urban radio").

In the '80s, the Boomers got around to producing that navel-contemplating, self-absorbed movie they always wanted to make (remember, it takes time to get movies done): *The Big Chill*. This, of course, produced a soundtrack that gave us a steady diet of that wonderful sixties music well into the mid-'80s. We now live in a world where every "Murphy Brown" episode opens with a sixties song (to many a more unforgivable "sin" than the existence of that bastard). Every other commercial apparently must have some 1960s tune to sell beer, cars, or whatever (at one point, during the 1997 NCAA championship game, no less than four [possibly five] consecutive commercials had a song from between 1968 and 1973 in its soundtrack). Literally, as this is being written, a 40-something farmer is driving around in his 1997 Nissan Altima, singing along to the sounds of the Monkees' "I'm a Believer." The Chambers Brothers' "Time Has Come Today," once a song chronicling youthful exuberance and the possibility of change (societal), is now the theme for Boomers putting away a financial next egg. Boomers loved the sixties so much, they won't let them die.

And the beat goes on—appropriately enough, did I forget to mention that Sonny Bono is now a member of Congress? The dominating cultural ethos of the Baby Boomers (this "'60s thing") is inextricably linked to their political governing mode. Woodstock was the love-in that so many of the Boomers running things now can't forget—or will let any of us forget, whether we lived it or not. Forget about the fact that many Woodstock performers died of drug overdoses; forget about the trash left in its wake; forget about the disease that is the product of their free love. For this privileged group, their memories are all peace, love, and understanding. Well, not quite: In the '90s, the elected leaders of the generation find themselves balanced somewhere between the temperaments of Woodstock and Altamont. They provoke confrontation while demanding to be loved. Result: Bill Clinton (key word: "change"), Republican Congress (key word: "revolution"). Can you say "government shutdown"? I thought you could.

"TALKING 'BOUT A REVOLUTION"

Yes, it's on. Undeclared though it is, a new Cold War exists. This one is generational. It has the most spoiled and self-indulgent generation in history on the one side and their dissed and deprived successors on the other. We may not have started the war (just like the Boomers "didn't start the fire." Yeah, right. And exactly what *were* you doing with those bras and flags?), but we had better be aware that it is going on or, just as we have been rolled in the past, we will be rolled in the future (as will our younger siblings).

The problem Boomers have with the generation that came right after them is what anyone would have upon suddenly noticing that their shadow was talking back to them. Shadows are supposed to be quiet. They are supposed to follow us without actually affecting anything. Shadows are seen, but not heard; observed, but not acknowledged. Yet, the only thing we have been able to do is scream.

Following in the wake of the SexDrugsRocknroll generation and its cultural domination has not been easy on the Shadow Generation. Having been bequeathed a legacy of AIDS, crack, and much hypocrisy, the Shadows seek refuge primarily in music as the predominant area of inventive experimentation. Cultural diversity ("subcultures"), irony, and an often brutal honesty are now the watchwords of Generation X.

Diversity and irony are almost evident in the name. Generation X was the name of a late-seventies punk rock band (lead singer: Billy Idol). However, it has also come to be symbolized by the many young people, black and white, who sport "X" hats in allegiance to Malcolm X. These same young people are as likely to consider themselves part of the Hip Hop Nation as they are Grunge Kids. They are the mixed-bag Americans.

Growing up as Shadows, the younger generation has attempted to create a cultural reality of its own. The Boomers however stand in the way, assert their prerogatives, and pull out the censors. The political spectrum from Left (Tipper Gore) to Right (William J. Bennett) condemns the musical choices of Generation X, on both aesthetic (grunge) and societal (rap) grounds. It occurs not at all to them that just as the music they listened to reflected a bright world open for exploration and indulgence (the Love Generation)—the world we grew up in was one of divorce, disease, and devastation. Should we be surprised that the musical giants of the Boomer generation—Janis Joplin, Jimi Hendrix, Jim Morrison—all died from accidental chemical-induced overdoses? They looked outward and kept striving to get to a higher plane, regardless of the costs. What about the giants of Generation X—Kurt Cobain, Tupac Shakur, and the Notorious B.I.G.? They die in acts of violence—one a suicide, the other two, homicide. Looking inward, and finding nothing, the Shadows turn upon themselves.

Despite the ascendancy of Ronald Reagan in the 1980s, the liberal ethic became the cultural orthodoxy, political correctness the secular theology, and sixties radicals the new establishment. With Boomers as programmers and the arbiters of what is "good" popular music, radio—the traditional medium for young people's music—became a closed avenue in the 1980s. Young people, black and white, learned that the only way to get "their" music heard would be to master the marketing side of music as well as the artistic side. This gave birth to independent record production and distribution. Furthermore, the harder-edged, upper tempo music, because radio ignores it, is "kicked to the curb" and spread via word-of-mouth, sales, and dance club exposure rather than the unifying airplay that drove much of '60s and '70s music.

This spirit of independence and ingenuity permeates the Shadow generation on multiple levels. It is a group that has been told all its existence that it is stupid (test scores have fallen consistently), unruly, and racist. Of course, this is all in relation to the Boomers who preceded us, the "perfect" generation that defined (and continues to define) what are the proper, "correct" ways to act, speak, sing, and dance. Frankly, not only should we be hesitant to condemn today's music but upon examination, we may actually discover that much of it is an appropriate cultural rejoinder to the overwhelmingly "Boomerish" culture of the 1960s. Rap, for example, is as much social commentary as it is dance music. In imparting information, it is the perfect style for the Information Age. Often harsh, yes, but then again the Shadows didn't grow up in the Summer of Love.

With the Boomer cultural hegemony now blossoming into a full-fledged political domination (Boomers are ascendant in the White House and Congress), is it any wonder that so many of the Shadow generation take to musical styles that the Boomers deride? Is it any wonder that we accept the silly kitsch of the seventies (the retro nightclub polyesters can be found jam-packed in a half dozen cities across the country) after having been bombarded with "serious" sixties culture all our lives? Perhaps rap, grunge, disco, and the other various forms of today's popular music deserves the title the "Sound of Young America"—1990s style.

What are we to understand from the music of the Shadows? Step back from the lyrics that suggest sex, violence, and mindless ennui. Look rather more toward the attitude. It is the sound of resistance. It is not necessarily the rejection of the American system, it is a rejection of the way the system has been rigged for the last twenty-plus years. And who is responsible for that? The answer is obvious.

"RIGHT HERE RIGHT NOW"

If we are to create a substantial reality of our own, those of us who live within the Shadows must hijack a Boomer m.o. We must marry our cultural inclinations as expressed in our musical selections—ideologically and racially diverse, direct, straight to the point, reality-based—into the political process. Otherwise, the Shadows will be ignored in every "positive" legislative item the Baby Boomers craft over the next twenty years. Let's remember, the "babies" begin retiring in 2010. Every decision they have made, every protest staged, and every political agreement they have hammered out has benefited them primarily. Look it up—all the way back to the 1960s. Why should we believe that their retirement plans would be any different'?

The big balanced budget agreement of 1997 was actually called, with a total straight face, the "deal of a generation" by one of the Baby Boomers who put it together. Well, yeah, if you happened to have a couple of kids (even better if they're about to go off to college), a nice portfolio you're thinking of cashing in, and other such amenities. "Deal of a generation," indeed. And we know which generation.

Therefore, the Shadows have two options. Either allow the Boomers to continue on their merry way and continue "fixing" problems (much of which they caused in the first place). Or, instead head out and fix them ourselves. Our second path also has two possibilities. We can act only in self-interest, as our mentors have done. Or, we can utilize our ability to be universally "in-touch" and "on-line" and develop solutions that can impact the greatest number of people.

With the rampant demand for more choices, the lasting impact of the tension between Boomers and Shadows will be that distinctions such as "alternative" or "cultish" and "mainstream" ultimately become meaningless. The Shadows have made so-called alternative music today's mainstream. We have mastered alternative forms of distribution. The old ways no longer apply. The Boomers incessantly "don't stop thinking about tomorrow," to quote the Clinton-Gore Fleetwood Mac anthem. The Shadows declare, "go your own way." Enough with the thinking, talking, and judging. Start acting.

There are solid lessons the Shadows can learn from our music and our culture. The attitude that typifies our generation is resistance to, independence from, and a rejection of Boomer cultural "values." Our generation is the one that will utter the truths that Boomers don't want to hear (and in many of our songs, we already have): The sixties are over; Woodstock was a bad trip; and, yes, Elvis is dead. Get used to it. You don't have to be a black nationalist rap group (or even a fan of one) to see why "Fight the Power" is a reasonable anthem for Generation X. And you don't have to apologize for joining the revolution.

4

The Birth of a Revolutionary Class

Lester C. Thurow

There were ancients in ancient times—according to the Bible, Methuselah lived to the age of 969—but they were very few in number. Historically, all human societies have been dominated by the young. But that is about to change.

A new class of people is being created. For the first time in human history, Western societies will have a large group of affluent, economically inactive, elderly voters who require expensive social services like health care and who depend upon government for much of their income. It is a revolutionary class, one that is bringing down the social welfare state, destroying government finances, altering the distribution of purchasing power and threatening the investments that all societies need to make to have a successful future.

Expenditures on the elderly have fundamentally altered our fiscal systems. In the 1960s, governments generated what was then called the fiscal dividend. However large its deficit, a government could generate a budget surplus simply by doing nothing for a few years. Now, the opposite is true. Even with rapid economic growth and no new programs, government spending rises faster than tax revenues.

Washington budget-cutting is almost irrelevant before this tidal force. As the numbers of the elderly rise, pension costs will soar and health care spending will explode, particularly as we employ expensive new technologies to help the elderly live even longer. Draconian budget cuts like those now being proposed by the Congressional Republicans bring only a small amount of breathing room.

Back in 1900, 4 percent of America's population was over 65. Now, about 13 percent is, even before the first baby boomer retires. In many countries the percentage of the population over 65 will double by 2025; in the United States, the elderly are expected to account for at least 20 percent of the population. And America faces what might be called the double-40 whammy. On average, those over 65 receive 41 percent of their income from government. And slightly less than 40 percent (38 percent to be precise) of the elderly receive 80 percent or more of their income from government. In contrast, only 35 percent receive money from private pensions.

This enormous transfer of resources has made the elderly into one-issue voters who exercise a disproportionate impact on the political process. Already the needs and demands of the elderly have shaken the social welfare state, causing it for all practical purposes to go broke. Today, spending on entitlements plus interest payments on the national debt (most of it accumulated in recent years to make payments to the elderly) take 60 percent of total tax revenue. (Excluding interest on the national debt, half the Federal budget goes to the elderly.) By 2003 expenditures on the elderly (plus interest payments) will take 75 percent, and by 2013 they will take 100 percent, if current laws remain unchanged

Over the past 25 years many entitlement programs have been paid for by reductions in military spending from peak Vietnam War levels. But even with the end of the cold war, there is not much room left for such shifts. Military spending is down to less than 4 percent of gross domestic product, and even if America were willing to take defense spending down to zero, the day of reckoning would be postponed by only a few years.

The elderly obviously don't want their benefits cut. The alternative is raising taxes, but the current 15 percent Social Security tax rate would have to be boosted to 40 percent by 2029 to provide the benefits that have been promised.

Not surprisingly, government spending on things other than the elderly is plummeting. Not counting expenditures on the elderly, domestic spending has fallen from 10 percent to 7 percent of G.D.P. in the last 20 years in the United States. Most important, expenditures on the elderly are squeezing government investments in infrastructure, education and research and development—from 24 percent to 15 percent of the Federal budget in 20 years.

Spending on the elderly is no longer an issue of equity or deprivation. In 1970 the percentage of the elderly in poverty was higher than for any other part of the population. Now there are fewer poor people among the elderly than among any other group.

Adjusting for things like household size, taxes and noncash benefits like health insurance and school lunches, the elderly have a median per capita income of a whopping 67 percent above that of the population as a whole. Looking at cash income alone in the 1960's, the average 70-year-old was spending only 60 percent as much as a 30-year-old. Today that 70-year-old is spending 20 percent more. The elderly also are much wealthier than the nonelderly. Those 65 to 74 have an average net worth of $222,000 versus $66,000 for those age 35 to 44. No public interest is served by making parents rich at the cost of making children poor.

While the elderly are not the spendthrifts they are sometimes made out to be, they quite understandably are not big savers for the future. Much of the decline in personal savings rates in the United States, from about 9 percent in the decades after World War II to 3 percent in the 1990's, can be attributed to the elderly or those about to be elderly. The near elderly, confident about their pensions, are saving less than they used to right before retirement. The elderly, knowing they have monthly pension checks and health coverage, are spending more during retirement.

While all of our economic resources are not going to be given to the elderly (police and fire departments, for instance, must be financed), no one knows how the growth of entitlements for the elderly can be held in check in democratic societies. Even now, when older adults are only 13 percent of the American population, they are so powerful that no political party wants to tangle with them.

Newt Gingrich could attest to that. His supposedly revolutionary Republican Congress never even talked about cutting Social Security. It focused solely on reducing the rate of increase in Medicare expenditures while balancing the budget. Nevertheless, the Republicans were savaged in the polls as the Democrats gleefully accused them of robbing the elderly of their hard-earned benefits.

That's today. Will democratic governments be able to cut benefits when the elderly are approaching a voting majority? A panel appointed by President Clinton reported that it could not agree on any specific proposals to slow the growth of Social Security, Medicare or other Government benefit programs, even though it could agree that the current programs would raise the Government deficit eightfold by 2030 if nothing was done.

Democracy is not yet a survival-of-the-fittest species. Universal suffrage is less than 100 years old. But it is going to meet the ultimate test in the elderly. If democratic governments cannot cut benefits that go to a majority of their voters, then they have no long-term future. No other investments can be made unless those benefits are brought under control.

The political problems are not created entirely by the political power of the ever more numerous elderly. All of us will eventually become old, and all of us, especially the near elderly, would rather use our own money for the luxuries of life and let the Government pay for our necessities when we are old. Less generous programs are ultimately less-generous programs for us and not just for them.

That holds even for the young. If the elderly have to pay more of their bills, then the young may have to pay more, or feel the guilt associated with not paying. Moreover, big bills for the elderly mean smaller inheritances.

The political message is simple. A policy of directing benefits to low-income elderly families reduces costs and improves economic efficiency by getting the money to those who need it most. But it quickly loses political support.

If one is looking for a group in need, it is not the elderly. The group with the highest proportion now in poverty is children under 18. Yet government spends nine times as much per person on the elderly (who vote) as it does on the young (who don't). Precisely the group that most needs investments if there is to be a successful American economy in the future is the group that is getting the least.

Leaving aside health care, advocates for the elderly argue that Social Security is running a surplus and, hence, needs no restructuring. But that is an illusion. If the Government is running an overall deficit, it is irrelevant if one sector has a "surplus" because it is credited with collecting more taxes than it needs. What matters is what is driving the expenditure side of the budget.

In the years ahead, class warfare is apt to be redefined as the young against the old, rather than the poor against the rich. As a young Frenchwoman said during a 1994 protest against government policies that would have lowered the wages of the young: "We have no future. That's why we're out here." In America the conflict is already clear. The elderly systematically vote against education levies when they have a chance. Better yet, they establish segregated retirement communities for themselves so that they will not have to pay for schools at all.

All successful societies need to make long-term investments in education, infrastructure and the basic research that leads to growth industries like biotechnology and new business opportunities on the Internet. How is this going to happen when the largest and most powerful voting bloc is the elderly, who know that they stand no chance of seeing the benefits of these investments? Quite simply, we have to generate values that allow us to go beyond the normal welfare calculus of capitalism to a mentality in which the satisfaction of building a better tomorrow outweighs the immediate appeal of greater and greater consumption.

5

End Special Tax Favors for Seniors

William Strauss and Neil Howe

*P*lus *ça change,* indeed!

For the 40 years the Democrats ruled the Congress, they constantly upped the ante in redistributing money from young to old. The mythology may be otherwise, but the cornerstone reality of today's "big government" is the huge growth in elder entitlements over that era of Democratic rule.

The numbers speak for themselves: In 1954, when the Democrats began their long congressional run, elder entitlements consumed 2.2% of the nation's gross domestic product. Today, they consume 7.7%—an increase of 5.5 percentage points. Over that same period, all other federal spending *actually declined* by 2.5% of GDP.

In the waning days of [the 1994] election campaign, the Democrats played the old Social Security card like they usually do, warning that the Republicans would take away Grandma's monthly check. But surprise! The old "third rail" of politics—"touch it and you die"—had no juice, and the GOP won anyway.

The aging World War II vets who care most about Social Security are the USA's most pro-Democrat generation. Now well up in their seventies, they're not the political force they once were.

Honesty about Social Security is an issue tailor-made for continuing the shift of young voters toward the GOP. Witness a recent Third Millennium poll confirming that more twentysomethings believe in UFOs than believe that Social Security will still be around when they retire.

So you would think the incoming Republicans would be rolling up their sleeves to slow down the flow of money from the hard-pressed young to the affluent old.

Wrong.

If the Republican Contract with America is turned into law, and if recent comments by Speaker Newt Gingrich and House Ways and Means Chairman Bill Archer are to be believed, the new GOP majority will continue the old New Deal coalition tradition of shoveling money up the age ladder, no matter how rich the elder beneficiaries might be.

Yes, they'll change the approach slightly. Rather than adding new elder-targeted benefits, they'll add new seniors-only tax cuts. They want to roll back the recently enacted and very limited tax on 85% of Social Security benefits paid to the most affluent seniors. This is the portion which was *not* previously taxed, despite what many seniors may think. Five-year cost: $17 billion.

The Republicans also want to eliminate the earnings test for beneficiaries in their late sixties, regardless of income. That's a big new benefit for the wealthiest age bracket in American history. Five-year cost: $7 billion.

True to the party's grass-roots credo, these Republican ideas are percolating up from the states. Ever since California passed Proposition 13 to curb property taxes back in 1978, Republicans at the state and local level have been the prime movers in pressing for seniors-only tax relief. Examples abound everywhere.

Nowadays, young home-buying Californians can pay as much as nine times more in property taxes than an older resident who has occupied the same house for 16 years or more. Proposition 13 wasn't written to favor the old, but do the math: It almost always does.

The most egregious GOP pro-senior tax giveaways can be found in Virginia, through a combination of enactments by Gov. George Allen and the Republican-led Board of Supervisors of Fairfax County, just outside Washington.

Effective in 1996, a sixty-five-year-old couple on maximum Social Security will pay no Virginia income tax on their first $59,728 of income—while a thirty-year-old working couple would pay tax after the first $7,400. And in Fairfax County, a sixty-five-

Disparity in Tax Burden

Here's how the 1996 tax burden of a 30-year-old homeowning couple with one child compares with a 65-year-old retired couple in Fairfax County, Va., a Washington, D.C., suburb, which has the highest median household income in the nation, according to the Census Bureau:

$30,000 Family Income

Young Couple		Retired Couple	
U.S. income tax	$2,127	U.S. income tax	$0
Social Security tax	$4,239	Social Security tax	$0
Va. income tax	$930	Va. income tax	$0
Real estate tax[1]	$1,188	Real estate tax[1]	$0
Total tax	$8,474	Total tax	$0
As % of income	28%	As % of income	0%

$60,000 Family Income

U.S. income tax	$6,837	U.S. income tax	$4,143
Social Security tax	$8,478	Social Security tax	$0
Va. income tax	$2,523	Va. income tax	$5
Real estate tax[2]	$2,377	Real estate tax[2]	$2,377
Total tax	$20,215	Total tax	$6,525
As % of income	34%	As % of income	11%

1. Based on $100,000 home; 2. Based on $200,000 home. Source: Bill Strauss and Neil Howe

year-old couple with an income of $30,000 pays no real estate taxes on their house, no matter how expensive it is. A young couple? No discount, no matter how poor they are.

Add this to the steeply pro-retiree bias in the federal tax code. (Remember: FICA—Social Security tax—is the biggest tax paid by 90% of workers under age thirty, and retirees don't pay it at all, no matter how rich they are.) What you get is this:

A thirty-year-old couple with a small child and a $30,000 income living in a $100,000 house in suburban Reston, Va., would pay a total of $8,474 in the "big four" taxes (federal income, federal FICA, state income, and local real estate).

Now picture a sixty-five-year-old couple with the same house and income (60% of which comes from Social Security). What would they pay in those four taxes? Zero. You read right: $0.00.

Do a similar calculation for couples with $60,000 incomes and $200,000 homes, and here's what you get: The young working couple pays $20,215 in "big four" taxes, and the retiree couple pays just $6,525.

Let's suppose the congressional GOP passes its new seniors-only tax rollback. If so, the total tax on $60,000-income Virginia retirees would fall to even less.

Yes, Virginia, there is a Santa Claus—for seniors only.

Not to be outdone, another new GOP governor, South Carolina's Jim Beasley, is proposing his own $50,000 seniors-only tax exemption. Georgia and other jurisdictions also have empty-nester laws benefiting homeowning seniors, but not younger people.

Money is money. Seniors-only tax benefits are "entitlements," too. Recognizing this, the Kerrey-Danforth Commission—a panel appointed by President Clinton and dominated by moderates from both parties—soon will come forward with much more potent anti-big-government medicine than the Republicans are now prescribing.

The Republicans risk missing out on a golden opportunity. The Democrats have allowed Social Security and Medicare to become giant pyramid schemes, siphoning tax money away from young people at ever-rising rates—even though today's younger generations stand no chance of getting anywhere near the deal dished out to today's seniors.

Young workers are paying *thirty times* more in taxes (in inflation-adjusted dollars) than they did in Congress's pre-Democratic era. Today's maximum FICA tax for a two-income twenty-five-year-old couple is $18,544. When today's seventy-five-year-olds were that age, that maximum was $120. (Adjust for inflation, and it was still only $611 in today's dollars.)

Clinton-style Democrats have made a shameless habit out of ignoring the truth about Social Security every time an election is near. They run negative ads the instant a Republican like Rick Santorum dares to suggest a commonsense reform (raising the Social Security retirement age) that would help balance the budget and benefit the young. What happened in Pennsylvania? Meet *Senator-elect* Santorum. Could a new trend be in the offing here?

Wake up, Newt & Co.: Four short years from now, in 1998, the generation born in the 1960s and '70s (the ones who rank Social Security below UFOs) will be the largest generational voting bloc in the USA. The day is coming when they vote, and vote big.

If the GOP is bound by contract to give a big, seniors-only tax cut, why stop there? If you *really* want to impress young voters, give a tax cut to UFOs. It would make just as much sense.

6

Herky-Jerky Bang-Bang

Russell Baker

They say young people don't read the papers anymore. There are scientific studies to prove it. Magnificently calibrated polls. Incredibly accurate laboratory simulations. Everything absolutely sure, statistic-wise. Young people numb.

Numb generation. Twenties, we had lost generation. Thirties hungry generation. Forties, war generation. Fifties, silent generation. Sixties, rebellious generation. Seventies, greedy generation. Eighties, generation of swine. All leading up to the numb generation.

Scientifically demonstrated. Impeccable polls. Astounding lab simulations. Today's youth: numb.

Why? Science fears today's youth suffer from herky-jerky brain. Effect of watching stroboscopic film pictures with bang-bang, clang-clang music.

Need new picture every half-second. Need new bang-bang, clang-clang. Need amp . . .

Bang-bang, clang-clang . . . lification. Bang-bang . . . More ampli . . .

Clang-clang . . . fication.

Bear with me, golden-oldie people. (Golden years and senior

---

citizenship, what a crock, eh, creakers?) Bear with me, middle-agers and thirtysomething people. I am trying to create in print something that might just possibly be read by somebody suffering from herky-jerky brain, in order to demonstrate why anyone so afflicted might give up ever reading anything.

How sad these poor young people should make us feel with their indifference to practically everything on the planet that is interesting, infuriating, maddening, exhilarating, fascinating, amusing and nutty.

Herky-jerky brain makes them vulnerable to the 10-second sound bite, which leaves them defenseless against demagogues. Unable to entertain two sequential thoughts, they are powerless to conclude that a politician saying "Read my lips " must be trying to distract their attention from whatever he has on his mind.

Skimming the papers, I am saddened to think of all they are missing. Here, for instance, is news that Canada is breaking up. Imagine a whole country coming apart, and it hasn't even had decades of Marxist governance to destroy it.

Here's an old Stalinist talking in Moscow. She yearns for the past, believe it or not, when Communism knew how to make Russians toe the line. For this woman, the golden age was a time when thinking for yourself could get you arrested in dead of night and exported as slave labor in the Arctic.

It's amazing what old-timers can pine for when sighing fondly over the good old days. Equally amazing is the absolute useless-ness of money in America as a way of measuring worth. Here are two stories demonstrating that money is essentially comic:

Donald Trump's bankers are forcing him to cut his living expenses to $450,000 per month, while Jose Canseco's employer has agreed to pay him some $450,000 per month for toiling in the baseball industry this year.

If you suffer from herky-jerky mind, but not so acutely that you can't read these two stories, you might say, "Trump is going to live just as well as Canseco, and he doesn't even have to spend all summer doing extremely difficult and nerve-wracking toil."

You would be wrong, lacking the brain organization to get you to the next thought; namely, that Canseco has to pay taxes on his $5.5 million whereas Trump will have the whole pile to spend.

The lesson here seems to be that America values bankrupt real estate speculators more than high-living baseball players. If your brain isn't going bang-bang, clang-clang, however, it might go one step further and marvel that America's bankers will lend the world's Trumps so much money that they have to keep financing them at $450,000 per month to save them from bankruptcy.

And you always thought bankers were so brilliant, didn't you, as they smiled so wisely at your laughable application for a roof-reshingling loan?

And there's so much more: Supreme Court recognizes right to die. Sure, but will New York City find a way to tax it? A dying-license fee, perhaps. Today's youth . . . ye of the numb generation . . . heed my words. Quit being numb, or you shall pay in pain when the next generation arrives. The next generation always reacts against the previous generation.

Be warned: If your numbness intensifies your dumbness, your destiny is a middle-age of bearing contemptuous sneers at your imbecility. Fight herky-jerky brain before it is too late.

But I shout down a rain barrel, don't I? Bang-bang, clang-clang.

Part Two

WHO HOLDS THE POWER?

Each generation wastes a little more of the future with greed and lust for riches.

—Donald Robert Perry Marquis

One of the most outspoken members of the U.S. Senate, Alan K. Simpson, spent 18 years taking on the national seniors lobby before his retirement in January 1997. As the chairman of the Subcommittee on Social Security and Family Policy, he continually clashed with leaders of AARP and the National Committee to Preserve Social Security and Medicare. He also relentlessly criticized then Social Security Commissioner Shirley Chater and other government officials who refused to acknowledge the seriousness of the problems facing entitlement programs.

Simpson is an astute commentator on the relative political strengths of each generation. In a candid, entertaining interview held with Harvard University graduate student Maya MacGuineas exclusively for this book, Simpson offers his critique of today's generational politics. To him, today's fight is a true mismatch, with youth in the weakest position.

Next, *Swing*'s Stuart Miller provides the obituary for the most incendiary and short-lived of the Generation X political groups, Lead . . . or Leave. Following, Jeff Shesol sizes up the remaining Xer organizations and finds a lack of seriousness and purpose. The only credible generational call to action for Generation X comes from the Preamble to the 1993 *Third Millennium Declaration*, which closes out the section.

7

Interview with Sen. Alan Simpson

Maya MacGuineas

M: Now that so much of public policy is being looked at through a generational lens or framework, how will generations be represented fairly when some of them are so much larger and so much more active than others?

S: It won't happen until they band together. They've got to band together. And there are many emerging groups, but it takes so much effort to reach even a 200,000 membership. Especially when you have these behemoth organizations like the AARP or the National Committee to Preserve Social Security and Medicare—or even the minor ones: The Silver-Haired Legislators and the Gray Panthers.

So, it's the sad and true part that nothing will get done until they [other generations] have [membership] numbers. And they won't have numbers until they can do something like what the AARP does, and that is try to lure people in. They've lured the seniors in by discounts and Royal Viking Cruises and wheelchairs and golf carts that collapse, and that's their advertising. And they know that. And then they finally, at the end, pop on what their driving energy is: to get something out of the federal treasury.

Really the young people at Third Millennium, who I regard highly, and you know what they're trying to do; they're trying to

This interview was conducted at the Kennedy School of Government, Harvard University, April 18, 1997.

figure what is the bait. What do you do, say we're going to have a national skateboard lottery? Or you're going to get [a] free skateboard if you do this? Or you're going to get fifteen records of Joe Banana and his bunch, music with appeal? Or Naughty Neal and His Nine Nasty Nosepickers or something? Something to lure them into the game. And that's gotta come. And market, market. Get the numbers through marketing.

M: So good public policy isn't enough.

S: Uh-uh.

M: What you need is a catch. And you need a way to get people involved for their own self-interest. And then get them involved in things that are beyond that.

S: Get them in first; get the numbers first. And then say, "Now, gang, that we got you all in here. That's why we gathered you all together in the elevator shaft . . ." And then just say, [Simpson whispers] "Here you are, guys, and here's what we're gonna do. What we have to do . . ."

M: What advantages do you think senior citizens have over the rest of the population, right now when it comes to the allocation of federal benefits?

S: Time—to go to Washington and pursue their cause. To wander into a congressman's office, while [at the same time] a poor guy thirty years old or twenty-five years old is hunkering down and working and doing his share. While the senior is thinking, "Well, I'll go to Arlington and visit the grave of my brother, and while I'm there"—and these are for the best of reasons—"I want to see Washington. I haven't been there. This is on our way to Florida." I mean, they have time.

And the [seniors] organization is telling them to, sure, drop by and see ol' Al Simpson. Tell him, we've heard what he's up to, with what he's trying to do with his ugly effort to screw us on Social Security. You get in there and tell ol' Al that he's really off the rail, and while you're there drop in and see Congresswoman [Barbara] Cubin. And then they find out who was working on your campaign and they get those people to come.

They have time. And they have the energy and they have been frightened enough to believe that any present, possible way to begin to correct the system is going to screw them in their next paycheck. Which is a rotten, phony lie, [that] anything we're trying to do is gonna take a nickel out of anybody's pocket who's over fifty-five.

M: And one thing Baby Boomers don't have is the time, because they're working. But they do have the positions. And a number of them hold the top, official, elected positions in Washington. Do you think they look out more for their generation and their generation's best interest? Or are they unduly influenced by seniors as well, because [of] their numbers and time? How do the Baby Boomers in their political role represent different generations?

S: Well ol' big boom Boomer himself sold his generation down the river: Bill Clinton. He should be the epitome of the leadership of the Boomers as to what's going to happen in the future and he just sold himself. He will go down as a failed president if he doesn't deal with the incremental reform—this year [1997], it's not an election year—with regard to Medicare and Social Security and assuring long-term solvency. I can't imagine a man who talks about compassion and caring, the children and the seniors and the veterans all day long, sits right there at the bridge of the ship, just letting it crash on the rocks.

M: So if you were giving advice to Bill Clinton or the next president, would your advice be that the way to leave a positive legacy for yourself is to reform these programs?

S: Yeah, the way to do it is to get up and give a speech that would just say, "My fellow countrymen, we've all been joshing you. The Republicans have been giving you a load of stuff, and I've been giving you a load of stuff, and the Democrats are giving you a load of stuff. And we're going to go back to the report of the [Social Security] Trustees." The Trustees, they are [Treasury Secretary Robert] Rubin and [Health and Human Services Secretary Donna] Shalala. I don't know who's taken [Labor Secretary Robert] Reich's place. These are the people telling us this.

They got rid of Shirley Chater [who was also a Trustee], who was the worst administrator of Social Security the world ever could've known. She never made a single recommendation to us. [Senator Daniel Patrick] Moynihan and I said, "You will never be confirmed by us. I shall never, ever vote to confirm you. You come before our committee; we say, 'You know the condition of Social Security. You know what's going to happen in 2029, and what would you have us do?' And we gave you independence. We separated you for the Executive Branch from the Congress and you do nothing. You are a massive atom of ineptitude."

And she would just sit and smile. And then she put out a bunch of crappy things to the school districts. It was a little education kit so little kiddies all throughout America could read that nothing has really happened to Social Security. It will be fine. And don't let these nasty old people tell you. . . . Anyway. So bad.

You know, Clinton could go on the tube and say, "Here's what we're going to do. Now relax and remember nobody is going to get hurt here. We're going to extend the age of Social Security over twenty years. You can't be hurt in that. COLAs [Cost of Living Adjustments], we're going to have to means test you. If you got more bucks, you're going to have to pay. But if you ain't got nothing, you ain't gonna pay nothing. And the CPI is not called breaking the contract. It's called saving us one trillion, two-hundred billion bucks in ten years. And Simpson retired with 66,100 bucks and is that fair? He put in 8 percent of his money and a postal worker in Denver retired putting in 7 percent and getting that kind of kickback back, with a COLA that goes with it. And guys, that's an unfunded liability." I think Americans are thirsting for that.

M: For the truth.

S: And somebody's going to come forward and give it. Now, they may get defeated. But, God, it would be refreshing.

M: Well, do you think young adults stand a chance of protecting Social Security and Medicare for the future, given the current political climate?

S: Not now. Here's [Senator] Pete Domenici, right at this moment working on trying to get the balanced budget and they can't get the figure on Medicare. And everybody knows it's just on terminal bloat. But they know they don't want to take on the American Medical Association and the American Hospital Association, and here we go again.

So, I do think things are better for your generation and that people are talking about it. And they really are. In a way I never saw ten years ago or even five. And maybe you're a part of the catalyst for that. But people are talking and people are talking in Congress about it. And that's helpful.

M: What is the most likely scenario you see for the future of entitlement reform? Who do you think will be the winners and the losers in the way that these programs are reformed to avert bankruptcy?

S: Well, the reform will take place because there will be panic at some point and time.

M: As we get closer to the bankruptcy date?

S: Yes. And the reform will take the place of the raising of the payroll tax. That will be the easiest one of all. You see, you can just say, "Now folks, you remember we told you that these doomsday bastards were off the rail and to prove that they are, all we're going to do now is raise the payroll tax three-fourths of one percent, which will raise blank billions of dollars. And you see, it wasn't as bad as you thought."

And meanwhile every business in America will think, "God Almighty, I'm on a margin of one to three percent between sending my kid to school or not. And now these sons-of-bitches have done a half, or quarter, even." I mean whatever it is, it's going to be made by Joe Six-pack.

M: Those wages will increase that much slower. Those people living paycheck to paycheck.

S: You got it. And meanwhile the seniors do not pay that. It's so phony.

M: And the payroll tax is the most regressive tax we have in our country.

S: It's surely—big time.

Or they might say, "Well, yes, we will affluence-test the COLA. But we certainly must set it at a hundred thousand [dollars]. We wouldn't want anyone to be punished who, just because it's America—and we've all paid our Social Security, all of us dear souls—and we certainly don't want to be greedy, but we certainly want it all back. We want all ours back. So, yes, we would give up our COLA if we make over a hundred thousand. Yes, we'll pay all of our premium on [Medicare] Part B if we make over seventy thousand, if we can. If we possibly can."

You're going to hear—I mean this is—the whining generation up above: "Breaking the contract. Seven bucks more a month—

what kind of a people are we that we should have to pay nine to seven bucks more a month?" Those kind of things will get us on the road to recovery—and we can't even get that.

M: Do you think the education of what we need to do will come from the government, the media, advocacy groups, where?

S: Well, I think it will come from the media because more and more young people are in the media. And more and more young people are figuring this out. I used to love to get interviewed by thirty-five-year-old people or forty-year-old interviewers: "Now, Senator, you seem to hate seniors. I'd like to know why you pick on seniors."

And I'd say, "Oh hell, don't worry about me, pal. I'll be smuggling it out of here in a sack." I said, "You'll be picking grit with the chickens when you're sixty-five. So just keep interviewing people and putting that bias on there. Hell, pal, in the year 2010, 60 percent of the domestic budget of the U.S. will be going to people over sixty, so the drinks are on me. Anybody with a rock for brains like that doesn't deserve to have a microphone in his hands." I did that. I've said that.

M: So in some ways it was the politicians educating the media, who then educate the public.

S: Yeah, let the media get back to their marvelous role, which is being biased. They're very good at it and they pretend they're not. Now go out and be youth-biased. And the next time they come out with a CPI recommendation, for God's sake, any reporter that goes and visits first with the American Association for Retired Persons and asks them to give their view deserves a horse flap. The dumb bastards. You've got to be stupid—and that's what they did.

That thing [the Boskin Commission report recommending a readjustment downward of the CPI] died in the womb, and it's a good piece of work. Well, yes, but they were all people on there who said it was overstated. Or, it was a breaking of the contract. They've got all the wedges, plowed in. Looks like Saint Sebastian with the arrows sticking out of it.

M: Great. Thank you very much for giving your time.

8

The Death of Lead . . . or Leave

Stuart Miller

There is a legend about the organization Lead . . . or Leave. It goes something like this:

It was an April night in 1992, and Rob Nelson and Jon Cowan sat in the Brickskeller, a Washington, D.C., pub, drinking beer and seething with frustration over their status as powerbroker wannabes. Cowan, who was then 26, had worked for a Congressman and a think tank; Nelson, a year older, had bounced from one job to another—trade commission, start-up magazine, government think tank. Both of them knew they wanted to have an impact on policy, even though they didn't have a plan in mind, and they also wanted to be political players, fast. The question was, how?

"We're mad and we're frustrated," Nelson complained as he gripped his beer. "What we need to do is stop waiting for other people to help us make it happen." What they needed, he said, was to "put something out there that would make us happy." Cowan looked at him skeptically. "What would that be?" he asked. The ensuing conversation eventually became the plan that turned Nelson and Cowan into Lead . . . or Leave, the twentysomething generation's most influential political action committee. Their plan

From *Swing Magazine* (November 1995): 56–61. Copyright © 1995 by Stuart Miller. Reprinted by permission of the author.

was to get political candidates to sign an oath to cut the deficit in half by 1996, or else leave office. Nelson and Cowan borrowed a pen from a passing Brickskeller waitress and scrawled out their advance strategy on a napkin. Within months they had opened an office on 20th Street. "That's how it began, in a tremendously random, haphazard way," Cowan says. "We didn't know what we would do after election day. It was very kind of homespun."

Cowan and Nelson portray themselves as part of the classic American success myth, in which humble outsiders triumph over the establishment. "We were incredibly persistent," Nelson says, remembering the early days when no one took Lead . . . or Leave seriously. Those days didn't last long. Only a few months after Nelson and Cowan hatched their beer-bar plan, Lead . . . or Leave had become a major force in the campaign. Before election day, Lead . . . or Leave became a pet cause of everyone from Paul Tsongas (who officially endorsed it) to Ross Perot (who generously funded it), and one hundred candidates signed the Lead . . . or Leave pledge, hoping to profit from the public's rage over the deficit, 1992's hottest election-year issue. Lead was the darling of the media, and its founders were hailed in the *New York Times*, the *Washington Post* and other influential papers as valiant spokesmen for the muchmaligned Generation X, even as revolutionaries saving America's future. Cowan and Nelson had hit the big time; within two years they had published a book, *Revolution X: A Survival Guide for Our Generation*, that boasted that Lead . . . or Leave had built a membership of a million people.

It is an impressive story that would be more impressive if it were altogether true. While it is true that Cowan and Nelson came out of obscurity and propelled themselves into the political foreground, it is not correct that they were a pair of innocents lassoing a whirlwind. While it is true that they were young, it is not exactly true that they created a youth movement. "This wasn't a group that was talking about, 'How do we get a bunch of other young people behind us,'" says a source who worked with Lead in the early days. "They really wanted to move it through the media." Even the simple story of the birth of their grand scheme in the Brickskeller seems suspect; Cowan now says he has only "vague" recollections of "a series of conversations" in bars and coffee houses. One certainty is that, as young and raw as they seemed, Cowan and Nelson were sophisticated enough to hire the Washington media firm Fenton Communications before their first press conference. Andrew Weinstein, Lead's communications director from July through November of 1994, says, "They were extremely intelligent, extremely creative—and very well versed in terms of how to use the media and politicians to achieve their goals."

That first press conference, held in early August at the National Press Club, made the deficit pledge part of the dialogue in the 1992 campaign. Although many politicians, including Bill Clinton, dismissed it as a gimmick, Lead quickly gained affluent and influential new friends—not only Perot but a posse of Republican moneymen such as Richard Dennis, Clyde Prestowitz, and Pete Peterson, the president of the antideficit Concord Coalition. The media frenzy produced a side effect that Cowan and Nelson had not foreseen: twentysomethings who cared less about the deficit than about rocking the system besieged them, asking to work for Lead . . . or Leave. "People were literally working in closets," Cowan says. "The energy was the kind of thing that you hear about when someone like Bobby Kennedy runs."

There is no question that Lead . . . or Leave did work—for a while. It widened public awareness of the deficit and raised youth interest in politics, and seventeen of the candidates who signed the Lead pledge won. But after the 1992 elections, Lead needed a reason to continue to exist. In 1993, Nelson and Cowan widened Lead's platform and attacked entitlements, using their political capital to confront Social Security spending and the American Association of Retired Persons. They published an op-ed piece in the *New York Times* advocating higher taxes on benefits for the wealthy elderly. "Older voters and politicians be warned: Younger Americans aren't going to let you continue destroying our country," they wrote. Lead's main goal, Nelson says, was not to lay out a specific plan, but to "challenge the institutional authority of the system." Opportunistically calling entitlement spending "our generation's Vietnam," the group held a rally on the AARP's steps and rode another wave of media adulation that transported it from "Nightline" to the cover of *U.S. News & World Report*.

As a result of the new coverage, more and more people who wanted to help make America better flocked to their banner. Lead hooked up with people who were organizing town hall meetings on the deficit. It started a curriculum for high school students called "Get Real," that had high school students discussing press coverage of the deficit and creating antideficit political cartoons and song lyrics. And in 1994, Lead held a Student Leadership

Summit in D.C., inviting hundreds of politically aware young people ·to interact with the likes of George Stephanopoulos and David Gergen. "We helped create a sense among young people that we could actually do something," Cowan says.

Ultimately, however, Lead tried to do too much, and lost its focus. In the fall of 1994, as Nelson and Cowan's book, *Revolution X*, was published, Lead broadened its mandate yet again, urging the government to launch "an unprecedented multibillion-dollar effort to crack down on violent crime; and a massive new investment program that can help save the next generation of impoverished youth." At the same time, Lead launched a new project, "Register Once," a drive to increase college campus polling places and to encourage voter registration. By early 1995, the media began to buzz with the question: How much of a role will Lead play in Election '96? In the eyes of the press, Lead had been the voice for the young generation, and Cowan and Nelson were its mysterious spokesmen. But no one asked who the two men behind the curtain were, or what right they had to speak for anyone else, until it was too late.

Jon Cowan had a comfortable Southern California upbringing. He went from a posh private high school in Brentwood to college at Dartmouth. "I was a pensive kid, I was labeled as too sensitive, too emotional," Cowan remembers. He was teased because he was very small. "I got picked on a lot," Cowan says. "I remember having my skateboard stolen. It's one of my most vivid memories." But he started riding horses at the age of five, and on horseback he became a different boy. "I learned that you can take on something really big and do it. I was a little kid and this giant animal was something I could really control." Cowan soon showed a knack for controlling the political animal as well, winning the eighth-grade class presidency by bringing his dog to the campaign. Even in high school he says he had a "gut sense" that he would one day be involved in public service. After Dartmouth, Cowan headed to Capitol Hill with visions of Robert F. Kennedy in his head. "Bobby Kennedy was my hero," Cowan says. "I came with the really specific idea that if there were another Vietnam War situation I'd want to be one of the people of my generation who knew what to do about it." In 1987, he began working for California Representative Mel Levine, and in 1988 he began to work at a think tank called Rebuild America, where he met Rob Nelson.

Nelson's childhood was less luxurious. He grew up between a

bar and a commune in an unconventional neighborhood in Milwaukee, and his parents were Christian Scientists—"the religion that doesn't believe in doctors," Nelson says critically. When Nelson was eight, he watched his younger brother die of scarlet fever because his parents would not seek medical care, an experience that he acknowledges "made me distrust authority." He has since left the religion. When Nelson was 13, his father, an urban planner, moved the family to a farm in rural Wisconsin. Nelson went to the local high school, got a B.A. at Principia, a small Illinois college, then earned a master's in international relations at Tufts University. Afterward, he went to Washington. His goals were similar to Cowan's, Nelson says, and adds with a touch of envy, "except he landed a job on the Hill with a member of Congress, and I didn't."

While Cowan and Nelson's partnership never wavered, by the fall of 1994 the Lead . . . or Leave organization was melting down. Eleven full-time workers and 12 interns in the large three-room office on 20th Street scrambled to fulfill one commitment after another, but many projects fell through. Lead had promised to add interactive educational software to its high school program, but it never happened. It had called for a national-debt rock concert to raise youth awareness about the deficit, but in the end, a different group sponsored the concert. It had tried to implement the Register Once campaign nationwide, but never made it work locally. "They only had one way of doing it for the whole country," complains Petri Darby, who became Arizona's volunteer state coordinator. When coordinators called Lead's offices in D.C. to ask practical questions, their calls were fielded not by Nelson and Cowan but by interns who knew little about the program. And . . . Lead was going broke. The older, wealthy donors who had supported the deficit attacks had no interest in backing a liberal voter registration group.

In the middle of these struggles, Cowan and Nelson left for their national book tour. While they were gone, the junior staff at the Lead offices confronted the communications director, Andrew Weinstein, and Lead's national field director, Tracy Newman. They had grumbled for months about the chaos of the organization, and now their discontent exploded into a roar, fueled by Cowan and Nelson's departure just when their guidance was needed the most. In the following weeks, several staffers, including Weinstein, quit, and before long, empty coffers forced Cowan and Nelson to lay off everyone else except Newman.

Finally, in May of 1995, after three years of press conferences, media campaigns, and grand plans gone awry, Lead closed its doors.

Cowan and Nelson admit now that they spread themselves too thin. They were torn between pleasing deficit hawks and pleasing young people who wanted to get involved on other issues. "We were dealing with so many people and so many different directions and agendas," Nelson complains. They lacked one particular cause to rally around. "It wasn't like there was a Vietnam War," he says. Many factors contributed to the fall of Lead . . . or Leave, but since the breakup, rising voices of detractors have criticized the duo as having half-baked crowd-pleasing ideas and of seducing a credulous press corps while leaving no substantive legacy. Economists point out that they never gave any detailed analysis of the deficit issue, the supposed cornerstone of their platform. Some young people complain about what they see as Cowan and Nelson's arrogance, while liberal critics accuse Lead of being neo-conservatives who only paid lip service to social issues. But the most frequent criticism centers on Lead's supposed penchant for deserting projects and distorting the truth.

One basis for such attacks is that the figures Lead circulated on their number of supporters cannot be verified. Lead early on replaced Fenton publicists with its own in-house operation, which dished out impressive figures. Lead claimed to have gathered a million members, and affiliations with 350 colleges—but these numbers were never backed up and they shifted wildly. Newspapers that wrote about Lead often published different accounts; in November of 1994, for example, the *Dallas Morning News* credited Lead with 25,000 members one day and with 50,000 the next. In fact, much of the credit for Lead's success goes to the media, which covered the group profusely and enthusiastically because Lead, as a young David taking on the Goliath of bad government, made such good copy. "I might have been a little gullible because [Lead] was so perfect for everything I needed," one reporter confesses. Many reporters hopped on the Lead bandwagon, accepting the past coverage as proof of its legitimacy.

Had they checked, reporters would have found many of the claims didn't hold up. Lead's much-touted figure of 1 million members was manufactured by adding up the number of students at every school affiliated with Lead. Such practices are legitimately employed by youth groups with paid memberships and elected leaders, as in the case of the United States Student Association (USSA), but Lead was never a bona fide student group and had no elected officers or membership meetings. Jeannette Galanis, the president of USSA, says that, as Lead metamorphosed into a voter's rights group in 1994, it wooed USSA member schools and counted schools as members if someone so much as agreed to receive printed information.

Cowan and Nelson refuse to divulge membership lists, but Cowan now says Lead peaked with 100,000 active members, and claims that reporters "deliberately misunderstand" the representation concept to juice their stories. And yet Cowan and Nelson repeat the "million members" claim in their own book. An ex-staffer calls the inflated numbers indefensible. "I don't think there are a million people who know what Lead . . . or Leave is." Paul Loeb, author of *Generation at the Crossroads,* a book about campus activism, agrees. He calls Lead's tactics "astoundingly shameless," and claims that he "never ran into a single member" during the research of his book. Cowan dismisses critics, refuses to talk on the record about complaints against Lead, and denies any controversy. According to Nelson, "We stepped on some people's toes, but it wasn't our problem." They say a few individuals, not schools, inadvertently landed on the list, but that any mistakes were honest ones. Galanis is not mollified. "It happened to too many schools, too many student body presidents," she retorts.

There were also questions about Cowan and Nelson's independence. Ever since the pair won the backing of conservative leaders after their press conference debut in August 1992, liberal commentators had doubted Lead's autonomy. Lead has steadfastly denied taking money from political organizations, and Cowan claims Lead did not adopt backers' positions. "I will unequivocally say we didn't get ideas from outside places," he says. "We didn't consult policy experts or generational experts." But the Social Security campaign that Cowan and Nelson suggest in their book and in the *New York Times* reflects the beliefs of backers like Pete Peterson, whom the book quotes, and their proposals often echo those of such zeitgeist commentators as Neil Howe and Bill Strauss, authors of the generational study *13th Gen.*

For the moment, Cowan and Nelson have stepped out of the spotlight. Nelson is at law school at Stanford, Cowan works for the department of Housing and Urban Development (HUD) as deputy assistant secretary for long-range planning. ("Essentially, saving the agency is what they asked me to do," he says. "I'm like a Dick Morris.") Jean Nolan, HUD's assistant secretary for public affairs, who hired Cowan, bursts out laughing at Cowan's self-aggrandizing job description. "How modest of him. . . . Oh, Lord . . . he'll be working on a communication team on long-range, big picture issues." When asked if he might run for political office one day, Cowan evades the issue, saying he'll "keep it wide open." Nelson, more blunt, as usual, says he will definitely seek office, and explains, "I have a vision. It's shaping and evolving. I have an obligation to step up to the plate."

Cowan and Nelson acknowledge they have made mistakes, but they say the mistakes were in the process, not in the end results. "The accusations didn't have to do with whether Lead . . . or Leave had an impact," Cowan says, and Weinstein agrees: "They really did touch a nerve." All the same, Heather McLeod, editor of *Who Cares,* an activism-oriented magazine, is not alone when she says that Lead may have done more harm than good and let a lot of young activists down. "The saddest thing is a lot of young people signed up with Lead and put their faith in them," she says, and now these young people "might be left feeling more disappointed and disillusioned with politics and 'youth politics' than before."

Next time, Cowan and Nelson both say, they will do better—and there will be a next time. The next incarnation of Lead . . . or Leave will concentrate on energizing focused young leaders in business, entertainment and politics, rather than on involving idealistic youthful volunteers with uncertain objectives. The new Lead . . . or Leave will be back for the 1996 elections, they promise, with an online dialogue for young leaders. They have already planned a gala Millennium Weekend for June of 1996. "You can't get everyone involved," Nelson says. "I used to think you could get everybody to do something, but I'd be more effective to get you and one other person to do a lot." No one can deny Lead's predilection for the Big Think, or its uncanny sense of what people want. But will people still follow Lead's call? Cowan confidently says yes: "We have a way of making that stuff happen."

Everyone's entitled to another chance, and the media loves a comeback—but for Cowan and Nelson, the goal in 1996 will be not to capture the public's attention, but to prove they deserve to keep it.

9

Fun in Politics? As *If.*

Jeff Shesol

"**Y**ou've reached Democrats with an Attitude," growls the voice on the answering machine. "The inauguration is over, but the fun is just beginning."

The Clinton White House might well dispute that last point, but it's hard to dampen the enthusiasm of Democrats with an Attitude, a fledgling national organization of young partisans. At a recent DWA bash on Capitol Hill, carefree pols barely old enough to drink were sipping free microbrews and shouting to be heard over thumping trip-hop. This is not your father's coffee klatch. DWA's logo (a Democratic donkey in Ray-Bans), motto ("Bite a Republican"), and even its toll-free number (1-800-FUN-DEMS) convey a simple but sassy message: Politics is fun, fun, fun.

Or, by their lights, it ought to be. "The Democratic party is using old methods to attract new members," explains Steve Johnson, 32, founder and director of DWA. "Precinct caucuses, conventions, issues meetings—young people don't like them much." What they do like, in Johnson's view, is, well, fun. "Fun events, fun logos, fun things. Politics needs to be made fun for them. First you get them active and then you feed them the issues."

In the 1990s, the notion of politics as pre-packaged, mass-marketed entertainment has seized young pols like an embarrassing fit of giggles; DWA is only the latest avatar. The group is half-right: Politics does need an attitude adjustment. But as a diagnosis for what afflicts young non-voters, this is sadly lacking. As a prescription for the disaffected or the disenfranchised, laughter may not be the best medicine.

A primer on the politics of fun begins with Lead . . . or Leave. In the heady days of the 1992 campaign, this twentysomething advocacy group promised a "Revolution X" and "guerrilla activism, '90s style—getting in the face of the media, getting in the face of the system."

Now, this was fun. Lead . . . or Leave founders Jon Cowan and Rob Nelson stormed Capitol Hill in T-shirts and backward baseball caps, straddled a Harley for the cover of *U.S. News & World Report* and wheedled endorsements out of Gen X celebrities like Christian Slater and Ricki Lake—all, ostensibly, in the name of deficit reduction. But the messy business of cobbling together a broader "youth agenda" was not fun; nor was it even possible in a group that professed to be beyond ideology. By the summer of 1995, a badly confused and poorly managed Lead . . . or Leave slipped from its ideology moorings, drifted aimlessly, and sank.

Meanwhile, on the road with Rock the Vote, the party continues. Rock the Vote has been luring young concert-goers to voter registration tables since 1990, positing rapper Queen Latifah as a sort of Pied Piper of participation and netting 500,000 new registrants in the past year. Thus candidates (usually challengers) now clamor for Rock the Vote rallies, knowing only that Rock the Vote has something to do with pop singer Sheryl Crow.

But while Sheryl Crow can lead young people to register, she can't make them vote. "Do they go to the polls? No," complains Mark Strama, Rock the Vote's 28-year-old program director, feeling perhaps a bit betrayed by all those fresh-faced Lollapaloozers who pledged to do their civic duty. For some, the music may be an "entry point" into political participation, as Strama contends. But for the vast majority, it is the first tentative step on a road to nowhere. According to Curtis Gans of the Committee for the Study of the American Electorate, the youth vote reached a new low in 1996, hitting its lowest point (under 30 percent of eligible voters) since 18- to 21-year-olds gained the franchise in 1971.

Playing to the crowd, in short, can be counterproductive.

*   *   *

Who said politics was supposed to be fun, anyway? Tabitha Soren and "MTV News," of course, as well as John Kennedy Jr.'s *George* magazine and any politician who makes wry reference to the macarena. Each, in its own way, portrays politics as just another facet of pop culture. Each bows to the conventional wisdom that young people are not citizens but consumers, and that democracy darned well better be sexy, funny, and entertaining if it's going to survive the next millennium.

Joining this glee club of forced frivolity, remarkably, is First Lady Hillary Rodham Clinton, who has probably had less fun in the last four years than just about anybody in Washington. Her exhortation to "make politics in America fun again!" is reprinted in bold type on the first page of DWA's mission statement.

It is unclear which previous era in American politics merits a laugh track. Politics were exciting but hardly "fun" when a young Hillary Rodham, on assignment for the House Judiciary Committee, analyzed the constitutional grounds for the impeachment of President Nixon, or when a young Bill Clinton reviewed the cases of increasingly desperate draft resisters for Sen. William Fulbright. Youth politics in the '60s and early '70s was, by and large, deadly serious. The Weathermen, Students for a Democratic Society, and Young Americans for Freedom were hardly in it for a good time (even if the Yippies were). Mrs. Clinton and her peers are nostalgic not for the politics of fun but the politics of passion.

But while the first lady's use of "fun" may actually translate to "seriousness of purpose," when her twentysomething audiences hear "fun," they break out the party hats and start testing the chandelier. Absent another Vietnam or Watergate, issues are a drag. Ideology is cause for embarrassment, like your mother's soft spot for the Great Society. But this time, it's not our parents who don't get it. It's us.

What young "post-partisans" (as well as avowed partisans like DWA) forget is that issues inflame passions, and passions drive and sustain participation—through brutal campaigns; long, boring nights of phone banking and canvassing; and years (perhaps decades) in the minority. DWA's Steve Johnson, a campaign veteran himself, acknowledges this. Promising to gird "Operation Attitude" with genuine issues, he entertains brief visions of picking up Lead . . . or Leave's tattered standard and leading the next youth crusade. But, when pressed, Johnson beats a quick retreat. "We haven't really worked as hard yet on the message," he says, admitting that "we're not going to solve the world's problems ourselves."

Fair enough; there's no reason to ask more of DWA than of Congress or the White House. But when politics is about attitude and not issues, young Democrats could become young Republicans as soon as the GOP throws a better party.

Fun, quite simply, is not enough to build a political cadre. "I like the motivation of these groups, I really do," says Curtis Gans. "We do need to make politics more fun. But these little organizational efforts are not going to have any impact until the macrocosm of American politics changes. You've got to remember, these young people got enfranchised in a period of disillusionment or extremism, in a time when our national values are shifting . . . away from participation, and toward self-seeking behaviors."

Recognizing this, at least one group of young pols has traded its party hats for green eye shades. Third Millennium, founded in 1993 by Robert Kennedy's youngest son, Douglas, is unexpectedly earnest in an age of irony. The group, which advocates fiscal responsibility so today's youth won't face old age penniless, publishes a 32-page manifesto that reads as if the Declaration of Independence had been drafted by interns at a think tank. There's no chest-pounding here, no "Revolution X" brewing, just "an extensive academic study" of state and municipal retirement plans and "a monograph" documenting the history of Social Security legislation. Upcoming public service ads will urge grandfolks to teach grandkids the value of a vote.

Don't expect Sheryl Crow to stage any rallies for partial privatization of the Social Security trust fund. This is "lethally boring" stuff, concedes Richard Thau, Third Millennium's 32-year-old executive director. "I might as well be talking about the pace at which ice melts." Third Millennium is more of a think tank than a grassroots advocacy organization, and Thau feels no obligation to sex up unsexy issues like pension reform for an audience that doesn't appear to be listening. "I am tremendously disappointed that my generation remains disengaged," Thau confesses, but he offers no glib means to engage his peers. Third Millennium fights for twentysomethings while, in a very real sense, it writes them off.

And that may be the key to its success. Instead of Lead . . . or Leave's spunk or DWA's sass, Third Millennium delivers principled, reasoned argument, hoping to persuade by the power of its ideas. Thau's generation may not be listening, but Congress is. Representatives of Third Millennium have testified 11 times on Capitol Hill, most recently in favor of adjusting the consumer price index. "Politicians like us because we're intelligent, lucid, and responsible," Thau surmises. "We don't walk around on the Hill wearing backward baseball caps and T-shirts."

But what does Third Millennium do when Congress shouts, "Show me the votes"? The group's *bête noire,* the AARP, can mobilize millions of senior citizens with an arched eyebrow. Third Millennium can't get its constituents to drop the remote. Still, by taking the issues seriously, Third Millennium has at least more hope of influence than thousands of young Democrats (or Republicans) with attitudes.

10

Preamble to the
Third Millennium Declaration

We stand at the edge of a new millennium. The superpower confrontation, which brought fear of the apocalypse into the lives of three generations, is over. We live in the richest, freest, and most powerful country the world has ever seen. Most excellent.

But we fear for the future.

Political and social time bombs threaten our fragile successes at home and abroad. Like Wile E. Coyote waiting for a 20-ton Acme anvil to fall on his head, our generation labors in the expanding shadow of a monstrous national debt. Racial, sexual and economic divisions have made fellow citizens brutal enemies. Our cities have fallen into a shameful state where ordinary acts of daily life have become painful struggles.

For too long, we as a nation have failed to exercise self-control. We've trashed the ethic of individual responsibility. We've exploited racial and sexual differences for political gains. Those in power have practiced fiscal child abuse, mortgaging our future, and the futures of those to come. Meanwhile, the engine of democracy has stalled, paralyzed by fringe issues.

It is time to take responsibility. The grave problems facing our country—economic stagnation, social fragmentation and the dete-

Reprinted by permission of Third Millennium: Advocates for the Future, July 1993, New York, NY.

rioration of the environment—demand solutions that transcend partisanship. We believe it is the challenge of our generation to move the country beyond partisan stagnation and focus on the real challenges at hand.

Those of us offering this declaration don't pretend to represent our entire generation. We recognize our generation's intense individualism as one of its strengths. The post-baby boom generation, born after 1960, is far too diverse to let one group represent it all. But we believe young people must initiate change. Our role in serving our country must be to stop the dumping of toxic policies on future generations.

The writers of this statement come from a wide array of backgrounds, careers and political persuasions, and not every one of us subscribes to every last letter in this statement. We are drawn together, however, by the belief that we can't let our differences—real as they are—excuse further inaction. Conservative, liberal, or none of the above, we unite in the sentiment that the time to act is now.

We look to President Abraham Lincoln, who, at another time when division threatened to destroy the country, pleaded for change: "The dogmas of the quiet past are inadequate to the stormy present. The occasion is piled high with difficulty, and we must rise with the occasion. As our case is new, so must we act anew."

Divisive issues such as abortion and the death penalty must recede to the background. It is up to us to direct our energies to the problems that threaten the future of our nation.

Our generation is often derided for its cynicism. We grew up amidst the betrayals of Vietnam, Watergate and the S&L scandal. We are witness to the highest divorce rate ever. We see neighborhoods across America battle lawlessness, drug abuse, dysfunctional families and substandard school systems. At the same time, divisive right-wing tactics fuel our country's worst fears and hatreds, while impotent left-wing dogma transforms us into a society of victims and dependents.

But if our common experience has jaded us, it has also added urgency to our outlook. We seek no sympathy and we ask for no handout. We know solving our problems will be tough, and we reject demagogues who tell us they can be solved without breaking a sweat. We must make the sacrifices necessary to address the dire problems facing our country.

To the new generation in power, we say: If you are ready to make the tough choices, we will support you. If you are ready to fight, we will join you. If you are ready to lead, we might in fact follow you. But if not, move out of the way.

The last thing we want is a generational war. We present this statement in the sincere hope that members of our generation—whatever their politics—can together chart a new direction for the country, and that members of all generations can embrace it.

Part Three

HOW GENERATIONS CYCLE

One generation passeth away, and another generation cometh: but the earth abideth forever.

—Ecclesiastes

The excerpts in this section provide the big picture on the interactions between generations.

William Strauss and Neil Howe's *Fourth Turning* posits that there are four prototypical generations that cycle continuously throughout American history. Within each cycle (which lasts between 80 and 100 years) there are four eras, or turnings, that last between 20 and 25 years each. These historians claim that the United States is in the midst of a "Third Turning" of a cycle that began right after World War II, and will culminate in a "Fourth Turning" crisis that will shake the U.S. to its foundations between 2005 and 2025.

The oldest excerpts in this book come from the *Atlantic Monthly* in 1911. In the February and May issues, writers Cornelia A. P. Comer and Randolph S. Bourne offer a fascinating look at how middle-aged Americans and young adults viewed one another nearly 100 years ago. Clearly, little has changed, except possibly for the style of language. The generations that battled then used such exquisite turns of phrase that one can easily lament the lack of nuance in today's debate.

11

Winter Comes Again

William Strauss and Neil Howe

America feels like it's unraveling.

Though we live in an era of relative peace and comfort, we have settled into a mood of pessimism about the long-term future, fearful that our superpower nation is somehow rotting from within.

Neither an epic victory over Communism nor an extended upswing of the business cycle can buoy our public spirit. The Cold War and New Deal struggles are plainly over, but we are of no mind to bask in their successes. The America of today feels worse, in its fundamentals, than the one many of us remember from youth, a society presided over by those of supposedly lesser consciousness. Wherever we look, from L.A. to D.C., from Oklahoma City to Sun City, we see paths to a foreboding future. We yearn for civic character but satisfy ourselves with symbolic gestures and celebrity circuses. We perceive no greatness in our leaders, a new meanness in ourselves. Small wonder that each new election brings a new jolt, its aftermath a new disappointment.

Not long ago, America was more than the sum of its parts. Now, it is less. Around World War II, we were proud as a people but modest as individuals. Fewer than two people in ten said yes

From *The Fourth Turning*, by William Strauss and Neil Howe, pp. 1–7. Copyright © 1997 by William Strauss and Neil Howe. Used by permission of Broadway Books, a division of Bantam Doubleday Dell Publishing Group.

when asked, Are you a very important person? Today, more than six in ten say yes. Where we once thought ourselves collectively strong, we now regard ourselves as individually entitled.

Yet even while we exalt our own personal growth, we realize that millions of self-actualized persons don't add up to an actualized society. Popular trust in virtually every American institution—from businesses and governments to churches and newspapers—keeps falling to new lows. Public debts soar, the middle class shrinks, welfare dependencies deepen, and cultural arguments worsen by the year. We now have the highest incarceration rate and the lowest eligible-voter participation rate of any major democracy. Statistics inform us that many adverse trends (crime, divorce, abortion, scholastic aptitudes) may have bottomed out, but we're not reassured.

Optimism still attaches to self, but no longer to family or community. Most Americans express more hope for their own prospects than for their children's—or the nation's. Parents widely fear that the American Dream, which was there (solidly) for their parents and still there (barely) for them, will not be there for their kids. Young householders are reaching their mid-thirties never having known a time when America seemed to be on the right track. Middle-aged people look at their thin savings accounts and slim-to-none pensions, scoff at an illusory Social Security trust fund, and try not to dwell on what a burden their old age could become. Seniors separate into their own Leisure World, recoiling at the lost virtue of youth while trying not to think about the future.

We perceive our civic challenge as some vast, insoluble Rubik's Cube. Behind each problem lies another problem that must be solved first, and behind that lies yet another, and another, ad infinitum. To fix crime we have to fix the family, but before we do that we have to fix welfare, and that means fixing our budget, and that means fixing our civic spirit, but we can't do that without fixing moral standards, and that means fixing schools and churches, and that means fixing the inner cities, and that's impossible unless we fix crime. There's no fulcrum on which to rest a policy lever. People of all ages sense that something huge will have to sweep across America before the gloom can be lifted—but that's an awareness we suppress. As a nation, we're in deep denial.

While we grope for answers, we wonder if analysis may be crowding out our intuition. Like the anxious patient who takes seventeen kinds of medicine while poring over his own CAT scan, we find it hard to stop and ask, What is the underlying malady really about? How can we best bring the primal forces of nature to our assistance? Isn't there a choice lying somewhere between total control and total despair? Deep down, beneath the tangle of trend lines, we suspect that our history or biology or very humanity must have something simple and important to say to us. But we don't know what it is. If we once did know, we have since forgotten.

Wherever we're headed, America is evolving in ways most of us don't like or understand. Individually focused yet collectively adrift, we wonder if we're heading toward a waterfall.

Are we?

IT'S ALL HAPPENED BEFORE

The reward of the historian is to locate patterns that recur over time and to discover the natural rhythms of social experience.

In fact, at the core of modern history lies this remarkable pattern: Over the past five centuries, Anglo-American society has entered a new era—a new *turning*—every two decades or so. At the start of each turning, people change how they feel about themselves, the culture, the nation, and the future. Turnings come in cycles of four. Each cycle spans the length of a long human life, roughly eighty to one hundred years, a unit of time the ancients called the *saeculum*. Together, the four turnings of the saeculum comprise history's seasonal rhythm of growth, maturation, entropy, and destruction:

- The *First Turning* is a *High,* an upbeat era of strengthening institutions and weakening individualism, when a new civic order implants and the old values regime decays.
- The *Second Turning* is an *Awakening,* a passionate era of spiritual upheaval, when the civic order comes under attack from a new values regime.
- The *Third Turning* is an *Unraveling* a downcast era of strengthening individualism and weakening institutions, when the old civic order decays and the new values regime implants.
- The *Fourth Turning* is a *Crisis,* a decisive era of secular upheaval, when the values regime propels the replacement of the old civic order with a new one.

Each turning comes with its own identifiable mood. Always, these mood shifts catch people by surprise.

In the current saeculum, the First Turning was the *American High* of the Truman, Eisenhower, and Kennedy presidencies. As World War II wound down, no one predicted that America would soon become so confident and institutionally muscular, yet so conformist and spiritually complacent. But that's what happened.

The Second Turning was the *Consciousness Revolution* stretching from the campus revolts of the mid-1960s to the tax revolts of the early 1980s. Before John Kennedy was assassinated, no one predicted that America was about to enter an era of personal liberation and cross a cultural divide that would separate anything thought or said after from anything thought or said before. But that's what happened.

The Third Turning has been the *Culture Wars*, an era that began with Reagan's mid-1980s Morning in America and is due to expire around the middle of the Oh-Oh decade, eight or ten years from now. Amid the glitz of the early Reagan years, no one predicted that the nation was entering an era of national drift and institutional decay. But that's where we are.

Have major national mood shifts like this ever before happened? Yes—many times. Have Americans ever before experienced anything like the current attitude of Unraveling? Yes—many times, over the centuries.

People in their eighties can remember an earlier mood that was much like today's. They can recall the years between Armistice Day (1918) and the Great Crash of 1929. Euphoria over a global military triumph was painfully short-lived. Earlier optimism about a progressive future gave way to a jazz-age nihilism and a pervasive cynicism about high ideals. Bosses swaggered in immigrant ghettos, the KKK in the South, the mafia in the industrial heartland, and defenders of Americanism in myriad Middletowns. Unions atrophied, government weakened, third parties were the rage, and a dynamic marketplace ushered in new consumer technologies (autos, radios, phones, jukeboxes, vending machines) that made life feel newly complicated and frenetic. The risky pleasures of a "lost" young generation shocked middle-aged decency crusaders—many of them "tired radicals" who were then moralizing against the detritus of the "mauve decade" of their youth (the 1890s). Opinions polarized around no-compromise cultural issues like drugs, family, and "decency." Meanwhile, parents strove to protect a scoutlike new generation of children (who aged into today's senior citizens).

Back then, the details were different, but the underlying mood resembled what Americans feel today. Listen to Walter Lippmann, writing during World War I:

> We are unsettled to the very roots of our being. There isn't a human relation, whether of parent or child, husband and wife, worker and employer, that doesn't move in a strange situation. We are not used to a complicated civilization, we don't know how to behave when personal contact and eternal authority have disappeared. There are no precedents to guide us, no wisdom that was not meant for a simpler age.

Move backward again to an era recalled by the oldest Americans still alive when today's seniors were little children. In the late 1840s and early 1850s, America drifted into a foul new mood. The hugely popular Mexican War had just ended in a stirring triumph, but the huzzahs over territorial gain didn't last long. Cities grew mean and politics hateful. Immigration surged, financial speculation boomed and railroads and cotton exports released powerful new market forces that destabilized communities. Having run out of answers, the two major parties (Whigs and Democrats) were slowly disintegrating. A righteous debate over slavery's westward expansion erupted between so-called Southrons and abolitionists—many of them middle-aged spiritualists who in the more euphoric 1830s and 1840s had dabbled in Transcendentalism, utopian communes, and other assorted youth-fired crusades. Colleges went begging for students as a brazen young generation hustled west to pan for gold in towns fabled for their violence. Meanwhile, a child generation grew up with a new regimentation that startled European visitors who, a decade earlier, had bemoaned the wildness of American kids. Sound familiar?

Run the clock back the length of yet another long life, to the 1760s. The recent favorable conclusion to the French and Indian War had brought eighty years of conflict to a close and secured the colonial frontier. Yet when England tried to recoup the expense of the war through taxation, the colonies seethed with a directionless discontent. Immigration from the Old World, emigration across the Appalachians, and colonial trade arguments all rose sharply. As debtors' prisons bulged, middle-aged people complained of what

Benjamin Franklin called the "white savagery" of youth. Middle-aged orators (peers of the fiery young preachers of the circa-1740 Great Awakening) summoned civic consciousness and organized popular crusades of economic austerity. The youth elite became the first to attend disciplined church schools in the colonies rather than academies in corrupt Albion. Gradually, colonists began separating into mutually loathing camps, one defending and the other attacking the Crown. Sound familiar again?

During each of these periods, Americans celebrated an ethos of frenetic and laissez-faire individualism (a word first popularized in the 1840s) yet also fretted over social fragmentation, epidemic violence, and economic and technological change that seemed to be accelerating beyond society's ability to absorb it.

During each of these periods, Americans had recently achieved a stunning victory over a longstanding foreign threat—Imperial Germany, Imperial New Spain (alias Mexico), or Imperial New France. Yet that victory came to be associated with a worn-out definition of collective purpose—and perversely, unleashed a torrent of pessimism.

During each of these periods, an aggressive moralism darkened the debate about the country's future. Culture wars raged, the language of political discourse coarsened, nativist (and sectional) feelings hardened, immigration and substance abuse came under attack, and attitudes toward children grew more protective.

During each of these periods, Americans felt well-rooted in their personal values but newly hostile toward the corruption of civic life. Unifying institutions, which had seemed secure for decades, now felt ephemeral. Those who had once trusted the nation with their lives were growing old and dying. To the new crop of young adults, the nation hardly mattered. The whole *res publica* seemed on the verge of disintegrating.

During each of these previous Third Turnings, Americans felt as if they were drifting toward a cataclysm.

And as it turned out, they were.

The 1760s were followed by the American Revolution, the 1850s by Civil War, the 1920s by the Great Depression and World War II. All these Unraveling eras were followed by bone-jarring Crises so monumental that, by their end, American society emerged in a wholly new form.

Each time, the change came with scant warning. As late as December 1773, November 1859, and October 1929, the American people had no idea how close it was. Then sudden sparks (the Boston Tea Party, John Brown's raid and execution, Black Tuesday) transformed the public mood, swiftly and permanently. Over the next two decades or so, society convulsed, and emergencies required massive sacrifices from a citizenry that responded by putting community ahead of self. Leaders led, and people trusted them. As a new social contract was created, people overcame challenges once thought insurmountable—and used the Crisis to elevate themselves and their nation to a higher plane of civilization: In the 1790s, they triumphantly created the modern world's first democratic republic. In the late 1860s, wounded but reunited, they forged a genuine nation extending new guarantees of liberty and equality. In the late 1940s, they constructed the most Promethean superpower ever seen.

The Fourth Turning is history's great discontinuity. It ends one epoch and begins another.

History is seasonal, and winter is coming. Like nature's winter, the saecular winter can come early or late. A Fourth Turning can be long and difficult, brief but severe, or (perhaps) mild. But, like winter, it cannot be averted. It must come in its turn.

Here, in summary, is what the rhythms of modern history warn about America's future.

The next Fourth Turning is due to begin shortly after the new millennium, midway through the Oh-Oh decade. Around the year 2005, a sudden spark will catalyze a Crisis mood. Remnants of the old social order will disintegrate. Political and economic trust will implode. Real hardship will beset the land, with severe distress that could involve questions of class, race, nation, and empire. Yet this time of trouble will bring seeds of social rebirth. Americans will share a regret about recent mistakes—and a resolute new consensus about what to do. The very survival of the nation will feel at stake. Sometime before the year 2025, America will pass through a great gate in history, commensurate with the American Revolution, Civil War, and twin emergencies of the Great Depression and World War II.

The risk of catastrophe will be very high. The nation could erupt into insurrection or civil violence, crack up geographically, or succumb to authoritarian rule. If there is a war, it is likely to be one of maximum risk and effort—in other words, a *total war.* Every Fourth Turning has registered an upward ratchet in the technology of destruction, and in mankind's willingness to use it. In the Civil

War, the two capital cities would surely have incinerated each other had the means been at hand. In World War II, America invented a new technology of annihilation, which the nation swiftly put to use. This time, America will enter a Fourth Turning with the means to inflict unimaginable horrors and, perhaps, will confront adversaries who possess the same.

Yet Americans will also enter the Fourth Turning with a unique opportunity to achieve a new greatness as a people. Many despair that values that were new in the 1960s are today so entwined with social dysfunction and cultural decay that they can no longer lead anywhere positive. Through the current Unraveling era, that is probably true. But in the crucible of Crisis, that will change. As the old civic order gives way, Americans will have to craft a new one. This will require a values consensus and, to administer it, the empowerment of a strong new political regime. If all goes well, there could be a renaissance of civic trust, and more: Today's Third Turning problems—that Rubik's Cube of crime, race, money, family, culture, and ethics—will snap into a Fourth Turning solution. America's post-Crisis answers will be as organically interconnected as today's pre-Crisis questions seem hopelessly tangled. By the 2020s, America could become a society that is *good*, by today's standards, and also one that *works*.

Thus might the next Fourth Turning end in apocalypse—or glory. The nation could be ruined, its democracy destroyed, and millions of people scattered or killed. Or America could enter a new golden age, triumphantly applying shared values to improve the human condition. The rhythms of history do not reveal the outcome of the coming Crisis; all they suggest is the timing and dimension.

We cannot stop the seasons of history, but we can prepare for them. Right now, in 1997, we have eight, ten, perhaps a dozen more years to get ready. Then events will begin to take choices out of our hands. Yes, winter is coming, but our path through that winter is up to us.

History's howling storms can bring out the worst and best in a society. The next Fourth Turning could literally destroy us as a nation and people, leaving us cursed in the histories of those who endure and remember. Alternatively, it could ennoble our lives, elevate us as a community, and inspire acts of consummate heroism—deeds that will grow into mythlike legends recited by our heirs far into the future.

"There is a mysterious cycle in human events," President Franklin Roosevelt observed in the depths of the Great Depression. "To some generations much is given. Of other generations much is expected. This generation has a rendezvous with destiny." The cycle remains mysterious, but need not come as a total surprise. Though the scenario and outcome are uncertain, the schedule is set: The next Fourth Turning—America's next rendezvous with destiny—will begin in roughly ten years and end in roughly thirty.

How can we offer this prophecy with such confidence? Because it's all happened before. Many times. . . .

12

A Letter to the Rising Generation

Cornelia A. P. Comer

From the dawn of time, one generation has cried reproof and warning to the next, unheeded. "I wonder that you would still be talking. Nobody marks you," say the young. "Did you never hear of Cassandra?" the middle-aged retort.

Many of you young people of today have not heard of Cassandra, for a little Latin is no longer considered essential to your education. This, assuredly, is not your fault. You are innocent victims of a good many haphazard educational experiments. New ideas in pedagogy have run amuck for the last twenty-five years. They were introduced with much flourish of drums; they looked well on paper; they were forthwith put into practice on the helpless young. It has taken nearly a generation to illustrate their results in flesh and blood. Have they justified themselves in you?

The rising generation cannot spell, because it learned to read by the word-method; it is hampered in the use of dictionaries, because it never learned the alphabet; its English is slipshod and commonplace, because it does not know the sources and resources of its own language. Power over words cannot be had without some knowledge of the classics or much knowledge of the English Bible—but both are now quite out of fashion.

As an instance of the working-out of some of the newer edu-

From the *Atlantic Monthly* 107, no. 2 (February 1911): 145–54.

cational methods, I recall serving upon a committee to award prizes for the best essays in a certain competition where the competitors were seniors in an accredited college. In despair at the material submitted, the committee was finally forced to select as "best" the essay having the fewest grammatical errors and the smallest number of misspelled words. The one theme which showed traces of thought was positively illiterate in expression.

These deficiencies in you irritate your seniors, but the blame is theirs. Some day you will be upbraiding your instructors for withholding the simple essentials of education, and you will be training your own children differently. It is not by preference that your vocabulary lacks breadth and your speech distinction. In any case, these are minor indictments, and, when all is said, we older ones may well ask ourselves whether we find our minds such obedient, soft-footed servants of the will as to make it clear that the educational procedure of our own early days is to be endorsed without reserve.

Your seniors also find themselves irritated and depressed because modern girls are louder-voiced and more bouncing than their predecessors, and because their boy-associates are somewhat rougher and more familiar toward them than used to be thought well bred. But even these things, distasteful as they are, should not be the ground of very bitter complaint. It requires more serious charges than these to impeach the capacity and intentions of those who are soon to be in full charge of this world. Every generation has—with one important abatement—the right to fashion its own code of manners.

The final right of each generation to its own code depends upon the inner significance of those manners. When they express such alterations in the fiber of the human creature as are detrimental to the welfare of the race, then, and perhaps then only, are our criticisms completely justified.

From the generation earlier than my own, still survive gentlewomen who are like old lace and opals, gentlemen all compounded of consideration and courtliness. Their graces are not due to their length of life, but to the lights by which they have lived. They are adorable. None of us born since the Civil War approach them in respect to some fine nameless quality that gives them charm and atmosphere. Yet, if we are not less stanch and unselfish than they, I take it we also have not failed in giving the world that nourished us its due.

Is the quality of the human product really falling off? That is the humiliating question you must ask yourselves. If the suspicion which runs about the world is true, then, youngsters, as you would elegantly phrase it, it is "up to you."

One of the advantages of living long in the world is that one steadily acquires an increasingly interesting point of view. Even in middle life one begins to see for one's self the evolution of things. One gets a glimpse of the procession of events, the march of the generations. The longer an intelligent being lives, the more deeply experience convinces him that there is a pattern in the tapestry of our lives, individual as well as national and racial, at whose scope we can only guess.

Yet the things we actually see and can testify to are profoundly suggestive. I know of my own knowledge how greatly the face of life in this country has altered since my own childhood. It is neither so simple nor so fine a thing as then. And the type of men of whom every small community then had at least half a dozen, the big-brained, big-hearted, "old Roman" men, whose integrity was as unquestioned as their ability, is almost extinct. Their places are cut up and filled by smaller, less able, often much less honest men. It is not that the big men have gone to the cities—for they are not there; it is not that they left no descendants—for in more cases than I care to count, the smaller, less able, less honest men are their own sons. These latter frequently make as much money in a year as their fathers did in ten, and show less character in a lifetime than their fathers did in a year.

The causes of this are too complicated to go into here, but so far as you young people just coming on the stage are concerned, the result of this change of type in American life and American men is to make life a far harder problem. The world is itself smaller; it is harder for the individual to live by his own light. The members of the body politic are much more closely knit together in the mesh of common interest today than ever before. While political scandals, graft, and greed have always existed, there never has been a time when low standards in business and politics have so assailed the honor and integrity of the people as a whole, by tempting them, through fear of loss, to acquiesce in the dishonesty of others. If better standards are to prevail, it is you who must fight their final battles. Your wisdom, patience, and moral earnestness are going to be taxed to the breaking-point before those battles are won. Have you the muscle for that fight?

Evidence in regard to the falling-off in the human product is necessarily fragmentary and chaotic. Let us run over a few of the points your elders have observed and recorded against you.

Veteran teachers are saying that never in their experience were young people so thirstily avid of pleasure as now. "But," one urges, "it is the season when they should enjoy themselves. Young people always have—they always will." "Yes," they answer, "that is true, but this is different from anything we have ever seen in the young before. They are so keen about it—so selfish, and so hard!"

Of your chosen pleasures, some are obviously corroding to the taste; to be frank, they are vulgarizing. It is a matter of ordinary comment that the children of cultivated fathers and mothers do not, nowadays, grow up the equals of their parents in refinement and cultivation. There must, then, be strong vulgarizing elements outside the home, as well as some weakness within, so to counteract and make of little worth the gentler influences of their intimate life. How can anything avail to refine children whose taste in humor is formed by the colored supplements of the Sunday paper, as their taste in entertainment is shaped by continuous vaudeville and the moving-picture shows? These things are actually very large factors in children's lives today. How should they fail of their due influence on plastic human material? Where the parents at the formative age saw occasional performances of Booth, Barrett, Modjeska, and "Rip Van Winkle," the children go to vaudeville, and go almost constantly. While most vaudeville performances have one or two numbers that justify the proprietors' claim of harmless, wholesome amusement, the bulk of the program is almost inevitably drivel, common, stupid, or inane. It may not be actually coarse, but inanity, stupidity, and commonness are even more potent as vulgarizing influences than actual coarseness. Coarseness might repel; inanity disintegrates.

"I don't approve," your fathers and mothers say anxiously, "but I hate to keep Tom and Mary at home when all the other children are allowed to go." These parents are conscientious and energetic in looking after Tom's teeth and eyes, Mary's hair, tonsils, and nasal passages, but seem utterly unconscious that mental rickets and curvature of the soul are far more deforming than crooked teeth and adenoids.

Our ancestors spoke frequently of fortitude. That virtue was very real and very admirable to them; we use the word too little; you, not at all. The saving grace of their everyday hardships has vanished. "Even in a palace, life may be well lived." One wonders how Marcus Aurelius would have judged the moral possibilities of flats or apartment hotels? When one gets light by pushing a button, heat by turning a screw, water by touching a faucet, and food by going down in an elevator, life is so detached from the healthy exercise and discipline which used to accompany the mere process of living that one must scramble energetically to a higher plane or drop to a much lower one.

When the rising generation goes into the militia, it is, old officers tell us, "soft" and incompetent, unpleasantly affected by ants and spiders, querulous as to tents and blankets, and generally as incapable of adapting itself to the details of military life as one would expect a flat-reared generation to be. The advocates of athletics and manual training in our schools and colleges are doing their utmost to counteract the tendency to make flabby, fastidious bodies which comes from too-comfortable living; but the task is huge.

Much more ado is made over this business of training the mind and body today than ever before. From the multiplied and unproved machinery of education, it would seem that we must be far in advance of our fathers. But where are the results in improved humanity? The plain truth seems to be that the utmost which can be done for the child today is not enough to counterbalance the rapidly growing disadvantages of urban life and modern conditions. Vast increase in effort and in cost does not even enable the race to keep up with itself. Forging ahead at full speed, we are yet dropping woefully behind.

Training is not a matter of the mind and body only. More fundamental to personality than either is the education of the soul. In your up-bringing this has been profoundly neglected—and here is your cruelest loss. Of the generation of your fathers and mothers it may be generally affirmed that they received their early religious training under the old regime. Their characters were shaped by the faith of their fathers, and those characters usually remained firm and fixed, though their minds sometimes became the sport of opposing doctrines. They grew up in a world that was too hastily becoming agnostic as a result of the dazzling new discoveries of science. It was a shallow interpretation that claimed science and religion as enemies to the death. So much is clear now. But, shallow or not, such was the thought of the [eighteen-]seventies. The rising generation of that day had to face it. A great many young people then became unwilling martyrs to what they believed the logic of the new knowledge. It was through inability to enlarge their ideas of Him, to meet the newly disclosed facts about His universe, that they gave up their God. They lost their faith because imagination failed them.

The clamor and the shouting of that old war have already died away; the breach between science and religion is healed; the world shows more and more mysterious as our knowledge of it widens, and we acknowledge it to be more inexplicable without a Will behind its phenomena than with one. But that period of storm and stress had a practical result; it is incarnated in the rising generation.

In the wrack of beliefs, your parents managed to retain their ingrained principles of conduct. Not knowing what to teach you, they taught you nothing whole-heartedly. Thus you have the distinction of growing up with a spiritual training less in quantity and more diluted in quality than any "Christian" generation for nineteen hundred years. If you are agnostic-and-water, if you find nothing in the universe more stable than your own life—what wonder? Conceived in uncertainty, brought forth in misgiving—how can such a generation be nobly militant?

Before it occurred to me to analyze your deficiencies and your predicament thus, I used to look at a good many members of the rising generation and wonder helplessly what ailed them. They were amiable, attractive, lovable even, but singularly lacking in force, personality, and the power to endure. Conceptions of conduct that were the very foundations of existence to decent people even fifteen years their seniors were to them simply unintelligible. The word "unselfishness," for instance, had vanished from their vocabularies. Of altruism, they had heard. They thought it meant giving away money if you had plenty to spare. They approved of altruism, but "self-sacrifice" was literally as Sanskrit to their ears. They demanded ease; they shirked responsibility. They did not seem able to respond to the notion of duty as human nature has always managed to respond to it before.

All this was not a matter of youth. One may be undeveloped and yet show the more clearly the stuff of which one is made. It was a matter of substance, of mass. You cannot carve a statue in the round from a thin marble slab; the useful two-by-four is valueless as framing-timber for ships; you cannot make *folks* out of light-weight human material.

When these young persons adopted a philosophy, it was naive and inadequate. They talked of themselves as "socialists," but their ideas of socialism were vague. To them it was just an "ism" that was going to put the world to rights without bothering them very much to help it along. They seemed to feel that salvation would come to them by reading Whitman and G. B. S., or even the mild and uncertain Mr. H. G. Wells, and that a vague, general good-will toward man was an ample substitute for active efforts and self-sacrifice for individuals. Somebody, some day, was going to push a button, and presto! life would be soft and comfortable for everybody.

Of socialism in general I confess myself incompetent to speak. It may, or it may not, be the solution of our acutely pressing social problems. But if men are too cheap, greedy, and sordid to carry on a republic honestly, preserving that equality of opportunity which this country was founded to secure, it must be men who need reforming. The more ideal the scheme of government, the less chance it has against the inherent crookedness of human nature. In the last analysis, we are not ruled by a "government," but by our own natures objectified, molded into institutions. Rotten men make rotten government. If we are not improving the quality of the human product, our social system is bound to grow more cruel and unjust, whatever its name or form.

"But of course you believe," said one pink-checked young socialist, expounding his doctrine, "that the world will be a great deal better when everybody has a porcelain bath-tub and goes through high school. Why—why, of course, you *must* believe that!"

Dear lad, I believe nothing of the kind! You yourself have had a porcelain bath-tub from your tenderest years. You also went through high school. Yet you are markedly inferior to your old grandfather in every way—shallower, feebler, more flippant, less efficient physically and even mentally, though your work is with books, and his was with flocks and herds. Frankly, I find in you nothing essential to a man. God knows what life can make of such as you. I do not. Your brand of socialism is made up of a warm heart, a weak head, and an unwillingness to assume responsibility for yourself or anybody else—in short, a desire to shirk. These elements are unpleasantly common in young socialists of my acquaintance. I know, of course, that a very passion of pity, a Christlike tenderness, brings many to that fold, but there are more of another kind. It was one of the latter who was horrified by my suggestion that he might have to care for his parents in their old age. It would interfere too much, he said, with his conception of working out his own career!

What can one say to this? The words "character" and "duty" convey absolutely nothing to young people of this type. They have not even a fair working conception of what such words mean. Did I not dispute a whole afternoon with another young man about the necessity for character, only to learn at the end of it that he didn't know what character was. He supposed it was "something narrow and priggish—like what deacons used to be." And he, mind you, was in his twenties, and claimed, *ore rotundo*, to be a Whitmanite, a Shavian, and a socialist. Also, he was really intelligent about almost everything but life—which is the only thing it is at all needful to be intelligent about.

The *culte du moi* is one thing when it is representative, when one rhapsodizes one's self haughtily as a unit of the democratic mass, as Whitman undoubtedly did; and quite another when it is narrowly personal, a kind of glorification of the petty, personal attributes of young John Smith, used by him to conceal from himself the desirability of remodeling his own personality; but that is what young John Smith, who calls himself a Whitmanite, is making of it. I knew one of these young persons—I trust his attitude is exceptional—who refused special training for work he wanted to do on the ground that he was "repelling interference with his sacred individuality."

Twenty years ago there were faint-hearted disciples of Whitman who took him as an antidote for congenital unassertiveness. His insistence on the value of personality supplied something needed in their make-up, and they found in wearing a flannel shirt and soft tie a kind of spiritual gymnastic that strengthened the flabby muscles of their Ego. The young Whitmanites of today have no flabby muscles in their Ego.

The same temperamental qualities operate when they name themselves Shavians. Their philosophy has been set forth lucidly in a recent *Atlantic* article.* Its keynote is the liberation of the natural will, with the important modifications that the natural will must hold itself to an iron responsibility in its collisions with other wills, must not obstruct the general good of society or the evolution of the race. To the unphilosophic eye, these modifications look suspiciously like duties—the old, old duties to God and man. Why go around Robin Hood's barn to arrive at the point where our

---

*"The Philosophy of Bernard Shaw," by Archibald Henderson, in the *Atlantic* for February 1909.—The Editors.

ancestors set out? If the exercise were mentally strengthening, the detour might be justified, but the evidence of this is decidedly incomplete.

It may easily happen that the next twenty years will prove the most interesting in the history of civilization. Armageddon is always at hand in some fashion. Nice lads with the blood of the founders of our nation in your veins, pecking away at the current literature of socialism, taking out of it imperfectly understood apologies for your temperaments and calling it philosophy— where will you be if a Great Day should really dawn? What is there in your way of thought to help you play the man in any crisis? If the footmen have wearied you, how shall you run with the horsemen?

In one way or another, every generation has to fight for its life. When your turn comes, you will be tossed on the scrap-heap, shoved aside by boys of a sterner fiber and a less easy life, boys who have read less and worked more, boys who have thought to some purpose and have been willing—as you are not—to be disciplined by life.

If you point out to one of these young Whitmanshaws the fact that the Ten Commandments are concrete suggestions for so conducting life that it will interfere as little as possible with "the general good of society and the evolution of the race," and that the Golden Rule is a general principle covering the same ground, he will tell you that the Ten Commandments and the Golden Rule are bad because they are promulgated on Authority, and nobody must take things on Authority—for Mr. Shaw says so! One must find it all out for himself. If you suggest that it is possible to regard Authority as the data collected by those who have preceded him along the trail, telling him what they found out about the road, so as to save him from trouble and danger; if you maintain that it is as unscientific to reject previous discoveries in ethics as in engineering, he may be silenced, but he will not be convinced, for his revolt is not a matter of logic but of feeling. He wants to do as he pleases. He desires to be irresponsible, and he will adopt any philosophy which seems to him to hold out a justification of irresponsibility, as he will adopt any theory of social organization which promises to relieve him of a man's work in the world. I am not exaggerating the shallowness of this attitude.

All educated young people are not "intellectuals." Most of them are perfectly contented without any articulate philosophy as an apology for their inclinations. There is also a considerable body of them who are already painfully commercialized even in their school-days. On the whole, the kind of young socialist who resents the idea of having to care for his parents in their helpless age is less of a menace to society as now constituted than the kind of young individualist who boasts how much money he acquired during his college course by making loans to his classmates upon the security of their evening-clothes and watches. The latter, hard as nails and predatory, has already molded himself into a distinctly anti-social shape; the former is still amorphous, still groping. There is yet a chance that he may make a man.

I am not a philosopher. I know only so much as the man in the street may know, the rough-and-ready philosophy that is born in us all. Just so long as any system of education or any philosophy produces folks that *are* folks, wisdom is justified of her children. That system has earned the right to stand. This point is not debatable. Even the new prophets concede it. For the end of all education, the business of all living, is to make men and women. All else is vain toil. The old conditions produced them; new do not.

Certain qualities go to the making of any human being whom other human beings esteem. Certain ingredients are as necessary to a man as flour and yeast to bread, or iron and carbon to steel. You cannot make them any other way. There is a combination of steadiness of purpose, breadth of mind, kindliness, wholesome common sense, justice, perhaps a flash of humor, certainly a capacity for the task in hand, that produces a worthwhile person. The combination occurs in every rank in life. You find it as often in the kitchen as in the parlor; oftener, perhaps, in the field than in the office. The people who are so composed have spiritual length, breadth, thickness; they are people of three dimensions. Everybody feels alike about them, even you youngsters. For this saving grace I have noticed about you—you do, after all, know whom to like when types are put before you in the flesh. Never by any chance do you waste your real admiration on the one-dimension people who, like points, have "position but no magnitude," or on the two-dimension people who, like planes, "have length and breadth but no depth." You frankly don't care much for the kind of creature your own ideas would shape. You want people to be stanch, patient, able, just as much as if you were not repudiating for yourselves the attitudes which produce these things.

Force, personality, the power to endure: these our fathers had;

these you are losing. Yet life itself demands them as much as it ever did. For though we may be getting soft and losing our stamina (another word which, like "fortitude," has gone out of fashion), the essential elements of life remain unchangeable. Life is not, and is not meant to be, a cheap, easy matter, even for flat-dwellers. It is a grim, hard, desolate piece of work, shot through with all sorts of exquisite, wonderful, compensating experiences.

Consider the matter of your own existence and support that you accept with such nonchalant ease. Every child born into the world is paid for with literal blood, sweat, tears. That is the fixed price, and there are no bargain sales. Years of toil, months of care, hours of agony, go to your birth and rearing. What excuse have you, anyhow, for turning out flimsy, shallow, amusement-seeking creatures, when you think of the elements in your making? The price is paid gladly. That is your fathers' and mothers' part. Yours is, to be worth it. You have your own salvation to work out. It must be salvation, and it must be achieved by work. That is the law, and there is no other.

Our rushing, mechanical, agitated way of living tends to hide these root-facts from you. Years ago I asked a young girl, compelled for reasons of health to spend her winters away from her home, how she filled her days. "It takes a good deal of time to find out what I think about things," she answered, explaining thereby, in part, the depth in her own character as well as the shallowness in whole groups of others. In simpler days, when there was more work and less amusement, there was more time for thinking, and thinking is creative of personality. Some of it must go to the making of any creature who counts at all, as must also some actual work. Also, and you ought to know this and to be able to rejoice in it, the other great creative elements in personality are responsibility and suffering. The unshapen lump of raw human material that we are cannot take on lines of identity without the hammer, the chisel, the drill—that comparison must certainly be as old as the art of moralizing, but it has not lost its force.

Sometimes you prattle confidently of growth by "development," as though that were an affair of ease. It is only experience, the reaction of our activities on the self, which develops; and experience has immense possibilities of pain. Have you forgotten what you learned in your psychology concerning the very kernel of selfhood? "We measure ourselves by many standards. Our strength and our intelligence, our wealth and even our good luck, are things which warm our heart and make us feel ourselves a match for life. But deeper than all such things, and able to suffice unto itself without them, is the sense of the amount of effort we can put forth . . . as if it were the substantive thing which we are, and those were but the externals which we carry. . . . He who can make none is but a shadow; he who can make much is a hero."

We are, obviously, here to be made into something by life. It seizes and shapes us. The process is sometimes very pleasant, sometimes very painful. So be it. It is all in the day's work, and only the worthless will try to evade their proper share of either pain or pleasure. To seek more of the former would be bravado, as to accept less would be dishonor. The whole matter is of such a simplicity that only the suspicion of a concerted, though unconscious, attempt of an entire generation to get the pleasure without the due pain of living, would justify such a definite statement of it here.

The other day I beheld a woman whose husband earns something less than two hundred dollars a month, purchasing her season's wardrobe. Into it went one hat at fifty dollars and another at thirty dollars. Her neighbors in the flat-building admired and envied. One of the bolder wondered. "Well, I can't help it," said Mrs. Jones. "I just tell Mr. Jones life isn't worth livin' if I can't have what I want." This, you see, was her way of "liberating the natural will."

The truth is that life isn't worth livin' if you *can* have what you want—unless you happen to be the exceptional person who wants discipline, responsibility, effort, suffering.

From the thought of Mrs. Jones and her hats, I like to turn to a certain volume of memoirs, giving a picture of New England life in the first half of the nineteenth century. It is an incomparable textbook on the art of getting the most out of living. It sets forth in such concrete, vivid fashion as to kindle the most reluctant imagination, the habits and virtues of a plain-living, high-thinking, purposeful day. The delightful lady who is the subject of it found three dresses at a time an ample outfit, and six days' sewing a year sufficed for her wardrobe; but she had "a noble presence and what would have been called stately manners had they not been so gracious."* Before the age of twenty she had read "all the authors on metaphysics and ethics that were then best known," and throughout life she kept eagerly in touch with the thought of the day. This

---

*Susan I. Lesley, *Recollections of My Mother* (Boston: Houghton Mifflin Co., 1889)

did not interfere with her domestic concerns, as they did not narrow her social life. If she arose at four a.m. to sweep the parlors, calling the domestics and the family at six, it was that she might find time for reading during the morning, and for entertaining her friends in the evening, as she habitually did some three times a week. She managed a large house and a large family, and her wit, cultivation, and energy enriched life for everybody who knew her. She had "no higher aim than to light and warm the neighborhood where God had placed her." She and her sisters "had never dreamed of a life of ease, or of freedom from care, as anything to be desired. On the contrary, they gloried in responsibility . . . with all the intensity of simple and healthy natures."

That day is gone, not to return, but its informing spirit can be recaptured and applied to other conditions as a solvent. If that were done, I think the Golden Age might come again, even here and now.

No generalizations apply to all of a class. Numerically, of course, many of the rising generation are fine and competent young people, stanch, generous, right-minded, seeking to give and to get the best in life and to leave the world better than they found it. I take it, any young person who reads the *Atlantic* will have chosen this better part—but, suppose you hadn't! Suppose you discovered yourself to be one of those unfortunates herein described? Deprived of the disciplinary alphabet, multiplication-table, Latin grammar; dispossessed of the English Bible, most stimulating of literary as well as of ethical inheritances; despoiled of your birthright in the religion that made your ancestor; destitute of incentives to hardihood and physical exertion; solicited to indolence by cheap amusements, to self-conceit by cheap philosophies, to greed by cheap wealth—what, then, is left for you?

Even if your predicament were, with but relief, dire as this, you would at least have the chance to put up a wonderful fight. It would be so good a thing to win against those odds that one's blood tingles at the thought. But there are several elements which alter the position. For one, the lack of a definite religious training is not irreparable.

This is not a sermon, and it is for others to tell those how to find God who have not yet attained unto Him, but it is certain that the mature world around you with which you are just coming into definite relation is morally very much alive just now. That its moral awakening is not exactly on the lines of previous ones, does not make it less authentic or contagious. Unless you are prematurely casehardened, it is bound to affect you.

Then—you are young. It is quite within your power to surprise yourselves and discomfit the middle-aged prophets of evil who write you pages of warnings. The chance of youth is always the very greatest chance in the world, the chance of the uncharted sea, of the undiscovered land.

The idealism of the young and their plasticity in the hands of their ideals have carried this old world through evil days before now. It has always been held true that so long as you are under twenty-five, you are not irrevocably committed to your own deficiencies. I wonder if you realize that for you, first among the sons of men, that period of grace has been indefinitely extended?

The brain-specialists and the psychologists between them have given in the last ten years what seems conclusive proof of the servitude of the body to the Self; they have shown how, by use of the appropriate mechanism in our make-up, we can control to a degree even the automatisms of our bodies; they have demonstrated the absolute mastery of will over conduct. Those ancient foes, Heredity and Habit, can do very little against you, today, that you are not in a position to overcome. Since the world began, no human creatures have had the scientific assertion of this that you possess. Many wise and many righteous have longed to be assured of these matters, and have agonized through life without that certainty. Saints and sages have achieved by long prayer and fasting the graces that you, apparently, may attain by the easy process of a self-suggestion.

Coming as this psychological discovery does, in the middle of an age of unparalleled mechanical invention and discovery, it is almost—is it not?—as if the Creator of men had said, "It is time that these children of mine came to maturity. I will give them at last their full mastery over the earth and over the air and over the spirits of themselves. Let us see how they bear themselves under these gifts."

Thus, your responsibility for yourselves is such an utter responsibility as the race has never known. It is the ultimate challenge to human worth and human power. You dare not fail under it. I think the long generations of your fathers hold their breath to see if you do less with certainty than they have done with faith.

13

The Two Generations

Randolph S. Bourne

I t is always interesting to see ourselves through the eyes of others, even though that view may be most unflattering. The recent "Letter to the Rising Generation" [see chapter 12 in this book], if I may judge from the well-thumbed and underscored copy of the *Atlantic* which I picked up in the College Library, has been read with keen interest by many of my fellows, and doubtless, too, with a more emphatic approval, by our elders. The indictment of an entire generation must at its best be a difficult task, but the author of the article has performed it with considerable circumspection, skirting warily the vague and the abstract, and passing from the judge's bench to the pulpit with a facility that indicates that justice is to be tempered with mercy. The rather appalling picture which she draws of past generations holding their breath to see what my contemporaries will make of themselves suggests, too, that we are still on probation, and so before final judgment is passed, it may be pertinent to attempt, if not, from the hopeless nature of the case, a defense, at least, an extenuation of ourselves.

The writer's charge is pretty definite. It is to the effect that the rising generation in its reaction upon life and the splendid world which has been handed down to it shows a distinct softening of human fiber, spiritual, intellectual, and physical, in comparison

From the *Atlantic Monthly* 107, no. 5 (May 1911): 591–98.

with the generations which have preceded it. The most obvious retort to this is, of course, that the world in which we find ourselves is in no way of our own making so that if our reactions to it are unsatisfactory, or our rebellious attitude toward it distressing, it is at least a plausible assumption that the world itself, despite the responsible care which the passing generation bestowed upon it, may be partly to blame.

But this, after all, is only begging the question. The author herself admits that we are the victims of educational experiments, and, in any event, each generation is equally guiltless of its world. We recognize with her that the complexity of the world we face only makes more necessary our bracing up for the fray. Her charge that we are not doing this overlooks, however, certain aspects of the situation which go far to explain our seemingly deplorable qualities.

The most obvious fact which presents itself in this connection is that the rising generation has practically brought itself up. School discipline, since the abolition of corporal punishment, has become almost nominal; church discipline practically nil; and even home discipline, although retaining the forms, is but an empty shell. The modern child from the age of ten is almost his own "boss." The helplessness of the modern parent face to face with these conditions is amusing. What generation but the one to which our critic belongs could have conceived of "mothers' clubs" conducted by the public schools, in order to teach mothers how to bring up their children! The modern parent has become a sort of Parliament registering the decrees of a Grand Monarque, and occasionally protesting, though usually without effect, against a particularly drastic edict.

I do not use this assertion as a text for an indictment of the preceding generation; I am concerned, like our critic, only with results. These are a peculiarly headstrong and individualistic character among the young people, and a complete bewilderment on the part of the parents. The latter frankly do not understand their children, and their lack of understanding and of control over them means a lack of the moral guidance which, it has always been assumed, young people need until they are safely launched in the world. The two generations misunderstand each other as they never did before. This fact is a basal one to any comprehension of the situation.

Now let us see how the rising generation brings itself up. It is perfectly true that the present-day secondary education, that curious fragmentary relic of a vitally humanistic age, does not appeal to them. They will tell you frankly that they do not see any use in it. Having brought themselves up, they judge utility by their own standards, and not by those of others. Might not the fact that past generations went with avidity to their multiplication table, their Latin grammar, and their English Bible, whereas the rising generation does not, imply that the former found some intellectual sustenance in those things which the latter fails to find? The appearance of industrial education on the field, and the desperate attempts of educational theory to make the old things palatable, which fifty years ago were gulped down raw, argues, too, that there may be a grain of truth in our feeling. Only after a serious examination of our intellectual and spiritual viands should our rejection of them be attributed to a disordered condition of our stomachs.

The author's charge that the rising generation betrays an extraordinary love of pleasure is also true. The four years' period of high-school life among the children of the comfortable classes, is, instead of being a preparation for life, literally one round of social gaiety. But it is not likely that this is because former generations were less eager for pleasure, but rather because they were more rigidly repressed by parents and custom, while their energy was directed into other channels, religious, for instance. But now, with every barrier removed, we have the unique spectacle of a youthful society where there is perfectly free intercourse, an unforced social life of equals, in which there are bound to develop educative influences of profound significance. Social virtues will be learned better in such a society than they can ever be from moral precepts. An important result of this camaraderie is that the boy's and the girl's attitude toward life, their spiritual outlook, has come to be the same. The line between the two "spheres" has long disappeared in the industrial classes; it is now beginning to fade among the comfortable classes.

Our critic has not seen that this avidity for pleasure is a natural ebullition which, flaring up naturally, within a few years as naturally subsides. It goes, too, without that ennui of overstimulation; and the fact that it has been will relieve us of the rising generation from feeling that envy which invariably creeps into the tone of the passing generation when they say, "We did not go such a pace when we were young." After this period of pleasure has begun to subside, there ensues for those who have not been prematurely forced into industry, a strange longing for independence. This feeling is most striking among the girls of the rising generation, and crops up in the most unexpected places, in families in the easiest circumstances, where to the preceding generation the idea of caring to do anything except stay at home and get married, if possible, would have been inconceivable. They want somehow to feel that they are standing on their own feet. Like their brothers, they begin to chafe under the tutelage, nominal though it is, of the home. As a result, these daughters of the comfortable classes go into trained nursing, an occupation which twenty years ago was deemed hardly respectable; or study music, or do settlement work, or even public-school teaching. Of course, girls who have had to earn their own living have long done these things; the significant point is that the late rapid increase in these professions comes from those who have a comfortable niche in society all prepared for them. I do not argue that this proves any superior quality of character on the part of this generation, but it does at least fail to suggest a desire to lead lives of ignoble sloth.

The undergraduate feels this spirit, too. He often finds himself vaguely dissatisfied with what he has acquired, and yet does not quite know what else would have been better for him. He stands on the threshold of a career, with a feeling of boundless possibility, and yet often without a decided bent toward any particular thing. One could do almost anything were one given the opportunity, and yet, after all, just what shall one do? Our critic has some very hard things to say about this attitude. She attributes it to an egotistic philosophy, imperfectly absorbed. But may it not rather be the result of that absence of repression in our bringing-up, of that rigid molding which made our grandfathers what they were?

It must be remembered that we of the rising generation have to work this problem out all alone. Pastors, teachers, and parents flutter aimlessly about with their ready-made formulas, but somehow these are less efficacious than they used to be. I doubt if any generation was ever thrown quite so completely on its own resources as ours is. Through it all, the youth as well as the girl feels that he wants to count for something in life. His attitude, which seems so egotistical to his elders, is the result of this and of a certain expansive outlook, rather than any love of vainglory. He has never known what it was to be molded, and he shrinks a little perhaps from going through that process. The traditional professions have lost some of their automatic appeal. They do conventionalize, and furthermore, the youth, looking at many of their representatives, the men who "count" in the world today, may be pardoned if he feels sometimes as if he did not want to count in just that way. The youth "who would not take special training because it would interfere with his sacred individuality" is an unfair caricature of this weighing, testing attitude toward the professions. The elder generation should remember that it is no longer the charted sea that it was to our grandfathers, and be accordingly lenient with us of the rising generation.

Business, to the youth standing on the threshold of life, presents a similar dilemma. Too often it seems like a choice between the routine of a mammoth impersonal corporation, and chicanery of one kind or another, or the living by one's wits within the pale of honesty. The predatory individualist, the "hard-as-nails" specimen, does exist, of course, but we are justified in ignoring him here; for, however much his tribe may increase, it is certain that it will not be his kind, but the more spiritually sensitive, the amorphous ones of the generation, who will impress some definite character upon the age, and ultimately count for good or evil, as a social force. With these latter, it should be noted, that, although this is regarded as a mercenary age, the question of gain, to an increasingly large number, has little to do with the final decision.

The economic situation in which we find ourselves, and to which not only the free, of whom we have been speaking, but also the unfree of the rising generation are obliged to react, is perhaps the biggest factor in explaining our character. In this reaction the rising generation has a very real feeling of coming straight up against a wall of diminishing opportunity. I do not see how it can be denied that practical opportunity is less for this generation than it has been for those preceding it. The man of fifty years ago, if he was intellectually inclined, was able to get his professional training at small expense, and usually under the personal guidance of his elders; if commercially inclined, he could go into a small, settled, self-respecting business house, practically a profession in itself and a real school of character. If he had a broader outlook, there was the developing West for him, or the growing industrialism of the East. It looks, at least from this distance, as if opportunity were easy for that generation. They had the double advantage of being more circumscribed in sheer outlook and of possessing more ready opportunity at hand.

But these times have passed forever. Nowadays, professional

training is lengthy and expensive; independent business requires big capital for success; and there is no more West. It is still as true as ever that the exceptional man will always "get there," but now it is likely to be only the exceptional man, whereas formerly all the able "got there," too. The only choice for the vast majority of the young men of today is between being swallowed up in the routine of a big corporation, and experiencing the vicissitudes of a small business, which is now an uncertain, rickety affair, usually living by its wits, in the hands of men who are forced to subordinate everything to self-preservation, and in which this employee's livelihood is in constant jeopardy. The growing consciousness of this situation explains many of the peculiar characteristics of our generation.

It has a direct bearing on the question of responsibility. Is it not sound doctrine that one becomes responsible only by being made responsible for something? Now, what incentive to responsibility is produced by the industrial life of today? In the small business there is the frank struggle for gain between employer and employee, a contest of profits vs. wages, each trying to get the utmost possible out of the other. The only kind of responsibility that this can possibly breed is the responsibility for one's own subsistence. In the big business, the employee is simply a small part of a big machine; his work counts for so little that he can rarely be made to feel any intimate responsibility for it.

Then, too, our haphazard industrial system offers such magnificent opportunities to a young man to get into the wrong place. He is forced by necessity to go early, without the least training or interest, into the first thing which offers itself. The dull, specialized routine of the modern shop or office, so different from the varied work and the personal touch which created interest in the past, is the last thing on earth that will mold character or produce responsibility. When the situation with an incentive appears, however, we are as ready as any generation, I believe, to meet it.

I have seen too many young men, of the usual futile bringing-up and negligible training, drift idly about from one "job" to another, without apparent ambition, until something happened to be presented to them which had a spark of individuality about it, whereupon they faced about and threw themselves into the task with an energy that brought success and honor—I have seen too much of this not to wonder, somewhat impiously perhaps, whether this boasted character of our fathers was not rather the result of their coming into contact with the proper stimulus at the proper time, than of any tougher, grittier strain in their spiritual fiber. Those among our elders, who, deploring Socialism, insist so strenuously on the imperfections of human nature, ought not to find fault with the theory that frail humanity is under the necessity of receiving the proper stimulus before developing a good character or becoming responsible.

Nor is the rising generation any the less capable of effort when conditions call it forth. I wonder how our critic accounts for the correspondence schools which have sprung up so abundantly within the past fifteen years. They are patronized by large numbers of young men and women who have had little academic training and have gone early into industry. It is true that the students do not spend their time on the Latin grammar; they devote themselves to some kind of technical course which they have been led to believe will qualify them for a better position. But the fact that they are thus willing to devote their spare time to study certainly does not indicate a lack of effort. Rather, it is the hardest kind of effort, for it is directed toward no immediate end, and, more than that, it is superimposed on the ordinary work, which is usually quite arduous enough to fatigue the youth.

Young apprentices in any branch where there is some kind of technical or artistic appeal, such as mechanics or architecture, show an almost incredible capacity of effort, often spending, as I have seen them do, whole days over problems. I know too a young man who, appointed very young to political office, found that the law would be useful to him, and travels every evening to a nearby city to take courses. His previous career had been most inglorious, well calculated by its aimlessness to ruin any "character"; but the incentive was applied, and he proved quite capable of putting forth a surprising amount of steady effort.

Our critics are perhaps misled by the fact that these young men do not announce with a blare of trumpets that they are about to follow in the footsteps of an Edison or a Webster. It must be admitted that even such men as I have cited do still contrive to work into their time a surprising amount of pleasure. But the whole situation shows conclusively, I think, that our author has missed the point when she says that the rising generation shows a real softening of the human fiber. It is rather that we have the same reserves of ability and effort, but that from the complex nature of the economic situation these reserves are not unlocked so early or so automatically as with former generations.

The fact that our fathers did not need correspondence schools or night schools, or such things, implies either that they were not so anxious as we to count in the world, or that success was an easier matter in their day, either of which conclusions furnishes a pretty good extenuation of our own generation. We cannot but believe that our difficulties are greater in this generation; it is difficult to see that the effort we put forth to overcome these difficulties is not proportional to that increase. I am aware that to blame your surroundings when the fault lies in your own character is the one impiety which rouses the horror of present-day moral teachers. Can it not count to us for good, then, that most of us, while coming theoretically to believe that this economic situation explains so much of our trouble, yet continue to act as if our deficiencies were all our own fault?

Our critic is misled by the fact that we do not talk about unselfishness and self-sacrifice and duty, as her generation apparently used to do, into thinking that we do not know what these things mean. It is true that we do not fuss and fume about our souls, or tend our characters like a hot-house plant. This is a changing, transitional age, and our view is outward rather than inward. In an age of newspapers, free libraries, and cheap magazines, we necessarily get a broader horizon then the passing generation had. We see what is going on in the world, and we get the clash of different points of view, to an extent which was impossible to our fathers. We cannot be blamed for acquiring a suspicion of ideals, which, however powerful their appeal once was, seem singularly impotent now, or if we seek for motive forces to replace them, or for new terms in which to restate the world. We have an eagerness to understand the world in which we live that amounts almost to a passion. We want to get behind the scenes, to see how the machinery of the modern world actually works. We are curious to learn what other people are thinking, and to get at the forces that have produced their point of view. We dabble in philanthropy as much from curiosity to see how people live as from any feeling of altruism. We read all sorts of strange philosophies to get the personal testimony of men who are interpreting the world. In the last analysis we have a passion to understand why people act as they do.

We have, as a result, become impatient with the conventional explanations of the older generation. We have retained from childhood the propensity to see through things, and to tell the truth with startling frankness. This must, of course, be very disconcerting to a generation, so much of whose activity seems to consist in glossing over the unpleasant things or hiding the blemishes on the fair face of civilization. There are too many issues evaded which we would like to meet. Many of us find, sooner or later, that the world is a very different sort of place from what our carefully deodorized and idealized education would have us believe.

When we find things simply not as they are painted, is it any wonder that we turn to the new prophets rather than to the old? We are more than half confident that the elder generation does not itself really believe all the conventional ideals which it seeks to force upon us, and much of our presumption is a result of the contempt we naturally feel for such timorousness. Too many of your preachers seem to be whistling simply to keep up your courage. The plain truth is that the younger generation is acquiring a positive faith, in contact with which the nerveless negations of the elder generation feel their helplessness without knowing just what to do about it except to scold the young.

This positive aspect is particularly noticeable in the religion of the rising generation. As our critic says, the religious thinking of the preceding generation was destructive and uncertain. We are demanding a definite faith, and our spiritual center is rapidly shifting from the personal to the social in religion. Not personal salvation, but social; not our own characters, but the character of society, is our interest and concern. We feel social injustice as our fathers felt personal sin. Settlement work and socialist propaganda, things done fifty years ago only by rare and heroic souls like Kingsley, Ruskin, and Maurice, are now the commonplaces of the undergraduate.

The religion that will mean anything to the rising generation will be based on social ideals. An essay like ex-President Eliot's "Religion of the Future," which in a way synthesizes science and history and these social ideals and gives them the religious tinge which every age demands, supplies a real working religious platform to many a young man and woman of the rising generation, and an inspiration of which our elders can form no conception. Perhaps it is unfair to call this religion at all. Perhaps it is simply the scientific attitude toward the world. But I am sure that it is more than this; I am sure that it is the scientific attitude tinged with the religious that will be ours of the rising generation. We find that we cannot keep apart our religion, our knowledge, our practice, and our hopes in water-tight compartments, as our ancestors did.

We are beginning to show an incorrigible tendency to work our spiritual assimilations into one intelligible, constructive whole.

It is to this attitude rather than to a softening of fiber that I think we may lay our growing disinclination to deify sacrifice and suffering. A young chemistry student said to me the other day, "Science means that nothing must be wasted!" This idea somehow gets mixed up with human experience, and we come to believe that human life and happiness are things that must not be wasted. Might it not be that such a belief that human waste of life and happiness was foolish and unnecessary would possibly be of some avail in causing that waste to disappear? And one of the most inspiring of the prophets to the rising generation, William James, has told us that certain "moral equivalents" of these things are possible which will prevent that incurable decaying of fiber which the elder generation so anxiously fears.

Another result of this attitude is our growing belief in political machinery. We are demanding of our preachers that they reduce quality to quantity. "Stop talking about liberty and justice and love, and show us institutions, or concerted attempts to model institutions that shall be free or just or lovely," we cry. You have been trying so long to reform the world by making men "good," and with such little success, that we may be pardoned if we turn our attention to the machinery of society, and give up for a time the attempt to make the operators of that machinery strictly moral. We are disgusted with sentimentality. Indeed, the charm of Socialism to so many of the rising generation is just that scientific aspect of it, its claim of historical basis, and its very definite and concrete organization for the attainment of its ends. A philosophy which gives an illuminating interpretation of the present, and a vision of the future, with a definitely crystallized plan of action with concrete methods, however unsound it may all be, can hardly be said to appeal simply to the combination of "a weak head, a soft heart, and a desire to shirk."

Placed in such a situation as we are, and with such an attitude toward the world, we are as interested as you and the breathless generations behind you to see what destinies we shall work out for ourselves. An unpleasantly large proportion of our energy is now drained off in fighting the fetishes which you of the elder generation have passed along to us, and which, out of some curious instinct of self-preservation, you so vigorously defend. We, on the other hand, are becoming increasingly doubtful whether you believe in yourselves quite so thoroughly as you would have us think. Your words are very brave, but the tone is hollow. Your mistrust of us, and your reluctance to convey over to us any of your authority in the world, looks a little too much like the fear and dislike that doubt always feels in the presence of conviction, to be quite convincing. We believe in ourselves; and this fact, we think, is prophetic for the future. We have an indomitable feeling that we shall attain, or if not, that we shall pave the way for a generation that shall attain.

Meanwhile our constructive work is hampered by your distrust, while you blame us for our lack of accomplishment. Is this an attitude calculated to increase our responsibility and our self respect? Would it not be better in every way, more constructive and more fruitful, to help us in our aspirations and endeavors, or, failing that, at least to strive to understand just what those aspirations and endeavors are?

Part Four

Do Demographic Trends Spell Disaster?

Demographics is destiny.
—Richard Easterland

We know how many Americans are alive today. Barring some unexpected calamity, we can be reasonably sure how many Americans will be in school, in the workforce, and in retirement in 30 years, when most of the Baby Boom will be over age 65. What does that portend?

Professor Susan MacManus of the University of South Florida–Tampa lays out the specifics with her chapter from *Young v. Old*. In 2030, according to U.S. Census projections, she says there will be more Americans over age 65 than under age 18. That's quite a shift, considering that today those under 18 outnumber those over 65 by a 2:1 ratio.

Former U.S. Commerce Secretary Pete Peterson looks at these numbers and asks in *Will America Grow Up Before It Grows Old?* one of the most important questions facing our country: "How will America prepare and pay for the growing dependency of our rapidly aging population?" He also contextualizes the question by looking at the coming "age wave" in other industrialized countries. What he discovers is not heartening.

Peterson, who served on the Bipartisan Commission on Entitlement and Tax Reform, has his own plan for addressing this question. Other members of the commission offered their own, which Peterson criticized as insufficient. Looking at the same demographic evidence, Chairmen Bob Kerrey and Jack Danforth devised a plan that gained the support of only a few other members of the 32-member panel. Labor leader Richard Trumka blasted it.

To date, Congress has not passed its own long-term plan to gird Social Security and Medicare for the Baby Boom's retirement, nor has President Clinton offered one for consideration.

14

The Nation's Changing Age Profile: What Does It Mean?

Susan A. MacManus

No amount of Grecian Formula can hide the fact that the population of the United States is rapidly graying. For decades, the United States was described as a nation of the young because the number of persons under the age of 20 greatly outnumbered those older than 65. But this is no longer true. Declining birthrates and longer life expectancies have aged our population. Suddenly, everyone from car makers, soft-drink manufacturers, and TV producers to political pollsters, pundits, and candidates have become aware of the country's changing age profile, and they are working fast to target their messages to distinct age-groups.

A simple flip through the TV channels affirms that age targeting has arrived. Whether it's "Sesame Street" or "Thirtysomething" or "The Golden Girls," a program for virtually every generation flashes before the eyes of Americans on a daily basis. Age targeting is just as evident in the public sector. From city hall to the county courthouse, the local school board to the state legislature, and onto the floor of Congress, different age-groups and their advocates wield their clout to influence the taxing, spending, and regulatory decisions made by governing entities at every level. Although most of the attention has been focused on the competi-

Pages 3–25 from *Young v. Old: Generational Combat in the 21st Century* by Susan A. MacManus. Copyright © 1996 by Westview Press. Reprinted by permission of Westview Press.

tion between the age extremes—that is, the young versus the old—the real strain in the future may be in relations between the middle-aged, or working-aged, population and the dependent segments, which are both the young and the old.

Ours is now an age-conscious nation in which perceptions of a widening generation gap and even outright generational conflict prevail. Stereotypes abound and undoubtedly influence individual opinions and the actions of public policy makers. But just how true is the notion of generational differences? Do older Americans really participate more actively in politics than their younger counterparts? Do the generations differ sharply in their opinions about government, public officials, taxing, and spending? Do the generations substantially disagree on most public issues and policies? Or do some issues tend to bring them together? If so, what are they? And will all this change over the next few decades?

These are questions *Young v. Old* addresses in what I believe to be the first extensive look at the impact of age on the U.S. political landscape as it has been painted in the past and will be designed in the future. I will test a host of age stereotypes through a longitudinal look at what's happening in the nation, coupled with a close inspection of generational differences over the past decade in Florida, a state widely accepted as the bellwether for the rest of the country. I will use national and Florida data as the basis of my forecast of what to expect in the political arena in the decades ahead.

I begin with a look at the demographic trends, past and projected, that have created this new fixation on age as a major determinant of political participation and public policy.

DEMOGRAPHIC TRENDS IN THE UNITED STATES

Most of those living in colonial times never survived to reach what we now commonly define as old age—65 and older. (Sixty-five is the age at which a person gains full eligibility for Social Security benefits.) During George Washington's day, half the U.S. population was younger than 16. But things were altered drastically over the succeeding two centuries as fertility, life expectancy, and immigration patterns changed. By 1990, fewer than one in four individuals (23 percent) was younger than 16, and 12.5 percent of all Americans were 65 or older.

The nation's age profile will continue to change. The Census

FIGURE 1. Old to Outnumber the Young by 2030

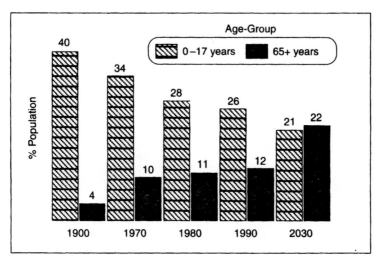

Source: U.S. Bureau of the Census. As reported in the *Tampa Tribune*, January 15, 1992, p. 3A.

Bureau predicts that by 2030, persons 65 and older will outnumber the young (see Figure 1). By 2050, more than one-fifth of the U.S. population will be 65 or older. Moreover, nearly 5 percent will be the "oldest-old," 85 years or more.[1] The median age will continue to rise well into the next century.[2]

Changes in the Median Age

In 1790, the median age of the population was roughly 16, meaning that half the population was younger than 16 and half was older. By 1990, the median age had jumped to 33. It is expected to rise to 39 by 2010 and reach 43 by 2050. It could even rise to 50 in 2050 if levels of fertility, mortality, and net migration are lower than currently projected by the Census Bureau.[3]

The Changing Age Pyramid

The nation's rapidly changing age profile can be visualized by looking at age-gender pyramids from 1905 to 2050, taken from the Census Bureau's *Sixty-Five Plus in America* report (see Figure 2).[4]

FIGURE 2. The Changing Shape of America's Age Profile: 1905–2050

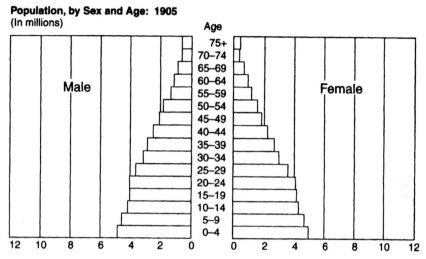

Source: U.S. Bureau of the Census, *Estimates of the Population of the United States, by Single Years of Age, Color, and Sex: 1900 to 1959,* Current Population Reports, Series P-25, No. 311, U.S. Government Printing Office, Washington, D.C., 1965.

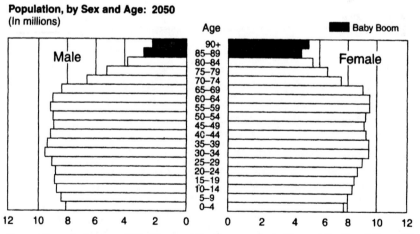

Source: Gregory Spencer, U.S. Bureau of the Census, *Projections of the Population of the United States, by Age, Sex, and Race: 1988 to 2080,* Current Population Reports, Series P-25, No. 1018, U.S. Government Printing Office, Washington, D.C., 1989 (middle series projections).

Age pyramids graphically display the relative size of successive generations, with the younger positioned beneath the older. The distribution of the population by age and gender in 1905 is often described as the classic age-sex pyramid—considerably wider at the bottom than at the top. In other words, the number of young persons greatly exceeded the number of old.

By 1945, the pyramid had begun to take on a different shape. The smaller-than-usual youth population reflected the lower birthrate of the 1920s, the Depression, and the World War II years.[5] By 1990, the age pyramid was even less steep than in 1945, and it had a middle-aged spread; the bulge represented the widely touted baby boomers, those born between 1946 and 1964. By 2050, the nation's age distribution will only slightly resemble a pyramid. All but the oldest-old age-cohorts will be nearly equal in size. (A cohort is a group of individuals born within the same time interval, usually five or ten years.)[6]

Shifting Societal Support Ratios

The nation's changing age profile has sparked concern among those representing the middle-aged portion of the population. The major source of anxiety becomes clear when we look at societal support ratios. These are the ratios of the number of youth (younger than 20) and elderly (65 and older) to every 100 persons aged 20 through 64, the principal ages for participation in the workforce. Such ratios, according to *Sixty-Five Plus in America*, are regarded as useful "indicators of potential change in the levels of economic and physical support needed" and as predictors "of the periods when we can expect the particular age distribution of the country to affect the need for distinct types of social services, housing, and consumer products."[7]

Working-aged individuals fear that they will be forced to increase their financial support of the dependent populations—the young and old—in the not too distant future. In 1990, the total support ratio (youth plus elderly in relation to the working-aged population) was about 70:100. Experts project that by 2050, the total support ratio will be 82:100.[8] This phenomenon is expected to occur across most racial and ethnic groups.

A big worry of today's younger workers is not just the projected increase in persons 65 and older but also the proportion of that increase that will be made up of those 80 years and older. This

FIGURE 3. Why the Young Have Their Doubts About Social Security

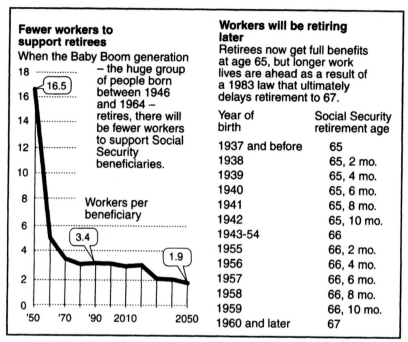

Fewer workers to support retirees

When the Baby Boom generation – the huge group of people born between 1946 and 1964 – retires, there will be fewer workers to support Social Security beneficiaries.

Workers per beneficiary

Workers will be retiring later

Retirees now get full benefits at age 65, but longer work lives are ahead as a result of a 1983 law that ultimately delays retirement to 67.

Year of birth	Social Security retirement age
1937 and before	65
1938	65, 2 mo.
1939	65, 4 mo.
1940	65, 6 mo.
1941	65, 8 mo.
1942	65, 10 mo.
1943-54	66
1955	66, 2 mo.
1956	66, 4 mo.
1957	66, 6 mo.
1958	66, 8 mo.
1959	66, 10 mo.
1960 and later	67

Source: Social Security Administration, House Ways and Means Committee. Reported in Gregory Spears, "Boomer Wave May Force Up Quitting Time," *The Tampa Tribune,* November 8, 1993. Reprinted with permission from *The Tampa Tribune.*

proportion will jump from 22 percent in 1990 to 36 percent by 2050. Because the oldest-old are the most likely to have health and disability problems and fewer economic resources, younger workers worry that the fast growth of this resource-shy but needy group will mean they will pay considerably higher taxes than their predecessors, leaving them less disposable income to support themselves and their families.

Younger workers, recognizing that they will be in their "golden years" in the coming decades, also worry about the shrinking size of the workforce relative to older individuals. Their primary concern is that the workforce will not be large enough to sustain the fiscal viability of the nation's Social Security system. By the beginning of the 1990s, there were only 3.4 workers for every retiree, down considerably from 40 in 1935.[9] There will be even fewer by the middle of the next century (see Figure 3).

Whether the focus is on median age, the shape of the age pyramid, societal support ratios, or shifts in the relative percentages of the youth and elderly populations, it is easy to see why so many prognosticators are forecasting dramatic changes in the relationships between young and old over the coming decades. From home to work to play, life will be different as these age changes, in turn, affect the relationships between men and women, racial and ethnic groups, different income and educational levels, rural and urban areas, and even one state and another.

Age Trends Create New Socioeconomic (and Ultimately Political) Realities

Aging does not affect everyone in the same way. For example, women tend to outlive men by an average of seven years. Life expectancy rates of whites exceed those of nonwhites, primarily because whites have higher incomes and better access to good medical care. The expected life spans of the more educated and affluent are longer than their poorer, less-educated counterparts. Rural areas have fewer numbers but higher proportions of older residents than metropolitan areas (as the young leave to find jobs in the cities). And the young elderly, those 65 to 74 years of age, in the Sunbelt states are younger, healthier, and wealthier than those left behind in the Snowbelt states of the Midwest and Northeast.

Even the concept of *old* is changing. "Twenty years ago, when somebody reached the age of 65, we thought they were old," says one Florida official who deals with concerns of the elderly. "Now we don't say that until they're over 80." Consider Flora Eskenazi, a 62-year-old New Yorker who divorced seventeen years ago, raised her children, enjoyed a career developing a chain of restaurants and selling real estate, and now is trying to figure out what to do for the next twenty or thirty years. "I feel like my life is just beginning," she says. One thing is sure, she adds, reflecting on her 87-year-old mother who lives alone in Miami Beach, "I don't want to live like that."[10]

At the other end of the spectrum, the young as a group are much more racially and culturally diverse than the nation's older population. This greater diversity can be traced to higher birthrates among minorities of childbearing age and the large number of youth in recent waves of immigrants, especially Hispanics and Asians. Today's teenaged females are much more likely to be single heads of households than were females from older generations. And children born in the 1980s and 1990s are more likely to be poor and experience more health problems than those born earlier. In fact, more than one-fifth of the children in the United States live in poverty. The long-term implications could be severe. As Lee Smith wrote in *Fortune* magazine: "A work force cheated of protein when it is young won't have the muscle required when it matures to keep the economy rolling."[11]

As youth become more racially and culturally diverse, so do the nation's elderly. From 1990 to 2050, the black elderly population will quadruple, and the number of Hispanic elderly will increase seven times. The combined Native American, Asian, Pacific Islander, Eskimo, and Aleut elderly group will more than triple. Unlike whites, minority elderly tend to rely more on family and neighbors for support. But because many minority households are already stretched beyond their fiscal limits, social programs in the community will become increasingly important.

Those who study the nation's changing age profile have identified many past and future consequences of the uneven aging of the nation's population.[12] Some of the most significant are discussed under the categories of home, work, and lifestyle that follow. . . .

Aging Differences and Home Life. Our traditional way of organizing ourselves into living arrangements continues to change (some would say decline). In 1940, nine in ten U.S. households were composed of married-couple families, but in 1992, only slightly more than half fit that description. This change reflects not only an increase in divorces in the postwar years but also a difference in life expectancy between men and women. At ages 65 to 69, elderly women outnumbered men five to four in 1990, but for those 85 years and older, women outnumbered men five to two. Interestingly, however, the life expectancy gap is narrowing. During the 1980s, the greatest improvements in life expectancy at age 65 were among white men.

With improved life expectancies for both men and women, middle-aged persons will increasingly find themselves "sandwiched" between their children and their aging parents. Indeed, the average American woman can expect to spend more years caring for her parents than she did caring for her children. At the same time, her own children may be slower to leave the nest than she might expect. Among never-married adults aged 18 to 24, for example, 58 percent were living with their parents in 1990, up from 48 percent in 1980. As a result, more Americans can expect to live in a three-, four-, or even five-generation household, creating real financial pressures on workers and delaying the accumulation of savings for their own retirement. Multigeneration households will also cause emotional and social stress, as Junior's rock music vies with Gramps's plea for quiet.

Given the potential for day-to-day living conflicts and their own need for independence, most elderly parents prefer not to live with their grown children. Healthier, relatively affluent elderly people are more likely to move to the Sunbelt soon after retirement, but most older citizens tend to stay where they have spent most of their adult lives. The least likely to move are the frail, the poor, and the oldest-old. If members of these groups move, it is usually to nursing homes or to be near their children. Actually, three-quarters of elderly parents live within twenty-five miles of their adult children. The vast majority—85 percent—have at least weekly contact with their grown children, and 58 percent say they see their grandchildren quite often.

Among the elderly, women generally fare worse than men. Most elderly men have a spouse to assist them, especially when their health fails, but the majority of elderly women do not. Among elderly Americans who live alone, four of five are women, and many are poor. Elderly women's poverty stems from many factors: low wages, a history of part-time jobs, lack of benefits, time taken out from the labor force to rear children or care for aging parents, age discrimination, and inequities in the Social Security system. This means that each day throughout the nation, millions of older women are asking questions such as: "If I pay the doctor, can I pay the rent?" and "Where will I go when I can't afford to stay here?" Out of necessity, older women will begin pooling resources and rooming together, not unlike the television characters in "The Golden Girls," to live more safely and inexpensively.

The vast majority of older homeowners plan to stay in their homes until the end of their lives. To do so, many will have to modify those homes to accommodate the disabilities that often come with increasing age. Only 5 to 6 percent of the elderly are in nursing homes at any given time, and most of these nursing home residents are the oldest-old (85 and older) women. Although the elderly can expect to live alone or with their families for most of their twilight years, more than half of all elderly women and one-third of all elderly men will spend time in a nursing home before they die.

Aging Differences: Work Life and Economic Status. For decades, the path to financial security in life was straightforward: go to college, get a good job, buy a house, retire with a pension. This path, which until recently applied primarily to white, middle-class males, may soon recede into history.

Although it's true that those with more education are more likely to earn higher incomes at each stage of their lives, a college diploma is no longer a one-shot proposition. Advancing technology and global market shifts demand that workers return to school periodically to update their knowledge or change their careers altogether. In addition, people who never attended college or dropped out to raise families are enrolling in classes to earn degrees or satisfy personal interests. Given these factors, it's not surprising that by 1990, 41 percent of all college students were older than 25, up from 25 percent in 1976.

But a college degree does not necessarily guarantee a good job. According to the Bureau of Labor Statistics, a fifth of those graduating from college in the 1980s ended up unemployed or working in jobs that did not require degrees. For graduates in the 1990s, that proportion may rise to 30 percent. The dismal job prospects prompted one popular Austin, Texas, restaurant, whose outdoor sign offers passing motorists a running satire of current events, to announce: "Attention 1994 graduates. Now you too can make less than our waiters." As mentioned earlier, younger workers can also expect the segment of dependent elderly to grow in the years ahead. Nearly a century ago, in 1900, there were about 7 elderly people for every 100 people of working age. As of 1990, the ratio had climbed to 20 for every 100, and by 2030, the ratio will rise to 38 per 100. As a result, some experts predict that workers will have to stay in the labor force longer, not retiring until they reach 70 or 75.

For older workers to stay on the job longer, age stereotypes will have to change. Currently, workers in their 50s and 60s often detect negative attitudes from employers about their health, productivity, and ability to learn new technology. In fact, increasing numbers of older Americans are filing age-discrimination charges with the Equal Employment Opportunity Commission. Moreover, when older workers lose their jobs, they stay unemployed longer than younger workers, suffer greater earnings losses in subsequent jobs, and are more likely to give up looking for work. And older

minority workers have higher rates of unemployment and dis-
couragement and lower earnings than do older whites.

For those who enjoy secure jobs and management positions, the
50s and early 60s can epitomize the prime of life. People in this
group, born before the postwar baby boom, often have paid off their
home mortgages and sent their children away to college or jobs, and
they still feel fit enough to play tennis or jog three times a week.
Flush with cash, they have become a key market for advertisers,
who have labeled them "well-off older people," or "woopies."
Indeed, Americans 50 and older control 70 percent of the country's
wealth, yet comprise only 25 percent of the population.

For many people, the decision to retire usually means
adjusting one's buying habits to fit a fixed income. But with good
health and grandchildren who delight in receiving gifts, retirees
often choose to continue working in some capacity. A 1987 study
found that 22 percent of older women and 24 percent of older men
continued to work in retirement, in the sense that they were
employed up to two years after first receiving Social Security
retired-worker benefits. In fact, according to a 1981 nationwide
poll by Louis Harris, about three-quarters of the labor force pre-
ferred to perform some kind of paid work after retirement. Among
workers 55 and older, 70 to 80 percent indicated an interest in part-
time work, a job that would allow a day or two a week at home,
and job sharing. These figures will grow as the population ages
and technology permits more in-home work.

For the present, however, most elderly families live on lower
annual incomes than younger families. In 1989, the median income
of families with household heads 65 and older was $22,806, which
is about two-thirds the median income of families headed by persons 25 to 54 years old ($36,058). Actually, 45 percent of elderly
households had a 1989 annual income below $15,000, and many
householders 75 or older are women without substantial survivor
or retirement benefits. Elderly income varies significantly not only
by gender but also by geographic region, marital status, and race.
Rural elderly in the southern states have the lowest median
incomes, for example. Elderly married couples are the most
affluent. Minority elderly have significantly lower incomes than
white elderly.

Of all income sources for the elderly, Social Security is the most
important, representing 79 percent of total income for poor elderly
households and approximately 36 percent for nonpoor households.

Some experts suggest that during the next thirty years, the income of Americans 65 and older may increase because of growth in pension coverage, increases in real earnings, and higher rates of labor force participation by women. Realistically, however, many older individuals will see few improvements in their economic status.

Though median income is lower for the elderly, their assets are greater. Gramps and Gram may own their home or other real estate, such as a farm, and may have accumulated substantial savings. The median net worth of household heads 65 and older was $73,471 in 1988, compared with a median net worth for all households (including elderly households) of $35,752. Of all age-groups, those 65 to 69 had the largest median net worth ($83,478). But even though the elderly as a whole have more assets than the nonelderly, many elderly households have little or nothing. In 1988, one in four elderly households had a net worth of less than $25,000, and one-seventh had a net worth below $5,000.

For the elderly, living alone carries a significant threat of lowered economic status. To wit: 24 percent of elderly people living alone are poor, compared with 14 percent of those who live with others. Those living alone in rural areas have the highest rates of poverty and near-poverty (defined as between 100 and 125 percent of the poverty threshold) compared to those in central cities and the suburbs. Furthermore, more than half of older blacks and two-fifths of older Hispanics who live alone are poor, in contrast to less than one-fifth of older whites who live alone. Despite the overall anticipated improvement in the economic status of older people, experts project that by 2020, more than two in five elderly people living alone will continue to be economically vulnerable—that is, they will have incomes below 200 percent of the poverty threshold.

Will women as a group face a rosier retirement than they do now? Certainly, they will have spent more of their adult years in the workforce. The average number of years women have served in the labor force has already risen from six years in 1900 to twenty-nine years today (or, put another way, from 13 percent of their life span to 38 percent). Additionally, more women will have worked in higher-income occupations once dominated by males, which means larger retirement incomes and better benefits.

Age Differences and Lifestyle. Never before in history have the vast majority of Americans been able to expect a third stage of life, a relatively long period of retirement after youth and working adulthood. Retirement can take various forms, but for many, it consists mainly of leisurely pursuits. As columnist William March wrote in the *Tampa Tribune*: "You pay for it with money you made while you were younger, and you try to do things you wanted to do then—travel, see your family, enjoy recreation, and have romance. Meanwhile, you hope your money and health hold out, and you hope society, still made up mostly of younger people, doesn't consider you irrelevant."[13]

Although often portrayed as sipping mint juleps at the country club after a round of golf, people 65 and older generally consume fewer goods and services than the nonelderly and spend slightly higher proportions of their budgets on essentials. For example, the elderly spent 59 percent of their 1989 consumption dollars on housing, food, and medical care, compared with only 50 percent spent by younger households on those items. The one commodity that the elderly spend more on (in actual dollars and as a percentage of total expenditures) than the nonelderly is health care and health insurance.

Quite simply, the elderly spend more on health care because they use it more. On average, an older person visits a physician eight times a year, compared with five visits annually by the general population. They are hospitalized more than three times as often, stay 50 percent longer, and use twice as many prescription drugs. Medicare pays less than half the average elderly person's total health care bill, and Medicare coverage terms require the elderly to pay part of their expenses, including a monthly premium for outpatient and physician services, a deductible for hospitalization, and the cost of all drugs.

At the same time, the elderly take better care of their health than the nonelderly. People 65 and older are less likely to smoke, be overweight, drink, or report that stress has adversely affected their health. (Their primary failing is a tendency to slack off on regular exercise.) Their moderate lifestyle no doubt reflects an effort to stave off heart disease, cancer, and stroke, the principal causes of death for three of four elderly people. Youth, by contrast, are more likely to die from accidents, violence (homicides), and cancer. Acquired immunodeficiency syndrome (AIDS) and suicide rates are also higher among the young.

Despite the fact that they spend more on health care, the elderly experience far fewer physical and mental limitations than is commonly believed. The 1990 census found than 62 percent of noninstitutionalized elderly Americans have no limitations that interfere with their daily lives. This means they manage their own homes, do paid or volunteer work, visit friends and grandchildren, and travel, among other pursuits. Of the remainder, 16 percent have a mobility limitation (they have trouble walking or moving about), and 12 percent have a self-care limitation (they cannot feed or dress themselves); only 7 percent have both.

A 1989 survey found that nearly 71 percent of elderly people living in an area with which they are quite familiar described their health, in comparison with others of their age, as excellent, very good, or good. Importantly, the perception of one's own health is directly related to income. About 26 percent of older people with incomes higher than $35,000 described their health as excellent, but only 10 percent of those with incomes below $10,000 did.[14]

Given this sense of well-being, many older persons make active and valuable contributions to their communities. A recent survey found that 4.9 million people who were 65 and older did some volunteer work for community organizations during one year.[15] "It's so satisfying to see some of these children develop," says one 73-year-old woman in El Paso, Texas, who worked with developmentally delayed preschoolers to prepare them for kindergarten. "Some come in not able to communicate at all and when they make progress, it's such a reward." More than two of every five older volunteers performed most of their work for churches and other religious organizations. On average, older volunteers worked more hours per week than did younger volunteers, and they also performed volunteer work during a greater number of weeks per year.

Activity sometimes slows down as the elderly enter the ranks of the oldest-old, those 85 and older. With increasing age, they may experience one or more of a long list of chronic ailments and debilitating conditions, such as deafness, blindness, osteoporosis, diabetes, hypertension, arthritis, incontinence, and the after-effects of stroke. The growing numbers of frail but not acutely ill elderly will give rise to new types of housing, including assisted-living centers. (Medicare does not cover chronic conditions, nor does it pay for long-term nursing care.) These numbers, plus the preference for staying in one's own community, will drive up expenditures for home health care—from $7.9 million in 1990 to an estimated $19.8 billion by the year 2020.

Gains in life expectancy have produced an unprecedented number of the oldest-old. In 1990, the Census Bureau counted more than 35,800 centenarians (people 100 and older), and four out of five of them were women. An informal measure of this group's growth comes from NBC's "Today" show, which has been airing birthday greetings to centenarians since the mid-1980s. The show now gets fifty requests a day, double the number received five years earlier. An assistant on the show who verifies the person's age before airtime notes, "We've had people who crossed the country in covered wagons."[16]

The degree to which these age-related differentials might be expected to affect public opinion and public policy varies, quite predictably, according to the relative size of various age-groups and subgroups within a particular political entity.

AGE CONCENTRATION PATTERNS: STATES, REGIONS, COUNTIES, AND CITIES

Tremendous differences in age concentrations exist across the nation's states, regions, counties, and cities. These concentrations changed significantly during the 1980s, when the U.S. population was highly mobile.

Concentrations of Older Persons

Every state experienced an increase in the number of elderly residents in the 1980s, primarily as a result of the general aging trend. However, the older populations in some states grew at a much faster pace than those in others. This variation in growth occurred for a variety of reasons, ranging from in-migration of the elderly (in the Sunbelt states), out-migration of the young (in the Farmbelt and Rustbelt states), low fertility rates, to some combination of these factors.

In an extensive look at the causes and consequences of elderly migration patterns, published in *American Demographics* magazine, Diane Crispell and William H. Frey observed that "America's elderly populations are growing in different places for different reasons."[17] The young-old (65- to 74-year-olds)—most of whom live with a spouse, are in good health, and are financially comfortable—are more likely to move than the old elderly (75 and older). During the 1980s, they moved to counties in the Sunbelt (coastal regions), the Southwest, and the Rocky Mountains. These regions were attractive not only "because of their low crime rates, unhurried and friendly atmospheres, temperate climates, and other amenities" but also because moving there often permitted retirees to be closer to their children and grandchildren. Generally, retiree movers prefer to relocate to small retirement communities, to the suburbs, and to rural areas rather than to large, densely populated cities or metropolitan areas. "We moved here because the water was pristine and the deer eat the roses in my yard every morning," says one 65-year-old who retired from a telephone company job in Houston to the Texas Hill Country town of Llano. Demographers forecast that these young-old movers of the 1980s will be more likely to stay put (or to "age in place") at their new residences for the rest of their lives. Their relative affluence makes them highly desirable residents because their spending in the local economy creates jobs and expands the tax base.

Other parts of the United States have not experienced such sharp increases in their older populations. States in the nation's heartland—those in the Farmbelt, Rustbelt, and oil patch—experienced either slow growth or a decline in their older populations during the 1980s. Crispell and Frey attributed this to the fact that "these places had struggling economies that could do little to attract or retain people," regardless of their ages.[18] In these states, the exodus of younger persons exceeded that of the elderly, leaving behind a disproportionate number of less-well-off older persons than in other states. The youth exodus explains why many midwestern states had relatively high percentages of older residents by 1990.

In that year, nine states had more than 1 million elderly residents: California, Florida, New York, Pennsylvania, Texas, Illinois, Ohio, Michigan, and New Jersey. The Census Bureau forecasts that by 2010, more than half (56 percent) of the nation's 39 million elderly will live in these same nine states plus North Carolina. From a political standpoint, the more interesting statistic is the percent of a state's population that is 65 or older. In 1990, Florida (18 percent) topped this list, followed by Pennsylvania (15 percent), Iowa (15 percent), Rhode Island (15 percent), West Virginia (15 percent), Arkansas (15 percent), South Dakota (15 percent), North Dakota (14 percent), Nebraska (14 percent), and Missouri (14 percent).

Concentrations of Younger Persons

The proportion of the U.S. population younger than 18 shrank between 1980 and 1990, from 28 percent to 26 percent, and is expected to fall to 21 percent by 2030. The states with the largest percentages of residents 17 or younger in 1991 were Utah (36 percent), Alaska (32 percent), Idaho (31 percent), New Mexico (30 percent), Wyoming (30 percent), Louisiana (29 percent), Mississippi (29 percent), Texas (29 percent), and South Dakota (28 percent).

Both the teenaged and young adult populations fell between 1980 and 1990. The number of 14- to 17-year-olds dropped 18 percent, and the number of those 18 to 24 fell 11 percent. These declines were not spread uniformly across the nation. In *American Demographics* magazine, demographer William Dunn reported that the drop was most marked in the Northeast and Midwest as families and young adults moved south in search of jobs and cheaper living costs.[19] In some areas of the South and West, the teenaged and young adult populations actually increased, not just because of in-migration from one state to another but also because of international immigration. (As previously noted, newly arrived immigrants are younger and have higher birthrates than resident Americans.)

Dunn's analysis of the 1990 census found that young adult Americans 18 to 24 years old (the youngest group of voting age) are clustered in college towns, military towns, and towns near the U.S.-Mexican border. These are places with more racially and culturally diverse populations. (Hispanic and black fertility rates exceed those of Anglos.)

The young teen population (14 to 17) is concentrated in rural and low-income areas, such as the Deep South, and there are high proportions of minorities in such areas. The largest proportion of teenagers occurs in Utah, where a high birth rate is consistent with the religious tenets of the large Mormon population. Importantly, however, Mormon teens are less likely to be poor than black and or Hispanic teens. The young teen population is smallest in high-cost tourist havens, job-poor areas of the agricultural Midwest, and urbanized and eastern states characterized by high living costs and small families.

Florida: A Bellwether State in Which to Observe Age Trends and Impacts

By 2010, California will still have the largest number of residents 65 or older, but Florida will have the largest percentage—20 percent, up from 18 percent in 1990. Three percent of Florida's population will be 85 or older by 2010, in contrast to 2 percent nationally. At the same time, Florida has a larger than average younger constituency. In recent years, the rate of in-migration among younger working-aged adults has exceeded that among persons 65 and over.[20]

Since the publication of John Naisbitt's *Megatrends* in 1982, Florida has been viewed as a "bellwether state"—a state in which social and political invention is common. By 1980, the author of *Megatrends* had already observed "growing tension between the state's older and younger residents" due to Florida's demographics. He predicted then that by about the year 1995, the entire U.S. population would soon have an age-to-youth ratio similar to Florida's. Naisbitt and other futurists have continued to argue that "by carefully watching what is happening now in Florida, we stand to learn a wealth of information about the problems and opportunities the entire nation will face in the future."[21] This is why many political and public policy analysts regard Florida as one of the best places in which to test various age-based theories about politics and public opinion, although the state's older population is somewhat younger, healthier, and wealthier than the elderly population at large.[22]

For many political analysts, Florida's older resident profile (younger, healthier, and wealthier) is seen as more of a pro than a con when studying generational political differences. Its profile is similar to that of several other Sunbelt states with fast-growing in-migrant retiree populations: Texas, California, Arizona, North Carolina, and Georgia.[23] Together, these six states contribute almost one-fourth of the total vote for president. They also have younger populations that are more racially and ethnically diverse than the nation as a whole, often as a consequence of immigration. Thus, although Florida's young and old populations are seen as slightly atypical, they are also seen as highly relevant and important politically—and a signal of what is to come in a growing number of states as the nation's population grows, ages, and diversifies.

Florida is also a good place to study generational political differences because of its cosmopolitan population and its highly competitive party makeup. It does not display the traits of its Deep South neighbor states. Nearly two-thirds (65 percent) of its 1990 residents were born in other states. Once dominated by Democrats, Florida has blossomed into a highly competitive two-party state.[24] By 1990, Democrats made up 52 percent of all registrants, Republicans 41 percent, and independents/third-party members 7 percent. The registration gap between Democrats and Republicans had narrowed even more by 1994: Democrats 49.8 percent, Republicans 41.6 percent, and independents/third-party members 8.6 percent. This party breakdown makes it possible to contrast the party affiliation trends of younger and older Floridians much more effectively than would be possible in a one-party state.

In Florida, as in most states, the youngest and oldest residents are unevenly concentrated in certain geographic areas. Historically, older residents, especially retirees moving to the state from other parts of the country, have tended to choose coastal counties in central and south Florida, which are warmer than those in the northern panhandle. The largest concentrations of younger persons, by contrast, are in the state's rural panhandle counties (which also have poorer populations and higher concentrations of minorities), in the predominantly agricultural counties in central and south Florida (which have higher concentrations of migrant workers), in the college towns (18- to 24-year-olds), and in the large and more racially and ethnically diverse urban areas (Jacksonville in Duval County, Miami in Dade County, and Tampa in Hillsborough County).

Florida's geographical age imbalances occasionally give rise to regionally based political conflict. State legislators representing districts with different age profiles tend to disagree on legislation perceived to have specific age-cohort impacts. The common belief is that Florida's older voters, like those in other states, are much more antitax and antigovernment than its younger ballot-casters. . . .

Part of the difficulty in testing such propositions is that social scientists often disagree about precise time lines used to define a generation, cohort, or life cycle. They even differ about which of these age groupings is more useful in understanding how age determines an individual's political behavior.

GENERATIONAL LABELS: AN INEXACT "SCIENCE"

Demographers, sociologists, psychologists, economists, historians, and political scientists rarely see eye to eye when it comes to defining and labeling a generation. When one considers that each of these disciplines emphasizes a different part of the human experience, one can more readily understand the inconsistency in labeling.

How Long Is a Generation?

No one agrees precisely on how many years compose a generation, primarily because birthrates, mortality rates, and social mores change. From a purely chronological perspective, a generation is defined as the average period of time from an individual's birth until the birth of that person's first child. Naturally, changing fertility and mortality rates, as well as shifts in social mores and lifestyle patterns, can alter this average period. Typically, however, time estimates of a generation have ranged from fifteen to thirty years.

Generation Has More Than Just a Temporal Meaning

In the words of one scholar, "Generations constitute an analytic entity not only because their members share a chronological coexistence but also because they are subject to common intellectual, social and political circumstances and influences."[25]

Like snowflakes, generational classifications are rarely identical (see Table 1). The purposes for which they are created and the criteria and data used to create them differ, based upon the creator's academic training.

A Historical Approach. One of the most popular recent studies, *Generations*, by William Strauss and Neil Howe, defined a generation as "a special *cohort-group* whose length approximately

TABLE 1. Three Classifications of Generations Born in the Twentieth Century

Strauss and Howe, *Generations*[a]		Torres-Gil, *The New Aging*[a]		MacManus, *Young v. Old*[b]	
Generation label	Birth years	Generation label	Birth years	Generation label	Birth years
G I	1901–1924	Swing	1900–1926	World War I	1899–1910
Silent	1925–1942	Silent	1927–1945	Depression/ World War II	1911–1926
Boom	1943–1960	Baby Boomers	1946–1964	Cold War/Sputnik	1927–1942
Thirteenth	1961–1981	Baby Bust (Boomerang)	1965–1979	Civil Rights/Vietnam/ Watergate	1943–1958
Millennial	1982–2003	Baby Boomlet (Echo)	1980–	Reagan	1959–1973

Notes   [a]The Strauss and Howe and Torres-Gil classifications include the nation's youngest generation (the under 18 nonvoters)

[b]The MacManus classification focuses exclusively on those of voting age (18 and over) as of 1991

Sources: William Strauss and Neil Howe, *Generations The History of America's Future 1584–2069* (New York: Quill, William Morrow, 1991), Fernando Torres-Gil, *The New Aging Politics and Change in America* (New York Auburn House, 1992)

matches that of a basic *phase of life* (or about twenty-two years over the last three centuries) and whose boundaries are fixed by *peer personality*" (italics added).[26]

In Strauss and Howe's scheme, each cohort-group is truly unique because "all its members—from birth on—always encounter the same national events, moods, and trends at similar ages." But all groups go through a four-phase life cycle. At each phase, a person takes on a different social role:

> *Youth* (age 0–21)—Central role: dependence (growing, learning, accepting protection and nurture, avoiding harm, acquiring values)
>
> *Rising adulthood* (age 22–43)—Central role: activity (working, starting families and livelihoods, serving institutions, testing values)
>
> *Midlife* (age 44–65)—Central role: leadership (parenting, teaching, directing institutions, using values)
>
> *Elderhood* (age 66–81)—Central role: stewardship (supervising, mentoring, channeling endowments, passing on values)

Any major event, such as social upheaval, war, or economic crisis, affects each age-group differently according to its central role in society at the time of the event.

In *Generations*, Strauss and Howe defined peer personality as "a common generational persona recognized and determined by (1) common age location; (2) common beliefs and behavior; and (3) perceived membership in a common generation."[27] Furthermore, each generation has "collective attitudes about family life, sex roles, institutions, politics, religion, lifestyle, and the future." Though Strauss and Howe saw each U.S. generation as unique, they also offered a theory that generations themselves are cyclical. In their scheme, one cycle takes about ninety years, or four generations.

1. A dominant, inner-fixated Idealist Generation. This generation grows up as increasingly indulged youths after a secular crisis; comes of age inspiring a spiritual awakening; fragments into narcissistic rising adults; cultivates principle as moralistic midlifers; and emerges as visionary elders guiding the next secular crisis. (A secular crisis occurs when society focuses on reordering the outer world of institutions and public behavior. A spiritual awakening occurs when society focuses on changing the inner world of values and private behavior.)

2. A recessive Reactive Generation. This generation grows up as underprotected and criticized youths during a spiritual awakening; matures into risk-taking, alienated, rising adults; mellows into pragmatic mid-life leaders during a secular crisis; and maintains respect, but less influence, as reclusive elders.

3. A dominant, outer-fixated Civic Generation. This generation grows up as increasingly protected youths after a spiritual awakening; comes of age overcoming a secular crisis; unites into a heroic and achieving cadre of rising adults; sustains that image while building institutions as powerful mid-lifers; and emerges as busy elders attacked by the next spiritual awakening.

4. A recessive Adaptive Generation. This generation grows up as overprotected and suffocated youths during a secular crisis; matures into risk-averse, conformist, rising adults; produces indecisive mid-life arbitrator-leaders during a spiritual awakening; and maintains influence, but less respect, as sensitive elders.[28]

The authors argued that each generation acts to correct its predecessor's excesses. In Strauss and Howe's classification scheme, the baby boomer generation (those born between 1946 and 1964) represents the idealist phase of one generational cycle; the baby boomlet generation (those born in 1980 and thereafter) is the reactive phase of the same cycle; the generation born between 1900 and the early 1920s represents the civic phase of the previous generational cycle; and the generation born between the mid-1920s and mid-1940s is the adaptive phase of a previous cycle.

The widely cited Strauss-Howe generational classification was historically based. It tracked eighteen generations through four centuries of U.S. history, beginning with the first New World colonists and ending with the "Thirteeners" born between 1961 and 1981. Relying heavily on historical archives, the authors attempted to define a generational life-cycle pattern that could be used to project the characteristics of future generations.

A Demographic Approach. Another widely cited generational classification was devised by demographer Fernando Torres-Gil in *The New Aging: Politics and Change in America.*[29] His time boundaries differed somewhat from those of Strauss and Howe. Focusing exclusively on the twentieth century, he identified five generations: (1) the "Swing" generation, born between 1900 and 1926; (2) the "Silent" generation, born between 1927 and 1945; (3) the baby boomers, born between 1946 and 1964; (4) the "Baby Bust," or "Boomerang," generation, born between 1965 and 1979; and (5) the "Baby Boomlet," or

"Baby Echo," generation, born between 1980 and the present. The Baby Echo generation consists of children of the baby boomers. Torres-Gil's classifications, largely generated from demographic or growth cycles, were devised to analyze, explain, and better understand age-group differences in terms of support for public policies affecting the elderly—now and in the future.

Torres-Gil, like Strauss and Howe, highlighted what he regarded as the major events—social, economic, political, and cultural—influencing the political outlook and behavior of three of the twentieth-century generations. For the Swing generation, the major events occurred in the 1930s and 1940s (the Depression and World War II). "This group," he said, "exhibits unique values and attitudes about government and the political process." They hold "traditional and conservative values of individualism, self-reliance, family, and patriotism, coupled with a belief that, in times of crisis, government has a responsibility to respond."[30]

The Silent generation, born in the 1930s and early 1940s but socialized throughout the 1940s and 1950s, grew up in a period of relative prosperity as the children of parents who vowed to make life easier for their kids than it was for them. Torres-Gil described this generation as "the group that is changing the definition of being old from poor and needy, to well-off and productive."[31] He also speculated that members of this generation will most likely bear the brunt of animosity from the younger generations because they are perceived to have achieved their prosperity at the expense of others. According to Torres-Gil, they are not as politically powerful and adept as their parents, those in the Swing generation. (Others disagree with this assessment.)

The boomer generation has been heavily influenced by the civil rights movement of the 1950s and 1960s, which, said Torres-Gil, "affected their view of individuals and government, making them more tolerant of differences." Watergate, Vietnam, and the Iran-Contra scandal "deepened their mistrust of government, public authority, and bureaucracies (e.g., business, labor unions)." Contrary to popular opinion, they are "far from being the liberal and radical generation painted in the '60s." According to Torres-Gil, "As a group, they share the values of their parents; they are generally patriotic and relatively moderate in their social views. . . . They tend to be more flexible politically and are more likely to act on issues and personalities rather than political parties or partisan politics."[32]

Pop Culture Classifications. In addition to the classifications assigned to them by scholars, generations sometimes pick up informal titles coined by the media or other elements in popular culture. Perhaps the most recent example is "Generation X," a label that comes from a novel of the same name by Douglas Coupland, who, in turn, borrowed the name from a British punk rock group.[33] Generation X refers to young Americans born between 1961 and 1975. These are the restless, disaffected "twentysomethings" who are trying to reconcile themselves to a United States of seemingly shrinking potential. They may express their dissent with the political system, for example, by simply not voting.[34] Whether Coupland's thesis is, in fact, true is something I investigate in *Young v. Old*.

A Political Approach. Analysts looking at variations in the political participation and policy preferences of different age-groups across time must focus on data gathered from those of voting age at the time of their analysis. Consequently, the youngest generation (not yet of voting age) is typically excluded from politically focused generational classifications. This approach was developed, defended, and popularized by political scientists Warren E. Miller, Arthur H. Miller, and Edward J. Schneider in their widely cited *American National Election Studies Data Sourcebook*.[35]

Political scientists' generational classification schemes are often different from those devised by other social scientists. Political scientists give much more weight to political events occurring at the time an age-group is politically socialized. Political socialization theories generally posit that the major events influencing a person's political being and behavior typically occur in the teens and early 20s (young adulthood).[36]

Where possible, the data presented in *Young v. Old* focus on the five age-groups (generations) of voting age in 1991, who were, in turn, eligible to vote in the 1992 presidential election. The labels given to each generation reflect what I believe to be the key political event(s) that occurred during their teens and early adulthood:

- World War I generation (born between 1899 and 1910); 81 and older in 1991
- Depression/World War II generation (born between 1911 and 1926); 65 to 80 in 1991
- Cold War/Sputnik generation (born between 1927 and 1942); 49 to 64 in 1991
- Civil Rights/Vietnam/Watergate generation (born between 1943 and 1958); 33 to 48 in 1991

- Reagan generation (born between 1959 and 1973); 18 to 32 in 1991

Although other political analysts studying age differences in political participation and policy preferences may not use these exact labels, the age breaks many use are quite similar because many of the national survey firms focusing on the opinions of the voting-age public use similar age-break categories.

Decades as Age Definers

Age-difference analyses are not limited to generational contrasts. Books, films, and pop culture today all focus on the intellectual, social, and political uniqueness of different decades—from the 1920s to the 1990s. Even an individual's passage from one decade to another is treated as a major event. A bunch of black helium balloons stuffed into the back seat of a car, for example, is a sure sign that someone is feting a person turning 40. Greeting card manufacturers, taking advantage of these perceived landmarks, target birthday cards to persons turning 21, 30, 40, 50, and 60, thus signifying that their lives will be forever different. The first example—associating a particular decade with events that permanently affect all who live through it—is a "period effect." The second example—being 21, 40, or 65, for instance—suggests that passing each milestone means one's interests and abilities change as one ages—a "maturational effect."

Different Ways to Look at Generational or Age Differences

One common thesis is that a person's opinions and political participation rates change as he or she ages. To test such a proposition, a researcher must track the same individuals over their lifetimes—in what is known as a *longitudinal approach*. This approach, also referred to as a panel study, is used to determine whether differences across age-groups reflect an aging, or maturational, effect. It is an expensive way to test age-based hypotheses because many Americans change addresses several times in their lives. The most extensive political panel study is part of the National Election Studies, conducted every two years by the Center for Political Studies at the University of Michigan.

Another common thesis suggests that today's young (or old) differ in important ways from yesterday's young (or old). This hypothesis is a little easier to test because one needs only the data from several points in time for the same age-group (or cohort), obtained by asking questions in an identical fashion. For example, to determine if today's 20-year-olds are more likely to be Democrats than were 20-year-olds in 1960, one would simply compare the percentage of 20-year-olds in 1990 who labeled themselves as Democrats with a similar figure for 1960. This is known as a time-lag approach to measuring age differences. If such differences emerge, they are attributed to a "period effect." A period effect usually means that some important political, cultural, social, or economic happening yielded diverse political outlooks and behaviors for same-aged persons at different points in time. Data from major public opinion polling firms, such as Gallup, Roper, CBS/New York Times, CNN, the University of Michigan's National Election Survey (NES), and the Florida Annual Policy Survey (FAPS), lend themselves to such an approach.

Most data reported in popular public opinion polls are also analyzed using a cross-sectional approach. One calculates political differences between young and old simply by comparing the views and participation rates of the younger voters with those of older voters at a particular point in time. Any differences between the groups that emerge are regarded as "cohort effects."

It is often quite difficult to separate out maturational, or life-cycle, effects from period and cohort effects because many participatory acts and opinions reflect a little of each.[37] In *Young v. Old*, I rely heavily on data collected in time-lag and cross-sectional modes since longitudinal panel data are rarely available. As previously noted, most public opinion firms collect data on questions of interest at a particular moment in time and rarely track the same individuals over time. Nonetheless, I often give life-cycle, or maturational, explanations for generational or age group differences that appear in cross-sectional or time-lag data because previous research has shown that certain behaviors and policy preferences change as one ages.

AGE TO BECOME A MORE WEIGHTY FACTOR

Regardless of the approach used to gauge age-group differences, it is almost impossible to state unequivocally that age alone explains political behavior. As Torres-Gil observed:

Belonging to an age cohort and identifying with a particular generation does not necessarily determine one's vote or political behavior toward another group. Taken alone, generational identity is an incomplete predictor of political view and participation. Other influences can carry greater weight, including level of education, racial and ethnic makeup, income and class status, and parents and families.[38]

However, as already noted, differences in the aging rate of groups defined by race, ethnicity, income, family status, and education certainly increase the likelihood that age will take on an equal or even greater weight in the not too distant future. I, like Torres-Gil, agree that age consciousness and age identification will intensify in the coming decades and that "the interaction of generations between and within themselves and with the political system will profoundly impact social, economic, political, and cultural institutions."

NOTES

1. Persons 65 and older are often classified into different age categories. Those 65 to 74 years of age are frequently labeled the *young-old*. Those 75 to 84 are referred to as the aged, and persons 85 and older are called the *oldest-old*. The term *frail elderly* is used to describe persons 65 and older with significant physical and cognitive health problems. These terms are primarily used for the sake of convenience and simplification, according to the U.S. Census Bureau in its report entitled *Sixty-Five Plus in America*, Current Population Reports, Series P-23, No. 178 (Washington, D.C.: U.S. Government Printing Office, August 1992). There is actually a great deal of variation in the usage of these terms by journalists and scholars.

2. For excellent overviews of age trends in the United States, see: U.S. Bureau of the Census, *Sixty-Five Plus in America*; U.S. Bureau of the Census, *Population Projections of the United States, by Age, Sex, Race, and Hispanic Origin: 1992 to 2050*, Current Population Reports, Series P-25, No. 1092 (Washington, D.C.: U.S. Government Printing Office, November 1992); and U.S. Senate Special Committee on Aging, in conjunction with the American Association of Retired Persons, *Aging America: Trends and Projections* (Washington, D.C.: U.S. Senate Special Committee on Aging, 1991).

3. In its 1992–2050 projections, the U.S. Census Bureau assumes that

age-specific fertility rates will be constant at slightly below 1990 levels for non-Hispanic whites, non-Hispanic blacks, and the non-Hispanic American Indians, Eskimos, and Aleuts. It assumes a 10 percent increase in fertility rates after the year 2000 for the Hispanic-origin and the non-Hispanic Asian and Pacific Islander populations because the share of their fertility contributed by the foreign born is expected to decrease. Convergence of the birthrates by race and origin is not assumed. Life expectancy is expected to increase slowly from 75.8 years in 1992 to 82.1 years in 2050. No race convergence is assumed. Net immigration is expected to remain constant throughout the projection at 880,000 per year (about 1,040,000 immigrants and 160,000 emigrants). This reflects the 1990 immigration law changes and current knowledge of emigration, undocumented migration, and movement to and from Puerto Rico. See: U.S. Bureau of the Census, *Population Projections of the United States, by Age, Sex, Race, and Hispanic Origin*, p. XI.

4. U.S. Bureau of the Census, *Sixty-Five Plus in America*.

5. According to the Census Bureau, "It is because of the relatively low birth rates of these years that growth in the size of the elderly population will be steady but undramatic until after 2011 when the Baby Boom begins to reach age 65"; (see U.S. Bureau of the Census, *Sixty-Five Plus in America*, p. 2–1).

6. Technically, the term *cohort* refers to persons born in the same year. The term *cohort-group* describes persons born in a limited span of consecutive years, often five or ten years. A generation is composed of different cohorts and cohort-groups and is usually given a label based upon a significant historical event that occurred during the young adult years of the group, for example, the Depression, the 1960s, and so forth. See William Strauss and Neil Howe, *Generations: The History of America's Future, 1584 to 2089* (New York: Quill William Morrow, 1961), and Fernando M. Torres-Gil, *The New Aging: Politics and Change in America* (New York: Auburn House, 1992).

7. U.S. Bureau of the Census, *Sixty-Five Plus in America*, p. 2–1.

8. The total support ratio is actually projected to decline somewhat in the 1990s and 2000s but then increase sharply by 2010, as the baby boomers reach their elder years and the number of persons of traditional working ages declines. However, some are concerned that the elderly support ratio will actually increase in the 1990s and 2000s and that the youth support ratio will dip. The common assumption is that the relative costs of supporting the elderly exceed those of supporting the young, although there have been few empirical tests of this proposition, according to Donald J. Adamcheck and Eugene A. Friedman, "Societal

Aging and Generational Dependency Relationships," *Research on Aging* 5 (September 1983), pp. 319–38. And youth advocates argue that even if this is true, society *ought* to spend far more on youth than it currently does, which would, in turn, reduce the amount that must be spent on the elderly in the long term.

9. Ken Dychtwald and Joe Flower, *Age Wave* (New York: Bantam Books, 1990).

10. Eskenazi, quoted in the *New York Times,* May 4, 1992.

11. Lee Smith, "The Tyranny of America's Old," *Fortune,* January 13, 1992.

12. U.S. Bureau of the Census, *Sixty-Five Plus in America*; Diane Crispell and William H. Frey, "American Maturity," *American Demographics* 15 (March 1993), pp. 31–42; and William Dunn, "Hanging Out with American Youth," *American Demographics* 14 (February 1992), pp. 24–35.

13. William March, "Longer Life Gives Chance to Enhance Quality of Old Age," *The Tampa Tribune,* September 29, 1992.

14. Reported in U.S. Bureau of the Census, *Sixty-Five Plus in America.*

15. Ibid.

16. Kay Mannello, quoted in Melinda Beck et al., "Attention, Willard Scott," *Newsweek,* May 4, 1992.

17. Crispell and Frey, "American Maturity," p. 32.

18. Ibid., p. 33.

19. Dunn, "Hanging Out with American Youth," pp. 24-25.

20. See James W. Button and Walter A. Rosenbaum, "Seeing Gray: School Bond Issues and the Aging in Florida," *Research on Aging* 11, no. 2 (June 1989), pp. 158–73; and Stanley K. Smith, "Population," in David A. Denslow et al., eds., *The Economy of Florida* (Gainesville: Bureau of Economic and Business Research, University of Florida, 1990), pp. 19-35.

21. John Naisbitt, *Megatrends: Ten New Directions Transforming Our Lives* (New York: Warner Books, 1982), p. 8.

22. See Walter A. Rosenbaum and James W. Button, "Is There a Gray Peril? Retirement Politics in Florida," *The Gerontologist* 29 (1989), pp. 300–306; and Charles E. Longino Jr., "From Sunbelt to Sunspots," *American Demographics* 16 (November 1994), pp. 22–31.

23. Longino, "From Sunbelt to Sunspots."

24. For good overviews of Florida's changing political environment, see Susan A. MacManus, ed., *Reapportionment and Representation in Florida: A Historical Collection* (Tampa: Intrabay Innovation Institute, University of South Florida, 1991); and Robert Huckshorn, ed., *Florida Politics* (Gainesville: University Presses of Florida, 1991).

25. Neil E. Cutler, paraphrasing Karl Mannheim, "The Problem of

Generations," in Paul K. Kecskemeti, ed., *Essays on the Sociology of Knowledge by Karl Mannheim* (London: Routledge & Paul, 1952), p. 282; see Cutler, "Aging and Generations in Politics: The Conflict of Explanations and Inference," in Allen R. Wilcox, ed., *Public Opinion and Political Attitudes* (New York: John Wiley, 1974), p. 441.

26. Strauss and Howe, *Generations*, p. 34. The authors acknowledged (p. 61) that the twenty-two-year definition is imprecise and always shifting a bit from one era to another.

27. Ibid., p. 64.

28. Ibid, p. 74.

29. Torres-Gil, *The New Aging*, pp. 12–16.

30. Ibid., pp. 13, 15.

31. Ibid., p. 15.

32. Ibid., p. 129.

33. Douglas Coupland, *Generation X* (New York: St. Martin's Press, 1991).

34. Frank Bruni, "Generation X," *The Tampa Tribune*, November 16, 1993.

35. This study lumped the voting-age population into five generations or cohorts: (1) those born before 1895, who came of voting age before or during World War I; (2) those born between 1895 and 1910, entering the electorate between the end of World War I and the Hoover-Roosevelt election of 1932; (3) those born between 1911 and 1926, who came of political age during the Roosevelt years and World War II; (4) those born between 1927 and 1942, who entered the electorate between 1948 and 1963; and (5) those born in 1943 or later, who entered the electorate no earlier than the Johnson election of 1964. See Warren E. Miller, Arthur H. Miller, and Edward I. Schneider, *American National Election Studies Data Sourcebook, 1952–1978* (Cambridge, Mass.: Harvard University Press, 1980), p. 8.

36. One popular college text on the U.S. government defined "political socialization" as "the process by which parents and others teach children about the values, beliefs, and attitudes of a political culture"; see James MacGregor Burns et al., *Government by the People*, 15th ed. (Englewood Cliffs, N.J.: Prentice-Hall, 1993), pp. 221–22. By one's early teens, political interest is fairly high and has been influenced greatly by family, school, and peers.

37. For excellent discussions of methodologies used to test these different kinds of effects, see Erdman Palmore, "When Can Age, Period, and Cohort Be Separated?" *Social Forces* 57 (September 1978), pp. 282–95; and Cutler, "Aging and Generations in Politics."

38. Torres-Gil, *The New Aging*, p. 17.

15

Will America Grow Up Before It Grows Old?

Peter G. Peterson

"A NATION OF FLORIDAS"

Been to Florida lately? You may not realize it, but you have seen the future—America's future two decades from now.

The gray wave of senior citizens that fills Florida's streets, beaches, parks, hotels, shopping malls, hospitals, Social Security offices, and senior centers is, of course, an anomaly created by our long tradition of retiring to Florida. Nearly one in five Floridians is over sixty-five—a higher share than in any other state.

But early in the next century, Florida won't be exceptional. By 2025 at the latest, the proportion of all Americans who are elderly will be the same as the proportion in Florida today.[1] America, in effect, will become a nation of Floridas—and then keep aging. By 2040, one in four Americans may be over sixty-five.

When we consider the great demographic shift that will shape the American future, we are speaking not of a mere transition but of a genuine *transformation*. As Baby Boomers become Senior Boomers, they will bring changes—economic, political, social, cultural, and ethical—that will transform American society.

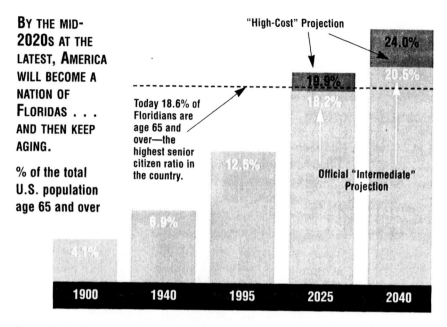

BY THE MID-2020S AT THE LATEST, AMERICA WILL BECOME A NATION OF FLORIDAS . . . AND THEN KEEP AGING.

% of the total U.S. population age 65 and over

"High-Cost" Projection

Today 18.6% of Floridians are age 65 and over—the highest senior citizen ratio in the country.

Official "Intermediate" Projection

4.1% 6.9% 12.5% 18.2% 19.9% 20.5% 24.0%

1900   1940   1995   2025   2040

Source: Census Bureau (various years) and Social Security Administration (1995).

This transformation will challenge the very core of our national psyche which has always been predicated on fresh beginnings, childlike optimism, and aspiring new generations. How we cope with the cultural dimensions of this challenge I will leave to others—to sociologists, political scientists, historians, and philosophers. I am none of these. I am a businessman who has long participated in public debates over the political economy of rising living standards. What concerns me most about America's coming demographic transformation is simply this: On our present course, we can't afford it. To avoid steep economic decline, we must forsake our consumption and deficit habits and once again reshape ourselves as a savings-and-investment society.

Today's political struggle to balance our federal budget may seem daunting, but it is only a gentle warm-up for the marathon we must run over the next half century as we confront the $17 trillion in unfunded entitlement benefits that have been promised to federal beneficiaries above and beyond the value of their tax contributions.[2] To put the number in perspective, this $17 trillion liability is *five times* greater than the official public debt and *seven times* greater than the total current assets of the federal government.

BY NORMAL ACCOUNTING STANDARDS, THE FEDERAL GOVERNMENT IS DROWNING IN A SEA OF RED INK.

Total assets and liabilities of the federal government, at end of FY 1995, in trillions of dollars

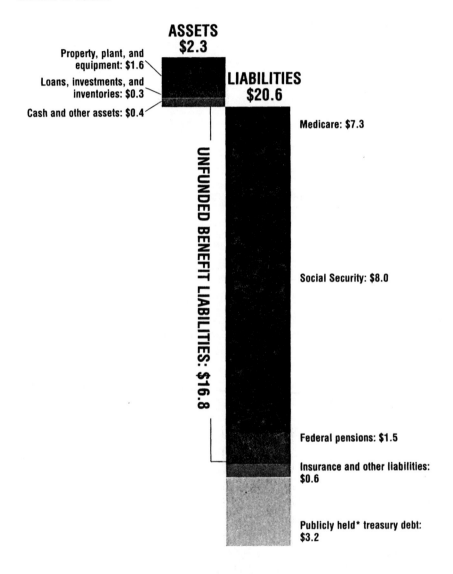

ASSETS
$2.3

Property, plant, and equipment: $1.6
Loans, investments, and inventories: $0.3
Cash and other assets: $0.4

LIABILITIES
$20.6

UNFUNDED BENEFIT LIABILITIES: $16.8

Medicare: $7.3

Social Security: $8.0

Federal pensions: $1.5

Insurance and other liabilities: $0.6

Publicly held* treasury debt: $3.2

Source: Office of Management and Budget (1996); Social Security Administration (1996); A. Haeworth Robertson, *Social Security: What Every Taxpayer Should Know* (1992); and author's calculations.
*Excludes debt held by the Federal Reserve system.

To provide for the largest generation of seniors in history while simultaneously investing in education and opportunity for the youth of the twenty-first century, we must reject the prevailing entitlement ethic and return to what I shall call our endowment ethic, which generated America's high savings, rapid economic growth, and rising living standards in the past. "Endowment" implies stewardship—the acceptance of responsibility for the future of an institution. But given our current emphasis on individual self-fulfillment, we must emphasize that in addition to endowing the future of our nation and its institutions, we must now endow our individual futures and those of our children, because no one else is going to do it for us. What I am talking about is "self-endowment."

But before any of this can happen, the challenge of our aging population must become central to the political dialogue. Americans must discuss it, debate it, confront it, and prepare for it. Only then can we avoid not only our impossible financial future but also the prospect of "generational warfare" between working-age taxpayers and the exploding number of retirees whom they will be asked to support.

So far, we have failed to face up. We are a nation in denial, one of whose classic symptoms is exaggerating the pain required by the cure. The historian Livy said of his fellow Romans, "We can bear neither our ills nor their cures." Coping with the economic effects of an aging population calls for major policy changes that will affect all of us, but these changes need not mean unbearable sacrifice for ourselves and our families. Yes, middle- and upper-income elders must forgo part of their federal benefits, but benefits to low-income elders need not be cut; indeed, in the plan I shall propose, they could even be raised. Yes, most working Americans will have to save a few percent more of their income, but in return they will enjoy a secure old age. It's not pleasant to acknowledge that a generational chain letter has run its course—and that we'll now have to start paying our own way—but such an admission will only foreshadow hardship and crisis if we fail to act soon.

Let me be clear: Having just passed my seventieth birthday, I am thrilled by what modern science has done to extend longevity. I am also delighted that in recent years we have pioneered new and active retirement lifestyles for seniors. But to maintain anything approximating today's opportunities for seniors in the future—*and to do so without doing a massive injustice to younger people*—we must make major changes in a system of public entitlements that now passes out huge windfalls regardless of need and, at the same time, substantially increase our meager level of private savings.

"Hope I die before I get old," sang the rock group The Who in their classic sixties anthem "My Generation." That statement, like so many slogans of the Baby Boomers' Peter Pan culture, was wishful thinking. The generation that once warned, "Don't trust anyone over thirty," is now beginning to pass fifty!

The real question is: Will America grow up before it grows old? Will we make the needed transformation early, purposefully, and humanely—or procrastinate until delay exacts a huge price from those least able to afford it and confronts us with an economic and political crisis to which there is no longer a win-win solution?

DEMOGRAPHICS IS DESTINY

A demographic time bomb is now ticking, set to go off in 2008, when the first Baby Boomers turn sixty-two and start to collect Social Security. As the huge generation of Baby Boomers whose parents brought them into the world with such optimism begins to retire, they will expect the munificent array of entitlements that our government guaranteed (again with so much optimism) to every retiring American without anticipating the ever-growing length of retirement due to rising life expectancy or the ever-rising expectations of independence, affluence, health, and comfort in retirement. But consider who is expected to pay for this late-in-life consumption: the relatively small "bust" generation in whose productive capacity we have largely failed to invest. Neither the founders of Social Security sixty years ago nor the founders of Medicare thirty years ago imagined America's demographic shape as it will unfold over the next several decades.[3]

Ponder the following:

- With seventy-six million members, the Baby Boom generation, born from 1946 to 1964, is more than 50 percent larger than my so-called fortunate generation, born between the mid-1920s and mid-1940s. To get some idea of how much the number of seniors will grow by the time the youngest Baby Boomers are in their seventies, think of the entire population of California today plus that of all the New England states combined. Or think of it this way: By the year 2040, the number of seniors will be at least double what it is today.

- In 1900, only one in twenty-five Americans was over sixty-five. The vast majority were completely self-supporting or supported by their families. By 2040, between one out of every five and one out of every four Americans will be over sixty-five, the vast majority supported to some degree by government.
- In 1960, 5.1 taxpaying workers supported each Social Security beneficiary. Today, there are 3.3. By 2040, there will be no more than 2—and perhaps as few as 1.6. In effect, every young working couple, in addition to their other tax burdens, will have to pay the Social Security and Medicare benefits of at least one unknown retired "relative. "
- The number of "young old," aged sixty-five to sixty-nine, is projected to double over the next half century, but the number of "old old," aged eighty-five and over, is projected to triple or quadruple, adding the equivalent of an entire New York City of over-eighty-five-year-olds to the population. Two-thirds of these old old will be women, and among these women, over four-fifths will be single, divorced, or widowed, the groups most likely to need extensive government assistance.
- In 1970, children under five outnumbered Americans aged eighty-five and over by twelve to one. By 2040, the number of old old will about equal the number of preschoolers, according to some forecasts. In 1970, there were just 1.4 million old-old Americans; by 2040, there could be 14.4 million—*ten* times as many.
- The extraordinary growth of the old-old population will add especially to federal health costs. This is because the average annual medical-care bill rises along a steep curve for older age groups. For hospital care, the ratio of public benefit spending on the old old relative to spending on the young old is 2 to 1; for nursing home care, it is over 20 to 1.[4] In other words, longer life spans add to health costs at an exponential, not just a linear, rate.
- In 2030, only about 15 percent of elderly Americans will be non-white. But about 25 percent of younger Americans will be non-white. This creates a potentially explosive situation

WHILE THE NUMBER OF WORKING-AGE ADULTS WILL GROW SLOWLY, THE NUMBER OF ELDERLY WILL SKYROCKET. BY 2040 THERE WILL BE ROUGHLY 40 MILLION MORE SENIOR CITIZENS THAN TODAY.

% growth in the population from 1995 to 2040, by age group

Age 65 and over

+129%
"High-Cost" Projection

+112%
Official "Intermediate" Projection

Age 20–64
+24%

Under age 20
+5%

Source: Social Security Administration (1995).

in which the largely white senior Boomers will increasingly depend on overtaxed minority workers.

- To provide the same average number of years of retirement benefits in 2030 that were contemplated when Social Security was originally set up in the 1930s, the retirement age would have to be raised from sixty-five to seventy-four. But this projection—daunting as it is—assumes that future gains in longevity will slow as average life expectancy approaches the supposed "natural limit" to the human life span. Many experts now question whether such a limit really exists. Summing up recent research at the National Institute on Aging, demographer James Vaupel goes so far as to suggest that we are now on the threshold of "a new paradigm of aging" in which *average* life expectancy could reach one hundred or more.[5]

Of course, the United States is not the only country facing an age wave. Indeed, the age waves in most European countries and Japan are approaching faster than ours and—at least to judge by official projections—will have an even worse impact on their public budgets and national economies.[6]

THERE WILL BE MANY FEWER WORKERS TO SUPPORT EACH SOCIAL SECURITY BENEFICIARY.

Covered workers per Social Security beneficiary

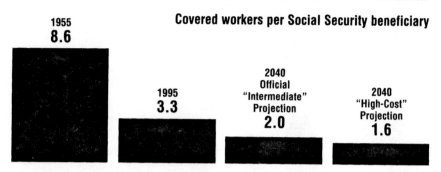

Source: Social Security Administration (1995).

I used to believe that most other industrial countries enjoy long-term defenses that we lack and that the prognosis for reform was much more favorable. Unlike the United States, it seemed to me, most can actually "budget" their public spending on health care and so have much greater control over this potentially explosive dimension of senior dependency. Unlike the United States, most generally tax public benefits as they do any other income. And unlike the United States, most have fairly healthy household savings rates (generally well over 10 percent of disposable income, versus about 5 percent here) and so can absorb public-sector deficits much better than we can.

And as for AARP-type senior lobbying, it is far less formidable in Europe. I was also under the impression that other countries, facing similar demographics, were much more proactive in solving the aging problem. Australia has made employer pensions mandatory, boosting coverage from under 40 to nearly 90 percent of the workforce. Iceland has means-tested its social insurance system. Germany has enacted—and France, Sweden, Italy, and the United Kingdom are debating—increases in the retirement age.

But having recently attended conferences in Europe and elsewhere on the *global* fiscal issues associated with aging, and having spent time discussing these matters with European leaders from Italy, France, Germany, and the U.K., I am no longer convinced the Europeans are in any better overall shape than we are.

Europe's problems manifest in different forms, to be sure. But they too have over-promised and under-funded entitlement pro-

AMERICA MAY EVENTUALLY HAVE AS MANY "OLD OLD" AGED 85 AND OVER AS PRESCHOOLERS UNDER AGE 5.

Millions of people, by age group

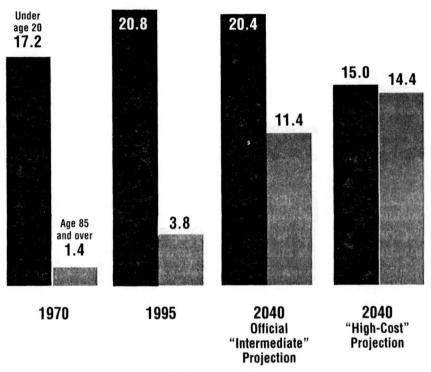

1970	**1995**	**2040** Official "Intermediate" Projection	**2040** "High-Cost" Projection

Source. Social Security Administration (1995).

grams on a massive scale. Indeed, as European experts quickly acknowledge, the unfunded liabilities of retirement programs in most European countries are significantly greater as a proportion of GDP than ours.* Several countries also face annual government deficits considerably larger than ours, such as Italy's at 7.5 percent of GDP, compared to "only" 2 percent in Washington. What's more, if we think our politicians are spineless in facing up to the aging problem,

---

*A 1996 World Bank study, *Global Capital Supply and Demand: Is There Enough to Go Around?* documents the "unsustainability of current Social Security policies." It reports that the present value of unfunded pension liabilities in major European countries ranges from 150 to 250 percent of GDP. "This means that the implicit social security debt is a multiple of an already large explicit public debt which . . . averages more than 70 percent of GDP in industrial countries, up from 40 percent just fifteen years ago."

Europe's coalition governments, fragile and shaky as they often are, are even less likely or able to take on tough long-term reforms.

Europe may lack a powerful counterpart to AARP, but its labor unions are far more powerful than American unions and extremely vociferous when it comes to the defense of entitlements. Thus, when the French government tried to bring a small measure of fiscal rectitude to that country's social security scheme in 1995, Paris was brought to a standstill with strikes and demonstrations.

At a recent conference in Italy, I heard Italian policy makers warn of an extremely bleak outlook based on zero (and perhaps negative) population growth, a "pension deficit" that already accounts for half the country's massive budget deficit and is growing worse by the day, and a public mentality accustomed and acculturated to extraordinary government generosity.

And Italy is not alone. These problems pervade European governments.

The issue of whose situation is worse—Europe's or America's —is obviously a pointless debate. The real point is that all over the industrial world, the demographics and political economy of aging are becoming Public Policy Issue Number One. This set of issues is on its way to becoming the transcendent domestic agenda throughout the developed world.

Japan's case is somewhat different. Although the aging society is a major issue in Japan, too (indeed, owing to Japan's unique demography the age wave hits in full force there much sooner than elsewhere), the Japanese are somewhat better equipped to handle the challenge. Their savings rates are not just high, but the highest in the developed world. And while one should not minimize the problem of creeping entitlement spending in Japan, they have never quite embraced the European or American lust for entitling everyone without regard to funding.

Most important, unlike Americans, the Japanese are unencumbered by the illusion that their people are entitled to live the last third of their adult lives in subsidized leisure: What government gives can also be taken back if such savings are deemed to be in the public's long-term interest. In 1986, when Japan enacted a major reduction in pension benefits, the Ministry of Health and Welfare issued a concise justification that cited "equity between the generations." Few if any objections were heard in a society where most of the elderly at all income levels live with their extended families. In a statement issued the day he assumed office, Japan's new

Prime Minister, Ryutaro Hashimoto, referred to the "imminent arrival of our Aging Society" as a priority imperative. Citing much greater life expectancy and a much reduced fertility rate, he went on to tell the Diet that Japan would have to "overhaul those social arrangements premised upon a life span of two score and ten to suit our new expected life span of fourscore."[7] Do we recall any American President ever making such a statement at *any* point in his term, let alone in the equivalent of an inaugural address?

Outside Europe, many developing countries are beginning to follow Japan's "Asian" model. Even many developing countries, with populations still much younger than our own, are preparing for their demographic future with astonishing resolution. In South Korea, where the household savings rate runs at about 35 percent, companies routinely flaunt such shop-floor banners as WORKING TO MAKE A BETTER LIFE FOR THE NEXT GENERATION. In Singapore, workers' account balances in the Central Provident Fund—Singapore's mandatory pension savings system—now total nearly three quarters of GDP. In Chile, the average worker owns $21,000 worth of assets in the fifteen-year-old national funded retirement system— a sum about four times the average annual Chilean wage. Argentina, Peru, and Colombia are following Chile's lead and setting up funded systems of their own. Here, nothing has been saved in any national retirement system for workers to own.

NOTES

1. This book is filled with demographic projections. With a few exceptions, the projections I use are the 1995 "Social Security Area Population Projections" prepared by the Office of the Actuary of the Social Security Administration (SSA). The basic numbers are published in the *1995 Annual Report of the Board of Trustees of the Federal Old-Age and Survivors Insurance and Disability Insurance Trust Funds*; some of the more detailed numbers are drawn from unpublished data supplied by the Office of the Actuary. As a rule, the numbers I cite refer to SSA's "intermediate" scenario, the benchmark used by most demographers, economists, and policymakers. This is a fiscally optimistic scenario that assumes modest gains in longevity, buoyant fertility rates, and high levels of net immigration. To give an idea of what our demographic future will look like if this "optimism" proves unfounded, I occasionally cite SSA's more prudent "high-cost" scenario.

2. This number is the combined unfunded benefit liability (at the end of fiscal year 1995) of the four major entitlement programs for which figures are available: civil service and military pensions, Social Security, and Medicare. The figures for federal pensions (a total of $1.5 trillion) are published in the *Budget of the United States Government: FY 1996*. The figure for Social Security ($8 trillion) was supplied by the SSA's Office of the Actuary; the figure for Medicare ($7.3 trillion) is based on calculations in A. Haeworth Robertson, *Social Security: What Every Taxpayer Should Know* (Retirement Policy Institute, 1992). These numbers do not offset liabilities by current trust-fund "assets," since such intragovernmental obligations do not represent true funding. If we counted them as assets to individual benefit programs we would have to turn around and count them as liabilities to the Treasury. The net effect on the federal government's balance sheet would be zero.

3. The demographic projections that follow come from the Social Security Administration's Office of the Actuary. (See note 1 above.) The one exception is for population by race, where I have used Census Bureau projections (SSA does not project race). See *Population Projections of the United States, by Age, Sex, and Hispanic Origin: 1993 to 2050*, Current Population Reports, series P25, no. 1104 (Bureau of the Census, 1993).

4. These figures are calculated by actuaries at the Health Care Financing Administration, which administers Medicare and Medicaid. See Daniel Waldo et al., "Health Expenditures by Age Group, 1977 and 1987," *Health Care Financing Review* (Summer 1989).

5. Cited in "New Views on Life Spans Alter Forecasts on Elderly," *The New York Times* (November 16, 1992).

6. My discussion of foreign retirement systems draws on numerous articles and studies, but especially the superb 1994 World Bank report *Averting the Old Age Crisis: Policies to Protect the Old and Promote Growth*.

7. For the 1986 communique, see Peter G. Peterson and Neil Howe, *On Borrowed Time: How the Growth in Entitlement Spending Threatens America's Future* (Institute for Contemporary Studies, 1988), pp. 21–23. The remarks of Prime Minister Hashimoto are quoted in two January 1996 press releases obtained from the Japan Information Center.

16

Bipartisan Commission on Entitlement and Tax Reform: Planning for the Future

Sen. J. Robert Kerrey and Sen. John C. Danforth

The following principles guided the development of the Kerrey-Danforth approach: Section 1 begins with a rationale for action; Sections 2 through 6 present the specific reform proposals; and Section 7 reaffirms the need to act now to address one of the most important fiscal issues facing this country.

1. We must plan for the future by addressing and solving our long-term fiscal problem head on.
2. We must lead by example—Congress cannot be exempt.
3. We must plan for the aging of America's population.
4. We must address rising health care costs by emphasizing market incentives and personal responsibility.
5. We must fulfill our promises to today's retirees and ensure the long-term solvency of Social Security. We do this by reducing the payroll taxes of today's younger workers in exchange for a revised long-term contract.
6. We must design a solution that is fair to all Americans.
7. We must act now to give people time to plan for the future and to avoid significant future revenue increases or benefit reductions.

From *Bipartisan Commission on Entitlement and Tax Reform: Final Report to the President,* January 1995 (Washington, D.C.), pp. 7–35.

1. WE MUST PLAN FOR THE FUTURE BY ADDRESSING AND SOLVING OUR LONG-TERM FISCAL PROBLEM HEAD ON.

The Commission's Interim Report graphically displays the need to address our future fiscal imbalance. The conclusion of the Report is clear and inescapable: If we do not plan for the future, entitlement spending promises will exceed financial resources in the next century. The current spending trend is unsustainable.

The problem, however, is not simply one of numbers. In addition to demographic problems created by the aging of America's population, we are also faced with human problems caused by the increasing inadequacy of Federal health care and retirement programs.

The American people expect their elected officials to plan for the Nation's future as they plan for their own future and that of their children. Recognizing and admitting our long-term fiscal problem is the first step toward addressing it. The effects of any problem-solving approach must be weighed against the effects of inaction. If we fail to act, we have made a choice that threatens the economic future of our children and our Nation.

—By 2012, unless appropriate policy changes are made in the interim, projected outlays for entitlements and interest on the national debt will consume all tax revenues collected by the Federal government.

—The supply of savings available for private investment, "net national savings," has dropped from more than 8 percent of the economy to less than 2 percent today. This decrease restricts American productivity and growth.

—By 2030, unless appropriate policy changes are made in the interim, projected spending for Medicare, Medicaid, Social Security, and Federal employee retirement programs alone will consume all tax revenues collected by the Federal government. If all other Federal programs (except interest on the national debt) grow no faster than the economy, total Federal outlays would exceed 37 percent of the economy. Today, outlays are 22 percent of the economy and revenues are 19 percent. (Chart I)

—By 2003, unless appropmate policy changes are made, fewer than 15 cents of every dollar will be available for nondefense discretionary programs that can raise productivity and contribute to economic growth. (Chart II)

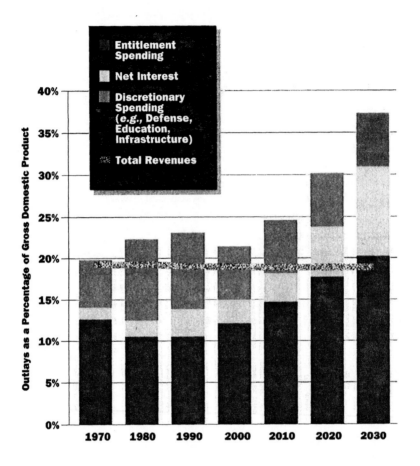

CHART I: THE PRESENT TREND IS NOT SUSTAINABLE

The gap between Federal spending and revenues is growing rapidly. Absent policy changes, entitlement spending and interest on the national debt will consume almost all Federal revenues in 2010. In 2030, Federal revenues will not even cover entitlement spending.

- Entitlement Spending
- Net Interest
- Discretionary Spending (e.g., Defense, Education, Infrastructure)
- Total Revenues

Outlays as a Percentage of Gross Domestic Product

40%
35%
30%
25%
20%
15%
10%
5%
0%

1970 1980 1990 2000 2010 2020 2030

2. WE MUST LEAD BY EXAMPLE— CONGRESS CANNOT BE EXEMPT.

The President and Congress must lead by example. Change must begin in Washington. It is essential that the Federal government reform its own entitlement programs before asking anything of the American people. In this spirit, the Kerrey-Danforth approach reduces the growth in congressional pensions and brings Federal civil and military retirement programs more in line with private sector standards. It includes the following proposals—

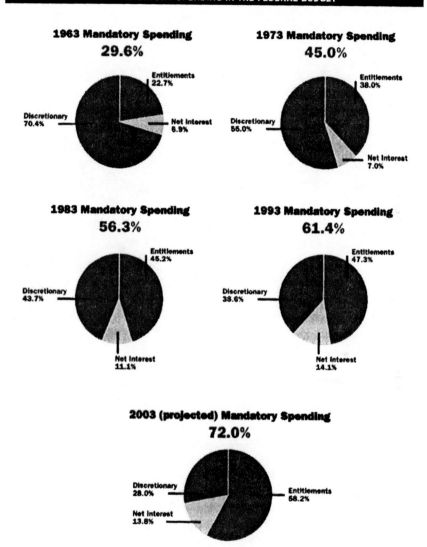

CHART II: GROWTH OF MANDATORY SPENDING IN THE FEDERAL BUDGET

1963 Mandatory Spending
29.6%

Entitlements 22.7%
Discretionary 70.4%
Net Interest 6.9%

1973 Mandatory Spending
45.0%

Entitlements 38.0%
Discretionary 55.0%
Net Interest 7.0%

1983 Mandatory Spending
56.3%

Entitlements 45.2%
Discretionary 43.7%
Net Interest 11.1%

1993 Mandatory Spending
61.4%

Entitlements 47.3%
Discretionary 38.6%
Net Interest 14.1%

2003 (projected) Mandatory Spending
72.0%

Discretionary 28.0%
Entitlements 58.2%
Net Interest 13.8%

- *Reduce pensions for Congress by up to 50 percent for each additional year of service.* This proposal would reduce congressional pension accrual rates to the rates applied to other Federal employees. It would apply to current Members of Congress and congressional employees for their remaining years of work and to all new workers hired after January 1, 1996.

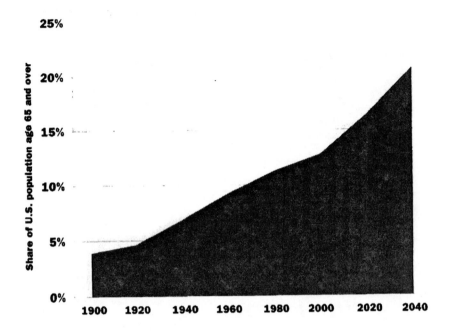

CHART III: THE SHARE OF THE POPULATION OVER 65 WILL CONTINUE TO GROW

- *Reduce Federal Employee Retirement System (FERS) benefits by up to 10 percent, and Civil Service Retirement System (CSRS) benefits by up to 5 percent.* This proposal would reduce the CSRS and FERS accrual rates by 0.1 percentage points for each year of work, effective January 1, 2000.
- *Raise the Federal retirement age to 60.* This proposal would gradually phase out eligibility for unreduced benefits for Federal workers before age 60, effective January 1, 2000.
- *Adjust CSRS and FERS benefit formula to "high-five" pay.* The benefit formula for both CSRS and FERS would be adjusted by changing the salary base from the employee's highest three consecutive years of pay to his or her highest five years, effective January 1, 2000.
- *Reduce the rate at which military retirement benefits accrue from 3.5 percent to 2 percent of basic pay for retirees with more than 20 years of service.* This proposal would reduce the addition to retirement pay for each year of service after 20 years from 3.5

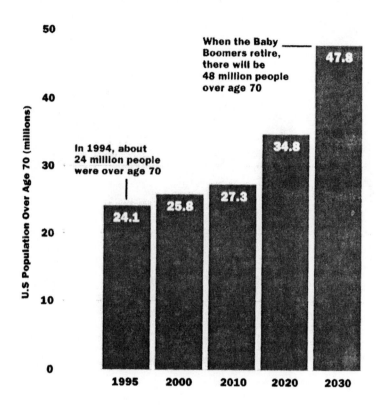

CHART IV: THE NUMBER OF AMERICANS OVER 70 WILL DOUBLE

percent to 2 percent per year. It would also drop the one-time increase in retirement pay at age 62 of 10 percent. It would retain the CPI minus 1 percentage point COLA that applies until age 62 and the one-time COLA adjustment at age 62. This proposal applies to military personnel hired after August 1, 1986.

3. WE MUST PLAN FOR THE AGING OF AMERICA'S POPULATION

America's population is growing older because of longer life expectancies and the aging of the Baby Boom generation. Federal

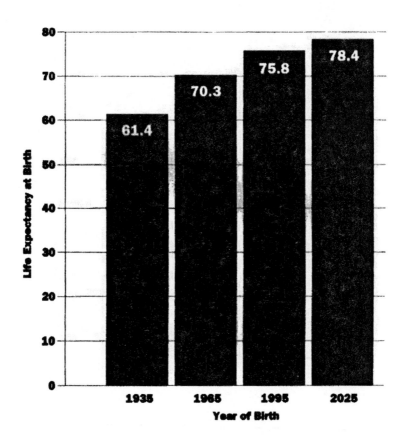

CHART V: AMERICANS ARE LIVING MUCH LONGER THAN WHEN SOCIAL SECURITY BEGAN

retirement and health benefits programs must be revised to adapt to these new realities.

—The share of the population over 65 has grown from fewer than 5 percent in 1900 to 13 percent in 1994, and is expected to reach 20 percent by the year 2025. (Chart III)

—The number of Americans over 70 will double in the next 35 years, from 24 million today to 48 million in the year 2030. (Chart IV)

—In 1935, when Social Security was established, the average American lived to 61 years of age. In 1994, the average American's life expectancy was 76. By 2025, it is expected to be 78 years of age. (Chart V)

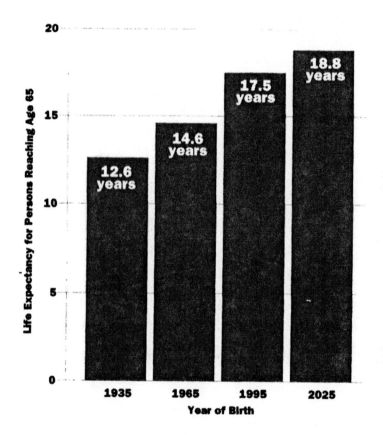

CHART VI: LIFE EXPECTANCY FOR PERSONS REACHING AGE 65

—In 1965, when Medicare was enacted, the average American expected to receive retirement and health care benefits for 15 years, up from 13 years in 1935. In the year 2025, benefits are expected to be provided for an average of 19 years. (Chart VI)

Social Security and Medicare benefits are funded primarily from payroll taxes on current workers. As the population ages and the Baby Boom generation retires, there will be fewer workers to support the increased number of retirees. In 1990, there were almost five workers to support each retiree. In 2030, there will be fewer than three workers to support each retiree. (Chart VII)

To plan for the changing demographics caused by longer life expectancies and the aging of the Baby Boom generation, the Kerrey-Danforth approach—

CHART VII: AN AGING POPULATION MEANS FEWER WORKERS TO SUPPORT EACH RETIREE'S BENEFITS

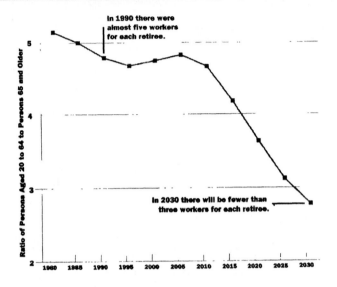

- *Retains the Social Security eligibility age at 62, and raises the age for retirement with full benefits from 67 to 70, phased in over 30 years.* This proposal would accelerate the phase-in period that is already in current law to age 67. In addition, the eligibility age would continue to rise by two-month increments until it reaches age 70 for those persons under age 28. *No one currently over the age of 50 would be affected, and the Early Retirement Age would remain at 62.*
- *Increases the Medicare eligibility age to 70 and allows seniors to enroll in Medicare at age 62 with a charge for early enrollment spread over life.* This proposed change would gradually raise the Medicare eligibility age to match the scheduled increases in the Social Security Normal Retirement Age. To ensure continued access to health insurance for older Americans, access would be expanded by allowing those age 62 to enroll in Medicare if they agree to pay for it. The charge would be spread over the actuarial life of the Medicare enrollee.

CHART VIII: MEDICARE PART A IS PROJECTED TO BE INSOLVENT BY 2001

To cover Medicare HI outlays, the payroll tax rate would have to increase from 2 9% today to more than 8% in 2030.

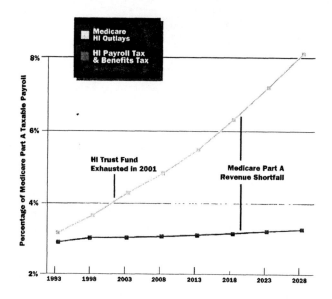

4. WE MUST ADDRESS RISING HEALTH CARE COSTS BY EMPHASIZING MARKET INCENTIVES AND PERSONAL RESPONSIBILITY

Federal health program spending has been increasing at annual rates averaging 10 percent or more during the past five years. According to the Medicare Trustees, the Hospital Insurance (HI) Trust Fund is projected to be insolvent by the year 2001. In the long run, spending on Medicare and Medicaid will triple as a percentage of the economy by 2030. (Chart VIII)

When Medicare Part A was enacted, it was a self-supporting system, financed solely by payroll tax contributions. Today, Part A coverage averages about $3,100 per enrollee, while the average enrollee pays only 32 percent of the cost (26 percent for couples with only one worker). As a result, the average enrollee collects benefits equaling approximately three times the amount contributed during his or her working life.

The Kerrey-Danforth approach creates incentives in the Medicare program to control costs and introduces market forces to allow greater flexibility and a wider variety of delivery systems.

CHART IX

GENERAL REVENUES WILL BE NEEDED TO SUBSIDIZE THE COSTS OF PART A UNDER CURRENT LAW

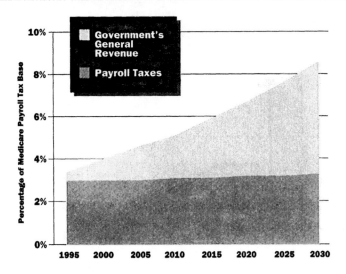

PART A COST INCREASES ARE SHARED UNDER KERREY-DANFORTH

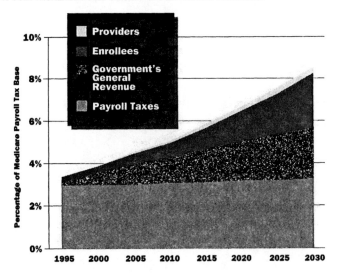

Individuals can make their own decisions about purchasing health care. Medicare enrollees would be given the option to stay in the current fee-for-service Medicare program or elect to enroll in an accredited private health plan paid for by a government voucher. The voucher would be equal in value to average fee-for-service per capita program costs. The above options are subject to the following program changes in Medicare Part A and B—

- *Add a graduated Part A premium.* Beginning in 2000 this proposal would require Medicare beneficiaries with incomes above 150 percent of poverty to pay a premium for Part A coverage. The premium would be graduated starting at 150 percent of poverty and peaking at $60 for persons with incomes at twice the poverty rate effective January 1, 2000. (Chart IX)

The share of Medicare Part B costs paid by enrollees as monthly premiums has been shrinking since the program began. When the program started the enrollee and the Federal government had a 50-50 partnership—each paid 50 percent of the cost. Today the Federal government pays 70 percent of Part B costs; by 2030 the government's share is projected to increase to 99 percent. (Chart X)

The Kerrey-Danforth approach would—

- *Index the Part B premium to program costs to keep the subsidy from increasing.* Part B premiums for 1994 covered about 30 percent of the cost of the Part B program. Beginning in 1996 this option would permanently index the Part B premium to maintain the 30 percent share of program costs currently paid by enrollees.
- *Raise the $100 Part B deductible to $300 and index it.* This proposal would increase the Part B deductible to $300 on January 1, 2000, and index it to medical care inflation thereafter.
- *Add a 20 percent coinsurance payment for clinical lab services and home health care.* Beginning in 2000 this proposal would establish a uniform coinsurance rate of 20 percent on home health services paid by Part A and Part B and laboratory services in excess of $10.

The Federal government also subsidizes a substantial part of health costs by allowing health insurance costs paid by employers to be deductible and exempt from income tax when received by

CHART X

TODAY, THE PART B SUBSIDY FOR EACH ENROLLEE IS 70% OF PROGRAM COSTS AND IS GROWING

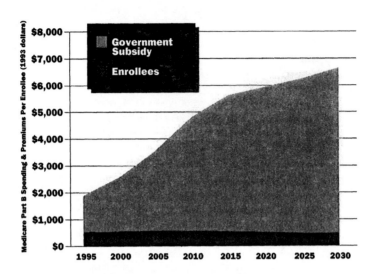

PART B COST INCREASES ARE SHARED UNDER KERREY-DANFORTH

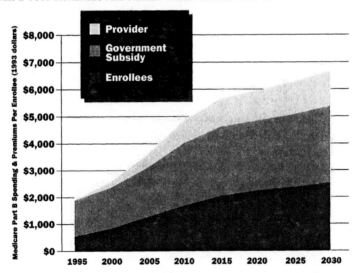

the employee. In 1994, the value of this subsidy was more than $50 billion. In addition to the program changes outlined above, the Kerrey-Danforth proposal would—

- *Cap the employer-paid health insurance deduction.* It would limit the amount of employer-paid health insurance and medical care that could be excluded from an employee's income for income tax purposes. The cap would be based on projected average health insurance premiums, effective January 1, 2000.

To attack waste, fraud, and abuse in the health care system, as well as to ensure that all participants in the health care system contribute to solving the problem, health care providers are asked to accept reduced payments.

- *Reduce Medicare provider payments.* This change could be implemented through reductions in provider payments such as adjusting inpatient capital payments to reflect better cost data, revising disproportionate share hospital adjustments, and eliminating formula-driven overpayment in hospital outpatient departments. These options would take effect January 1, 2000.

5. WE MUST FULFILL OUR PROMISES TO TODAY'S RETIREES AND ENSURE THE LONG-TERM SOLVENCY OF SOCIAL SECURITY. WE DO THIS BY REDUCING THE PAYROLL TAXES OF TODAY'S YOUNGER WORKERS IN EXCHANGE FOR A REVISED LONG-TERM CONTRACT

The aging of the population will strain major entitlement programs, particularly Social Security. When the Baby Boom generation begins to retire in 2008, the cash now surplus from Social Security will rapidly decline. According to the Social Security Trustees, by 2013 benefit payments will exceed dedicated tax revenues. Cash flow shortfalls in Social Security will then increase the Federal deficit rapidly unless policy changes are made. Trust Fund insolvency is also projected by 2029. (Chart XI)

There are two ways to prevent insolvency: (1) raise taxes or (2) revise long-term promises to today's younger workers. The

CHART XI: SOCIAL SECURITY TAX COLLECTIONS EXCEED CURRENT BENEFITS BUT AREN'T ENOUGH TO FUND FUTURE PROMISES

Revenue short falls will rise to more than 4% of payroll by 2030. To cover Social Security outlays, payroll taxes would have to increase from 12.4% today to more than 16.5% in 2030.

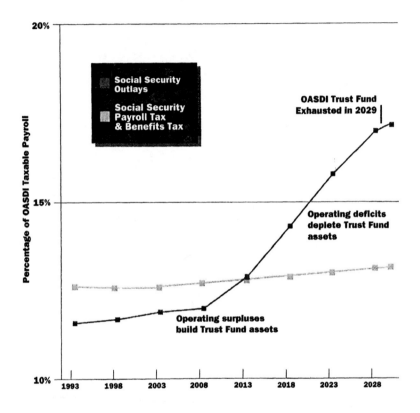

Kerrey-Danforth approach chooses the second option. In so doing, the Kerrey-Danforth approach restores long-term solvency to Social Security.

Under current rules, Social Security benefits grow faster than inflation. This means that each generation is promised greater benefits (even if they earn the same real wages) than the preceding generation. Greater benefits require higher taxes on future workers. For example, if each generation of a family has wages of $24,000 per year (in 1994 dollars), each generation is promised 12.5 percent greater benefits than its predecessor (e.g., benefits increase by 25 percent in constant dollars over 60 years). (Chart XII)

CHART XII: EACH GENERATION GETS GREATER BENEFITS EVEN IF THEY HAVE THE SAME WAGES

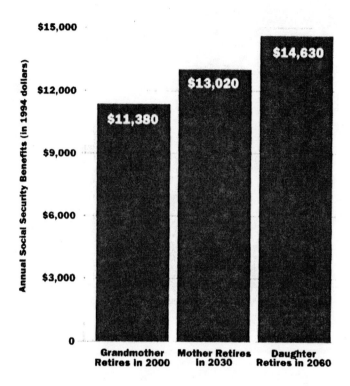

The Kerrey-Danforth approach promises that each generation will be treated equitably, by—

- *Indexing the Social Security "bend points" for inflation instead of average wage growth.* Effective in 1998 for new recipients only, this proposal would index the bend points in the benefit formula for inflation as measured by CPI instead of adjusting them for average wage growth.
- *Reducing growth of benefits to mid- and upper-wage workers by adding a third bend point.* This proposal would modify the benefit formula over a 50-year period beginning in 2000, gradually reducing the growth in benefits paid to workers with average and above-average earnings. No person age 55 or older would be affected, and in the first two decades after it takes effect, the impact would be minimal.

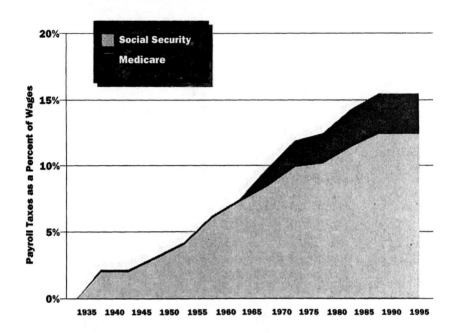

CHART XIII: PAYROLL TAX RATES HAVE GROWN STEADILY

COMBINED EMPLOYER AND EMPLOYEE TOTAL

Americans are not saving for their futures—the current national savings rate of 1.7 percent is lower than historical rates and the savings rates of other major industrial nations. With the government taking increased amounts of wages through payroll taxes, this should come as no surprise. Since 1937, payroll taxes have increased from 2.0 percent of wages to 15.3 percent today. (Chart XIII and Chart XIV)

If no policy changes are made, payroll taxes must increase to 24.6 percent by 2030 to support the Medicare and Social Security programs. As the payroll tax rate has increased, so has the wage base for both Social Security and Medicare taxes. The Kerrey-Danforth approach reduces the Social Security payroll tax by 1.5 percentage points ($57 billion in the year 2000—one of the largest tax cuts in history) and requires that Americans invest that money for their family's health and retirement needs. Accordingly, the Kerrey-Danforth proposal promotes savings and personal responsibility for the future by—

CHART XIV: ANNUAL MAXIMUM TAXABLE EARNINGS FOR SOCIAL SECURITY

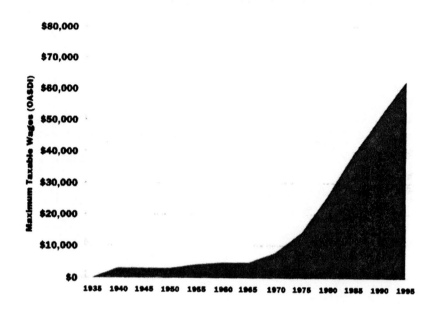

- *Providing a 1.5 percent Social Security payroll tax DECREASE and required contribution to personal savings/IRA.* This proposal would reduce the Social Security payroll tax for those under age 55 and require mandatory contributions to personal retirement accounts. Contributions to the individual's personal account would not be deductible, and earnings on the account would be taxed upon withdrawal. Withdrawal would be allowed only upon disability or retirement. This payroll tax decrease affects all workers in the Social Security system, and has no effect on benefits. . . . This proposal would take effect January 1, 2000. (Chart XV)

6. WE MUST DESIGN A SOLUTION THAT IS FAIR TO ALL AMERICANS

We must all share the costs of planning for the future. As previously noted, Members of Congress, congressional and civil service

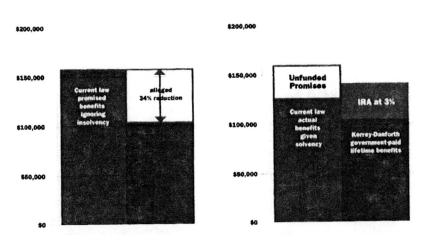

CHART XV

SOME MISTAKENLY CLAIM THAT KERREY-DANFORTH CUTS SOCIAL SECURITY BY 34% ...

BUT THEY IGNORE BOTH PROJECTED INSOLVENCY AND THE RETURN ON IRAS

Source: Social Security Trustees; C. Eugene Steuerle & Jon M. Bakija, *Retooling Social Security for the 21st Century* and calculations by the staff of the Bipartisan Commission on Entitlement and Tax Reform.

A 25-year-old male born in 1970 who earns average wages can retire at age 67 in the year 2037. Under current law, he is promised lifetime benefits of $158,267 (in 1995 dollars). The Social Security Trustees project that the Trust Fund will be insolvent by the year 2029. The Trust Fund will then shift to a pay-as-you-go system. Thus, only 79% of this worker's promised benefits will be provided, absent changes in the law. The lifetime government-paid benefits delivered to this person by the Kerrey-Danforth package would be worth $104,456. In addition, under Kerrey-Danforth, the worker invests 1.5% of each paycheck in an IRA. If he receives a real 3% rate of return on his IRA, he will have an additional $36,661 in private savings when he retires. His total benefits (government + private) would be ($104,456 + 36,661) $141,117. His actual benefits under current law will be $124,589. Even if his IRA earns only the 2.3% real return assumed by the Social Security Trustees, his total benefits would be $135,516. If he earns 4%, his total benefits would be $151,326. Furthermore, if he dies before age 62, his surviving relatives would inherit the value of his IRA.

employees, and military personnel all contribute under the Kerrey-Danforth approach. In addition, other entitlement programs must be evaluated to ensure that our tax dollars are spent judiciously. Accordingly, the Kerrey-Danforth approach asks for a 10 percent reduction in entitlement programs such as veterans compensation, agriculture, and welfare. After the reduction, the proposal caps the growth in these programs. The proposal would—

- *Cut other entitlements by 10 percent in 2000 and cap at CPI plus population growth thereafter.* This option would require a 10 percent reduction in all other entitlements from the 1999 level of spending (i.e., about a $20 billion cut). Programs affected include Supplemental Security Income, Food Stamps, Aid to Families With Dependent Children (AFDC), veterans' pensions and compensation, farm price supports, and unemployment compensation. The proposal would take effect starting in fiscal year 2000.

Re-evaluate the Consumer Price Index (CPI) to ensure that it more accurately reflects increases in the cost of living. The Bureau of Labor Statistics is currently reviewing the methodology used to calculate the CPI. Many economists and technicians believe the current CPI formula overstates cost-of-living increases by between 0.2 and 0.8 percentage points. The Kerrey-Danforth approach would reduce increases in the CPI by one-half of one percentage point and direct the Bureau of Labor Statistics to evaluate the current formula.

- *Adjust the CPI to better reflect inflation.* A number of Federal programs are adjusted annually based on increases in inflation as measured by the CPI. The CPI is based on a "market basket" of goods and services purchased by a representative urban worker. Adjusted every 10 years, the current market basket was last revised in 1987 using data for the period 1982 to 1984. As a result, the CPI does not capture annual changes in the pattern of consumer preferences. In addition, the CPI may not adequately measure the consumer benefit derived from improvements in the quality of existing goods or from the introduction of new goods. This proposal would require the Bureau of Labor Statistics to modify the CPI formula to reflect changes in the cost of living more accurately. These changes would apply to cost-of-living adjustments for Social Security and Federal retirement, veterans' compensation, and indexation in the Federal individual income tax (i.e., income brackets, exemptions, and deductions). A revised formula for the CPI could take effect January 1, 1998.

The burden of reform should be distributed based on ability to pay. Those who can afford to shoulder a greater portion of the burden should. The Kerrey-Danforth proposal would—

- *Means test Medicare, veterans compensation, and unemployment insurance.* This option would be phased in over five years, starting in 2000. The sum of income from government payments, earned income, and unearned income would determine the rate of benefit reduction for these three programs. The option would gradually reduce benefits for families with incomes over certain thresholds. For example, reductions would start at $0.10 for each additional dollar of income between $40,000 and $50,000; rise to $0.20 for each additional dollar of income between $50,000 and $60,000; and increase thereafter up to $0.85 for each additional dollar of income above $120,000. Regardless of income level, all beneficiaries would continue to receive a benefit. High-income beneficiaries, however, would see their benefits reduced.
- *Limit itemized deductions to 28 percent.* Itemized deductions would be limited to a rate of 28 percent regardless of the marginal tax rate applicable to the taxpayer. This would only affect couples whose incomes exceed $91,850 in 1994 dollars. This new provision would take effect January 1, 2000.

While asking all Americans to share in the costs of planning for our future, the Kerrey-Danforth proposal would make participation in the Social Security system mandatory for virtually all workers—

- *Include State and local workers in the Social Security system.* Starting in 2000, new state and local workers and those with five or fewer years of service would be required to participate in the Social Security program.

7. WE MUST ACT NOW TO GIVE PEOPLE TIME TO PLAN FOR THE FUTURE AND TO AVOID SIGNIFICANT FUTURE REVENUE INCREASES OR BENEFIT REDUCTIONS

Americans must have time to plan for and adjust to necessary policy changes. Most elements of the Kerrey-Danforth approach do not begin before the year 2000, and are phased in over at least five years. The changes in Social Security are phased in over much longer periods of time. Although most of these policies do not take effect until the next century, allowing people time to plan dictates that action should occur soon. If the President and Congress choose inaction, demographics and the growth of health care costs will cause future solutions to the problem to be both draconian and politically fractious.

Although the short-term fiscal outlook has improved, the long-term situation requires immediate attention. For the next five years, the Federal deficit is projected to average 2.5 percent of the economy, its lowest level since the 1970s. After 1998, however, Federal spending is projected to grow faster than revenues, causing Federal deficits to rise rapidly.

The costs of inaction are already apparent. Current long-term interest rates are high due to expectations of future spending policies. Moreover, funds needed for appropriate and essential government functions are being diminished by the rising costs of entitlement programs and payments on debt. If the President and Congress solve the Nation's long-term spending problems, families and businesses will enjoy lower interest rates and expanded investment opportunities that are vital to a strong economy in the next century.

> "I recognize it is difficult to deal with a problem whose symptoms are hard to detect and whose full-blown effects seem to be years or decades away. But financial markets have a way of bringing future problems into the present."
> —Alan Greenspan, Chairman, Board of Governors of the Federal Reserve System (July 15, 1994)

The Present Trend Is Not Sustainable . . .

FUTURE IMPACT OF CURRENT LAW

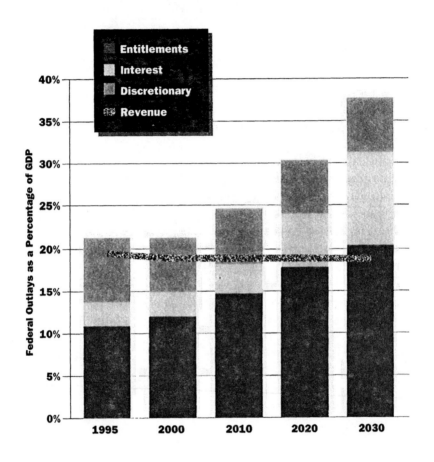

KERREY-DANFORTH ADDRESSES
AND SOLVES THE PROBLEM

FUTURE IMPACT OF KERREY-DANFORTH

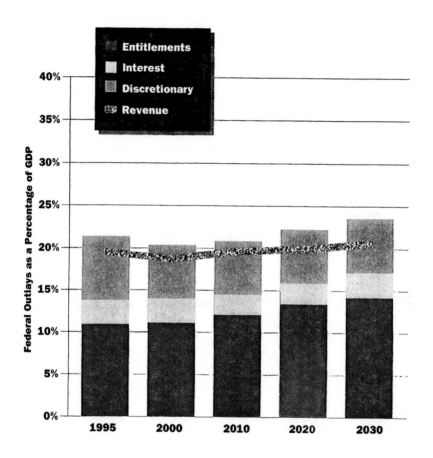

THE SOCIAL SECURITY TRUST FUNDS ARE
THREATENED WITH INSOLVENCY . . .

FUTURE IMPACT OF CURRENT LAW

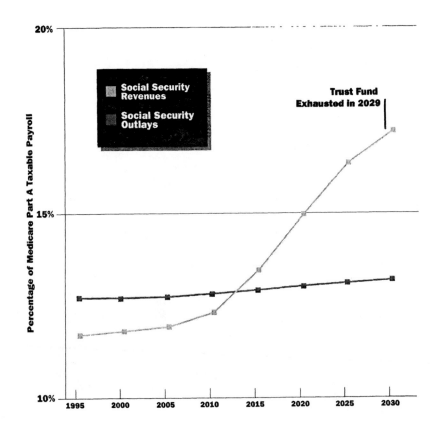

KERREY-DANFORTH ENSURES THE
LONG-TERM SOLVENCY OF THESE PROGRAMS

FUTURE IMPACT OF KERREY-DANFORTH

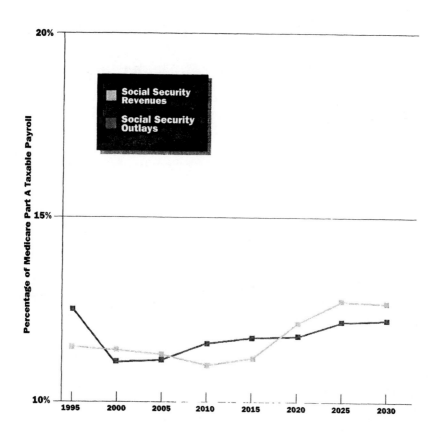

17

Bipartisan Commission on Entitlement and Tax Reform

Statement of Commissioner Richard L. Trumka

W hen I was appointed by the President to serve on the Bipartisan Commission on Entitlement and Tax Reform, I welcomed the opportunity to work with you to explore ways to balance projected Federal revenues with expected expenditures for health and social insurance programs. In our work together we agreed that there is a need to address the rapidly increasing cost of health care; to strengthen the long-term financing of Social Security and Medicare; to encourage a course that reduces long-term deficits; to encourage increased savings and investment; and, by doing this, to secure a better future for our children and our Nation.

While I agreed with some of the initial findings, I dissented from the sweeping conclusions of the Interim Report that couched the problem of future Federal budget deficits almost entirely in terms of the size of the Baby Boom generation and their future retirement benefits. The one-sided Interim Report took very little account of the effect of runaway health care costs on the Federal budget or of the tax revenues lost from unjustifiable tax loopholes enjoyed by corporations and wealthy individuals. Moreover, I felt that lumping social insurance and entitlement programs together

From *Bipartisan Commission on Entitlement and Tax Reform: Final Report to the President*, January 1995 (Washington, D.C.), pp. 146–52.

was a major analytical mistake. Each program has different revenue sources, different budgetary outlooks, and very different effects on the productive capacity of the economy.

Last week, I joined seven members of the Commission who were unwilling to sign a letter that restated the findings contained in the Interim Report and outlined several principles for reforming entitlement programs. I continue to believe that there is a need for greater balance than either our deliberations or the computer game achieved. We need far less rhetoric about our so-called entitlement crisis and a more balanced discussion of the benefits, costs, and challenges arising from the Nation's commitment to provide Social Security, Medicare, and other entitlement programs.

I regret that the approach was one-sided and that the needs of working Americans were overlooked in our discussions. This can be seen in the way we defined problems associated with entitlement spending, and in the recommendations of Senators Kerrey and Danforth to radically restructure and reduce Social Security and Medicare protection. These recommendations were advanced without spending so much as one hour of our year-long deliberations assessing the implications of these and other policy options on the everyday lives of average American families.

My proposal is based on my conviction that health care costs must be dealt with before any major restructuring of Medicare and Medicaid can be considered. In addition, I will show that actuarial balance can be achieved in the Social Security program without departing from its basic principles.

1. THE BIPARTISAN COMMISSION: A ONE-SIDED GAME

What has been hailed as the crowning achievement of the Commission—the computer game—is a metaphor for all that is wrong with the Commission. I regret that Commission members were not asked to vote on the computer game, nor were we given any input into its design.

For all its complexity, Americans playing the game can manipulate only one side of the budget equation. They can save money by cutting Social Security, Medicare, unemployment insurance, and programs for the poor. However, the computer game does not show the increased costs on employers, States, and households that will result from the decreased protection for the middle class and the increased poverty of others. In addition, while the game allows the player to cut domestic income support programs, it is not programmed to show what cutting defense, raising taxes on the wealthy or corporations, closing loopholes, or systematically controlling health costs would do for the Federal budget.

Lumping all entitlements together as one large problem creates a false sense of crisis and distracts us from addressing the real budget issue, skyrocketing health care costs. The rising cost of health care, including Medicare and Medicaid, not overall entitlement spending, is the major cause of the projected growth in the Federal deficit.

Rather than addressing the need to control health care costs, our discussions focused on cutting Medicare and Medicaid, which will only shift costs to beneficiaries, employers, and hospitals, and reduce the quality and quantity of care to those who need help the most. *Projected long-term deficits are driven primarily by rapidly increasing health care costs. But even here, the Commission overstated the effect of the Baby Boom generation on the Federal health care budget.*[1]

The two major programs—Social Security and Medicare, which together account for 60 percent of entitlement spending—have long-range financing problems, but for different reasons and in different ways. Social Security has not contributed one cent to the deficit or the debt of the United States. It is in fact a contributory program that is entirely supported by its own funding.

Contrary to the views advanced by Commission documents, Social Security is in good financial condition. Since 1937, when Social Security first collected earmarked contributions from employers and employees, $4.3 trillion has been paid in and $3.9 trillion has been paid out, including administrative expenses (now running at one cent for each dollar of benefits). This leaves nearly $400 billion in reserve.

By only looking at the cost side, the Commission's report ignores the fact that Social Security keeps 45 million people out of poverty and many millions more from near poverty. But it is more than a poverty program. Social Security is the only pension system for 6 out of 10 workers in private industry and is the base on which other retirement systems and individual savings are built, making it equally important for employers.

Families are protected by Social Security insurance against the total disability or death of a worker. The $12.1 trillion in life insurance protection provided by Social Security exceeds by $1.3 trillion the financial protection provided by all other types of private life insurance combined. It is a mistake to think of Social Security as primarily for the elderly. It is family protection for all, providing benefits for nearly 3 million children every month.

The Commission advanced a list of over 50 options, many of them dealing with Social Security. But at no point—not at its meetings or in its Staff work—did the Commission carefully examine how altering Social Security and other entitlement programs might affect the security of average families.

The computer game and many of the Commission's documents imply that entitlements and the growing number of older Americans are "THE PROBLEM"—the causes of Federal deficits and reduced savings and the real threat to the well-being of the economy and our children. This explanation of our current economic and budgetary problems is wrong and leads inescapably to irrational reductions in Social Security, Medicare, Medicaid, and other critical programs.

2. THE KERREY-DANFORTH PROPOSAL: UNDERMINING THE WELL-BEING OF WORKERS AND THEIR CHILDREN

The Kerrey-Danforth proposal fails to live up to the Senators' own promise not to hurt younger generations or current retirees and to balance long-term spending with revenue. By cutting the payroll tax, the proposal forces cuts in Social Security far beyond what is needed to maintain the solvency of the Trust Funds. In fact, their expenditure cuts are three times greater than would be needed to bring Social Security into balance. This package represents a fundamental attack on the idea of Social Security, arguably the most fundamental attack in its 60-year history.

a. The Effects of Raising the Social Security Retirement Age to 70

Raising the retirement age proposal represents a 20 percent benefit reduction, even for people who retire at age 70. Older workers in poor health, widows, widowers, and spouses with limited resources will bear the brunt of these changes. Raising the age will have an especially severe impact on low-income workers, who generally have shorter life expectancies, are generally in worse health, and have fewer employment opportunities. For example, the life expectancy of African-American males has actually been declining and is now 65.

If increasing the retirement age causes one-half of those aged 65 and over to look for work, the economy would have to create millions of additional jobs in the next decade alone. Raising the retirement age will generate millions of new workers, but it will not generate the 25 million additional jobs that will have to be produced by the year 2030 to accommodate these extra workers. *In other words raising the retirement age could create a deficit of another sort: a jobs deficit.* As a result, young people could face higher rates of unemployment and lower pay.

b. Raising the Medicare Retirement Age

Raising Medicare eligibility age is even more devastating than raising the Normal Retirement Age for Social Security. Making 65- to 69-year-olds ineligible for Medicare will leave millions of older Americans without health insurance and at risk of impoverishment due to an unexpected hospitalization or other health emergency. Many people in this age group have one or more chronic health conditions and are uninsurable in the private market. Even if private insurance coverage is offered, many people will find it too expensive to purchase.

The Kerrey-Danforth proposal would allow people under age 70 to purchase Medicare, an option that simply amounts to a further cut in Social Security. Given the high rate of poor health among minority and low-income individuals, an increase in the Medicare eligibility age will be particularly harmful to minority and low-income persons.

c. Other Medicare Proposals

The Kerrey-Danforth proposal also raises premiums; creates a new tax; raises deductibles and copays; reduces Medicare provider payments; and caps employer-provided health insurance. Together, these proposals would mean an enormous benefit cut for many of today's elderly and disabled, violating the promise made by the Chairman not to harm current beneficiaries.

Under these proposals, by the year 2000, middle-income beneficiaries would pay $1,000 more in out-of-pocket expenses for Medicare. The elderly already pay more than any other group on health care. In fact, they pay half of their own medical costs even when covered by Medicare.

Moreover, deductible and coinsurance increases are regressive and fall hardest on sick persons who lack Medigap or Medicaid coverage, individuals who are normally just above Medicaid eligibility levels. Providers have been squeezed to the point that many are already reluctant to accept Medicare beneficiaries.

The Kerrey-Danforth proposal also includes a cap on employer deductions for contributions to employee health insurances. This will cause many employers to ratchet down coverage and in effect would penalize workers who have already given up wages to maintain their health care benefits. Our government should be enacting policies that expand access to health care, not erecting additional obstacles.

Finally, the proposal calls for means testing and the partial privatization of Medicare—yet another tragic retreat from America's progress toward universal health insurance. Means testing would transform Medicare into a welfare program, rendering it more expensive to administer and making it more vulnerable to political attack. Upper-income retirees who lose benefits may opt to leave the system altogether, thereby eroding the universal support it now enjoys.

d. The Kerrey-Danforth Social Security Cuts

The Kerrey-Danforth proposal would cut Social Security benefits by the following amounts: 33 percent of low-wage earners (under $10,000 per year); 43 percent for average-wage earners (between $25,000 and $40,000 per year); and 50 percent for maximum-wage earners (over $60,600). Without question, this is the most extraordinary package of Social Security cuts ever produced.

Another factor overlooked by the Commission is interaction between the Social Security system and employer retirement planning. In fact, it is likely that if Social Security and Medicare were cut, private sector costs would increase. For example, private industry would incur much greater costs to induce people to retire.

e. Mandatory IRAs—Partial Privatization

The Kerrey-Danforth plan would compel people to direct 1.5 percent of the Social Security payroll tax to individual savings accounts—the so-called mandatory IRAs. On an individual level, personal savings accounts are popular. Unlike Social Security, IRAs allow individuals to see their savings grow. But savings accounts are not insurance, and shift an enormous risk to the individual. Even with today's average return on savings, a 50-year-old making the average wage today would have only $7,379.62 by the time s/he is 62.[2]

Among the biggest losers will be the disabled, whose benefits will be based on a smaller Social Security benefit. A worker's account will provide sufficient retirement income only if s/he does not die or become disabled before the account has had sufficient time to grow; if s/he is employed continuously; does not make bad investment decisions; and leaves the workforce when the market is strong.

The only clear winners are money management firms. If these mandatory IRAs existed in 1993, $39 billion would flow out of the OASDI Trust Fund into the hands of private sector financial managers. In three years the total would be over $126 billion.

f. The Kerrey-Danforth Proposal
Places False Hope in the Private Pension System

Sixty percent of retirees have no retirement income other than Social Security. Middle-class workers (annual earnings between $25,000 and $40,000) expect to get about 57 percent of their total retirement income (including earnings) from Social Security. As we pointed out, the Kerrey-Danforth proposal would cut these benefits by over 43 percent.

The private pension system and private savings cannot make up for this. In fact, the trends in private employer-provided pensions point in the opposite direction. Participation in employer-provided voluntary pensions held steady at around 45-46 percent throughout the 1970s and 1980s, but declined to 44 percent in 1993. Only 39 percent of current workers have defined benefit plans they can count on.

g. Women Retirees Face Special Problems

The Kerrey-Danforth proposal takes a backward step away from gender equity because it disproportionately hurts women workers and retirees. There are three reasons women are particularly harmed by Social Security cuts: women are more likely to be lower-income workers; they depend more heavily on their spouses for retirement income; and women live longer than their husbands. For these reasons, women experience higher rates of poverty in old age and get a larger percentage of their income from Social Security.

By the time today's 38-year-old female reaches age 65, she has a 40 percent chance of living alone and in poverty at some point in her old age. The Kerrey-Danforth proposal greatly increases their chances of living in poverty and makes a bad problem worse.

The Kerrey-Danforth proposal lacks any analysis of the critical role Social Security plays in the lives of older women. Before Congress moves ahead with Social Security reforms, I hope it will take account of the following facts about the income needs of older women: (1) nearly three out of four of the Nation's elderly poor are women; (2) one in four women over age 65 depend on Social Security for 90 percent of retirement income; (3) women are largely left out of the private pension system—women are half as likely to receive a pension as men; and (4) non-married women 65 and older experience poverty at three times the rate of older couples.

h. The Kerrey-Danforth Proposal and National Savings and Investment

Rather than achieving their goal of increasing national savings, the creation of mandatory IRAs may actually lower national savings by eliminating from the savings pool the fees that will be collected by IRA managers. Moreover, once people have individual accounts they will likely cut back their saving elsewhere.

Means testing will also discourage private savings. Savings are already taxed as income; if Medicare benefits are reduced because workers have assets, the tax rate may become so high that workers will not bother to save.

Finally, the Commission's analysis hinges on the unsupported assumption that increasing national savings will in turn increase investment. However, the link between national savings and job-producing investment is theoretical at best.

There are other equally plausible scenarios that were never explored. Not once did the Commission seriously address how Federal spending—even if it requires deficits—could increase productivity and economic growth by investing in education, basic research, and infrastructure. In fact, the historical evidence points in this direction—in times when Federal spending is high, business confidence tends to be high and investment spending increases. Investment spending by business is not necessarily related to the Federal deficit.

Furthermore, the proposition that savings automatically leads to more investment is refuted by one of the major tenets of modern economics. Supply does not create its own demand. The forces that make capital available for investment are not the same as those that produce enough business optimism to spur investment.

i. Entitlement Cap

The Kerrey-Danforth proposal cuts programs designed to help the poor by imposing a cap on future spending for entitlement programs other than Social Security and Medicare. While I agree that the welfare system is in need of reform, for the benefit of both recipients and taxpayers, it is unlikely that there will be major savings from this effort.

Moreover, any savings to the Federal government will likely be matches by increases in spending by the States. The fact is, programs designed for the poor need to be better financed, not cut. We should begin by patching the leaks in our tax system—for example, by closing tax loopholes for the well-off and subjecting all other tax expenditures to a rigorous review.

NOTES

1. The Interim Report wanted to prove that demographics alone causes entitlement spending to exceed sustainable levels in the year 2030. This is simply not the case. It is uncontrolled growth in health care costs, not the size of the Baby Boom generation, that is the problem. The Interim Report assumes our Nation will be unable to control health care costs. As a result, the Commission overstated the implications of population aging on Federal deficits.

In order to separate the effects of population aging and unreasonable health care costs the Commission Staff had to make some assumptions. The Staff had to decide what portion of future health care costs would be the result of more people using health services and how much could be attributed to extraordinary health care cost inflation due to expensive technology, waste, and the health market's power to raise prices.

The Interim Report makes the argument that even if we reform health care—even though there is no particular plan in mind—the Medicare and Medicaid portion is still too high. The Staff decided it is reasonable to reform health care so costs grow "no more than the general growth rate of the economy." We agree. The difference between our view and the Staff view is what "the general growth rate of the economy" means.

The economy grows at about 2 percent a year (adjusted for inflation). The CBO is projecting large growth in the middle of the 1990s (about 2.3 percent a year) and a tapering off by about 1.3 percent a year between 2010 and 2070. We use these projected growth rates in the GDP as "the general growth rate in the economy." Using the cost of Medicaid and Medicare in 1994 we projected how much increasing numbers of people would cause spending in these categories to increase over time. Then we presumed that health care costs would go up by the growth rate of the economy. We get health care costs that are pretty high in terms of GDP, but they eventually fall to 5.5 percent of GDP, compared to the 4.5 percent of GDP today.

On the other hand, the Commission staff used a much larger number to inflate health care. Instead of the real growth rate of the economy, they used the real growth rate of the economy *and* the inflation rate and then divided it by the number of workers, which makes the index grow even more. Having health care costs grow by the rate of inflation plus the real growth rate in the economy is just too high. Our reforms should do better. Their estimate is 7.2 percent in 2030.

We do not know how much we can succeed in curbing the rate of increase in health care costs. But neither does the Commission. By assuming a rate that is very large, the Commission skewed the representation to make the future size of the elderly group, and not skyrocketing health care costs, appear to be the problem.

2. We assume a 2 percent wage growth and fund earnings of 7 percent.

Part Five

SOCIAL SECURITY AND MEDICARE IN THE TWENTY-FIRST CENTURY

The test of our progress is not whether we add more to the abundance of those who have much; it is whether we provide enough for those who have too little.

—Franklin D. Roosevelt

This last section of the book catapults the reader into the cutting edge of the debates over overhauling entitlement programs. The numbers offered by Eugene Steuerle and Jon Bakija have occupied a central position in the debate over Social Security, and have offered intellectual heft to the case for overhauling the government's largest program.

Yet, there appear to be two schools of thought forming. As articulated in the *Newsday* editorial "The Sky's Not Falling, The Sky's Not Falling," Social Security needs just some minor tinkering to be fixed, such as an increase of 2.2 percentage points in the FICA tax. But the Concord Coalition challenges that idea in its *Facing Facts* publication, saying these steps would be insufficient.

In a *Washington Post* op-ed, Twentieth Century Fund President Richard Leone attempts to reassure young adults that they needn't worry about their futures and that elderly Baby Boomers would not wreck the economy or Social Security. This, too, is disputed by Concord Coalition economists, who beseech Generation Xers to "listen up."

Finally, three of the members of the 1994–96 Social Security Advisory Council, Robert Ball, Ed Gramlich, and Carolyn Weaver, offer the *New York Times* their recommendations for fixing the Social Security system. Notice how, given the same evidence, they come to vastly different conclusions.

18

How Social Security Redistributes Income

C. Eugene Steuerle and Jon Bakija

S ocial Security is the largest transfer program in the United
States, each year redistributing hundreds of billions of dollars
between generations. It also reallocates the shares of income
enjoyed by different income groups within each generation. Yet the
nature of this redistribution remains a mystery to the vast majority
of the American public. Although it is widely recognized that the
Social Security payroll tax by itself is mildly regressive—it tends to
take a larger percentage of income from low- and moderate-wage
workers than it does from those with high incomes—less well
understood are the progressive features of the benefit formula.
Very few Americans know the exact ways in which their retirement benefits are related to the value of their lifetime contributions
or whether the program as a whole is progressive or regressive on
a lifetime basis.[1]

Although in theory the relationship between benefit payments
and taxes within Social Security might be viewed as a compromise
between the two principles of progressivity (or redistribution
according to need) and individual equity (or fair returns on all
contributions), in practice the system's development has not been
so precise. The relationship has varied over time in ways not

always consistent with either of these principles. Historically, a large amount of the redistribution caused by Social Security has been arbitrary or even regressive in nature. In the future, on the other hand, redistributive patterns will change in ways that may have a profound effect on the equity and political popularity of the system. A clear understanding of how benefits, taxes, and net redistribution change over time, therefore, is essential if one is to make an informed judgment about options for long-run reform.

ANNUAL BENEFITS

Real Value of Benefits

Annual Social Security benefits have risen dramatically in real (inflation-adjusted) terms since the inception of the program. During Social Security's early decades, increases in real benefit levels resulted from a combination of wage growth and a variety of ad hoc legislative actions. As recently as 1972, for example, all benefits were increased across-the-board by 20 percent. Since 1974, annual benefit amounts for retirees have been automatically indexed to keep pace with inflation. Since the late 1970s, moreover, the benefit formula has been indexed in a way that keeps average real benefit levels growing for each successive cohort of retirees at roughly the same rate as economy-wide wages. Thus, so long as there is real wage growth, real benefit levels continue to increase for every new generation of recipients.

To illustrate how benefit levels change in value over time, figure 1 displays the real (inflation-adjusted) Old-Age and Survivors Insurance (OASI) benefit paid in the first year of retirement for a set of hypothetical workers and their spouses. . . . Note that for a "two-earner" couple, a high-wage husband is assumed to have an average-wage wife, while average- and low-wage men are both assumed to be married to women with low-wage earning histories.

Substantial increases in the real value of annual benefits can usually be seen for each successive cohort of retirees at each income level and marital status. Consider, for example, the OASI benefits going to single workers retiring at age 65 in 1990. Annual benefits for high-, average-, and low-wage workers are worth about $13,600, $9,700, and $5,900, respectively, in constant 1993 dollars. In real terms, these amounts are 2.7 to 3.1 times as large as

Figure 1. OASI Benefit in First Year of Retirement (in Thousands of Constant 1993 Dollars)

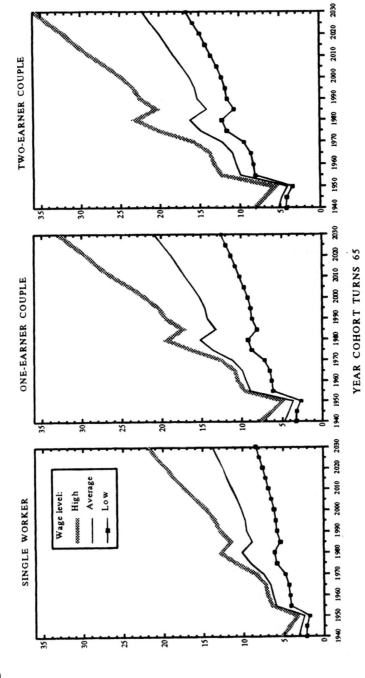

Notes: Figure depicts OASI benefit in first 12 months of retirement, assuming retirement at OASI Normal Retirement Age. Couples are assumed to be the same age. Data cover cohorts born every five years beginning in 1875.

the annual benefits received by these workers' counterparts in 1940. Benefits for married couples, of course, are much larger than for single individuals.

The path of benefit growth has not always been smooth. Early in the program's history, real benefit levels were often eroded by inflation during the years between legislative acts. The year 1950 represents a low point for the real value of benefits because no action had been taken to offset the effects of inflation during the 1940s; a large benefit increase implemented for all recipients in 1952 compensated for this. More recently, benefit values have sometimes declined slightly from one group of retirees to the next during recessions or periods of transition to a new benefit calculation procedure.[2] The general trend in benefit levels, nonetheless, exhibits a steep upward slope. Recall that for most people retiring after the introduction of automatic indexing in the early 1970s, the basic benefit level remains constant in real value after the first year of retirement. Those retiring in earlier years often benefited from rising real postretirement benefits despite years of inflationary decline between legislative enactments.

Reasonable projections suggest that the real value of Social Security benefits will continue to climb steadily for future retirees if current law remains intact. Under the best-estimate economic assumptions of the Social Security Administration, for example, we calculate that an average-wage worker retiring at age 67 in 2032 can be expected to receive a basic annual benefit, excluding spousal and other benefits, of about $13,900 in constant 1993 dollars. Thus, as a result of growth in real wages, the purchasing power of his or her benefit would be approximately 42 percent greater than that of a similar worker who retired in 1995. For a high-wage worker, the increase is expected to be almost 61 percent in real terms.[3] If this high-wage worker were married to someone earning the average wage, he or she could expect to receive combined benefits equal to about $35,700 (in constant 1993 dollars) upon retiring in 2032. This would be about 53 percent higher than the $23,300 going to such a couple retiring in 1995.

Income taxation of Social Security benefits can be expected to offset some portion of the benefit growth, as the unindexed taxation thresholds decline in real value over time. Budget legislation in 1993, which increased the maximum portion of benefits that can be included in taxable income to 85 percent and also raised the top income tax rate, will also offset some of this growth. The average tax rate on Social Security benefits can be expected to rise gradually from around 2 percent in 1993 to perhaps 7 percent or 8 percent by 2030.[4] The reduction for a very few individuals at the very highest income levels could rise to about a third of benefits,[5] but most recipients will continue to face only modest burdens, if any, from benefit taxation.[6]

A second factor that could offset some real growth in OASI benefits is a rise in the cost of SMI premiums, which are subtracted directly out of Social Security checks. In 1993, SMI premiums reduced the annual OASI benefit going to each recipient by about $493, which amounted to about 5 percent of the benefit paid to a newly retired average-wage worker. If SMI premiums were to be maintained at 25 percent of program costs, they would rise by 2030 to more than $1,700 annually (in constant 1993 dollars) under the HCFA's intermediate projections.[7] This would amount to about 12 percent of an average-wage worker's cash OASI benefit.

When increased taxation of benefits and higher SMI premiums are taken into account, the SSA's best-estimate projections still suggest that Social Security benefits will normally provide a more comfortable standard of living during the next century than they do today. For example, the real after-tax, after-premium value of OASI benefits for newly retired average-wage workers rises by 22 percent between 1995 and 2030 if we assume the average tax rate on benefits, and that SMI premiums grow as just described.[8]

Although these projections predict a fairly healthy growth in the value of Social Security benefits, a recent poll indicated that almost a third of nonretired Americans considered it "very likely" that Social Security payments would no longer be available at all when they retire (Yankelovich, Skelly, and White, Inc., 1985). Although fears that the nation will not be able to afford any Social Security benefits are unfounded, there are valid reasons to be skeptical of the benefit projections reported here. First of all, the system's imbalance makes it likely that Congress will reduce the rate of future benefit growth. Second, long-term economic projections of real wage growth—the source of real benefit growth under Social Security formulas—are always uncertain. Despite these caveats, even with pessimistic assumptions about future wage growth and congressional action, the real value of cash benefits for most future retirees is still likely to be higher than today's benefit levels. The real value of health benefits, moreover, is expected to grow also.

Replacement Rates

The "replacement rate" is a measure of the percentage of a worker's previous annual wage that is replaced by Social Security benefits. Most commonly, replacement rates are expressed as a percentage of wages in the last year preceding retirement, or as a share of the average wage in the three highest-earning years. Maintaining "adequate" and stable replacement rates over time for workers at all earnings levels has been a primary goal of policymakers throughout much of Social Security's history.[9]

Figure 2 illustrates how replacement rates for hypothetical workers have evolved over time and are expected to change in the future. . . . The figure shows OASI benefits paid in the first full year of retirement as a percentage of earnings in the year prior to retirement, after adjusting for inflation.[10] Replacement rates for low- and average-wage workers retiring today and in the future are somewhat higher than the historical norm. Rates for high-wage workers, in turn, are higher than at the inception of the program, but slightly lower than typical of the 1950–80 period.[11]

According to Robert J. Myers, former chief actuary of the Social Security Administration, the 1939 Social Security formula was set so that a worker earning the average wage and retiring at age 65 today would receive—in the absence of changes in wage and price levels—a replacement rate of approximately 40 percent.[12] This is almost exactly the same percentage as determined under the newer formulas. Thus, replacement rates have, in a sense, been kept more stable throughout time than is indicated by figure 2.

Various indexing provisions in the current benefit formula are designed to keep this particular replacement rate fairly constant for workers retiring at the Normal Retirement Age in the future—at about 53 percent for a single low-wage worker, 40 percent for an average-wage worker, and 26 percent for a high-wage worker. Rates for workers with spouses or dependent beneficiaries, of course, are much higher.

This traditional replacement rate measure provides a useful illustration of the value of Social Security benefits relative to wages prevailing near the time of retirement. It helps us see how a standard of living can be maintained over time. It should, however, be interpreted with caution. First of all, the traditional measure does not take into account that people typically face much lower taxes after retirement than before. OASI replacement rates would look

Figure 2. OASI Replacement Rates

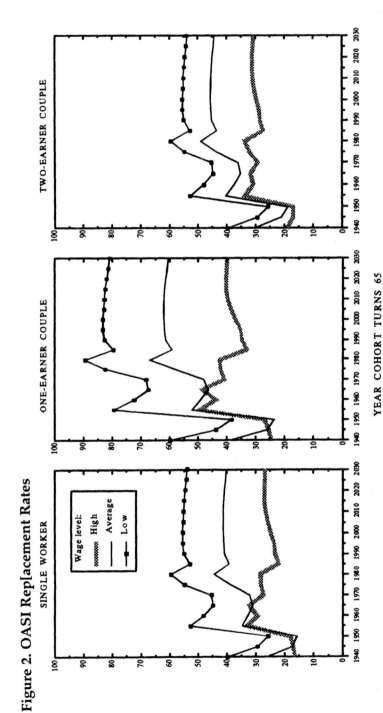

Notes: Figure depicts OASI benefit in first 12 months of retirement as percentage of earned income in preceding 12 months, after adjusting for inflation. Assumes retirement at OASI Normal Retirement Age. Couples are assumed to be the same age. Data cover cohorts born every five years beginning in 1875.

significantly higher if expressed as a percentage of after-tax earnings. Second, a number of other burdens, such as child-care, work expenses, rent, and mortgage payments, also tend to have less effect on the disposable incomes of the elderly than the nonelderly. Adjusting for these factors would make Social Security replacement rates look even better.[13] Third, replacement rates are much higher for those receiving spousal benefits. Fourth, pensions and property income often add substantially to the well-being of middle- and higher-income workers when they retire, thus adding to their "replacement" income. Fifth, the traditional replacement rate compares benefits to income in one of a worker's highest-earning years.[14] Replacement rates would be much higher if expressed as a percentage of a person's normal preretirement standard of living.

It is also important to remember that constant replacement rates often mean that the real purchasing power of benefits is growing substantially from one cohort of retirees to the next. This is particularly important in a budgetary context. Our current budget process treats any growth in most programs as an "increase," even if it only offsets inflation, because nominal expenditures have risen. At the same time, any change that reduces Social Security replacement rates is considered a "cut," even though the program may be growing significantly in real terms. A government budgetary process needs to focus, instead, on how real expenditures and real growth in all programs should be allocated.

The use of the replacement rate as a criterion for setting policy is problematic, moreover, because it does not follow logically from basic principles. A replacement rate is a nice target, perhaps, but it is not a principle.[15] . . . Benefits for middle- and upper-income individuals are justified primarily on the grounds of "individual equity" (i.e., those who contributed to the system should get back a fair return on their investment). Redistribution to lower-income workers, in turn, is justified on grounds of "progressivity" (i.e., by the presumed neediness of some recipients relative to others in society). The replacement rate criterion, however, goes well beyond the simple requirements of both individual equity and progressivity. It suggests that participants at all income levels should receive an "adequate" percentage replacement of past income that is not necessarily related to what they contributed to the system or to their need. Thus, when Social Security policy is set by simple reference to "replacement" rates, middle- and high-income persons can be granted large redistributions beyond what they contribute, as well as beyond their need. Indeed, as we shall see, this is exactly what happened.

MOVING TO A LIFETIME PERSPECTIVE

How does the Social Security system redistribute income? The preceding discussion of benefit levels and replacement rates reveals something about how Social Security outlays are distributed among retirees in any given year, but not the complete picture. A more thorough understanding of Social Security's redistributive nature requires moving to a *lifetime* perspective, that is, examining how Social Security benefits actually compare in value with tax contributions over a lifetime for people of different generations, income levels, and family types. A number of researchers have tackled this question using a wide variety of techniques.[16] Our approach builds on methodologies developed by Nichols and Schreitmueller (1978), Pellechio and Goodfellow (1983), Myers and Schobel (1983 and 1993), Hurd and Shoven (1985), and Boskin et al. (1987), among others. Essentially, it involves using standard actuarial procedures to compare the value of the annuity provided by Old-Age and Survivors Insurance with the value of a private annuity or pension that could be purchased with a worker's lifetime OASI contributions.

Assumptions and Methods

Our approach calculates the *annuity value* (also known as the "actuarial present value") of all OASI contributions made by a worker and his or her employer over a lifetime,[17] given certain assumptions about wage level, family type, probability of death, and year of birth. The employer's portion of the payroll tax is included here, since it is analogous to contributions made to a pension or annuity plan on a worker's behalf. We can then compare these contributions with the full annuity value of the OASI benefits that a worker and his or her dependents or survivors may receive over a lifetime. If the system were to meet the "individual equity" standard perfectly, these two amounts would be identical: an "actuarially fair" annuity would have been purchased through one's contributions. To the extent that the system is progressive on a lifetime basis, one would expect the value of benefits to exceed that of contributions for low-wage workers and to fall short of contributions for higher-wage workers.

To measure and compare contributions and benefit payments occurring at many different points in time, an annuity calculation must adjust all possible payments for the effects of inflation, interest, and probability of occurrence. We compensate for inflation by converting all amounts into their real value in constant 1993 dollars, using the consumer price index.[18] Next, to account for interest, all benefits and taxes are converted to their equivalent present value at age 65. Essentially, this means taking the value of lifetime tax contributions and adding the interest that these contributions would have accumulated by age 65. Likewise, all benefit payments after age 65 are converted to the amount that would have to be invested at age 65 to yield the benefit stream realized.[19] Our analysis calculates present values at the same age for every cohort, so that fair comparisons may be made among different generations. We use a real (after inflation) interest rate of 2 percent[20] for all past and future years, which seems reasonable when compared to average real interest rates over time for safe investments.[21] Social Security is an extremely safe investment that is uniquely resistant to economic fluctuations and inflation and receives favorable tax treatment.

Finally, an annuity calculation must adjust values according to their probability of occurrence, which in this case depends on the likelihood of survival. We make two types of calculations here. The first examines the actuarial present value of lifetime benefits and taxes *assuming survival to age 65.* In this fairly common type of calculation, the tax number is simply the total value of lifetime OASI tax contributions, plus interest, for someone in this group who exhibits a particular pattern of lifetime earnings. The benefit number is determined by multiplying the present value of each possible benefit payment by the probability that someone will be alive to receive that payment, given that he or she has already survived to age 65. For example, a woman who was alive at age 65 in 1970 had about an 80 percent chance of surviving to age 75, so the value of a benefit at age 75 is multiplied by 0.8. Dependents and survivors benefits are similarly weighted according to probability of occurrence. All possible benefit payments through age 110 are adjusted in this manner and then summed together. This procedure expresses the value of Social Security benefits in terms of a "lump sum" of money that someone would have to pay to purchase a similar annuity from a private insurance company at age 65. Calculations of this sort are very useful for examining the obligations that Social Security incurs and its responsiveness to the needs of those who do survive to retirement.

Our second calculation takes into account the chance of death in all years after age 21. Some people may contribute to the system for many years, but receive no retirement benefits because they die before reaching retirement age. Their survivors, on the other hand, may be eligible for benefits that partially offset this loss. Taking these factors into account is useful when trying to compare the insurance protection provided by Social Security with the value of contributions *over an entire lifetime*.[22] This approach has the advantage of measuring how the system treats *all* adult members of a cohort, not just those fortunate enough to survive to old age.

In this second calculation, we continue to adjust for inflation and interest as before, but weight each year's benefit or tax payment according to the probability that someone will be alive in that year, assuming only that they were alive at age 21 (in effect, that they were old enough to join the system in the first place).[23] For example, a male born in 1920 had, on average, an 89 percent chance of surviving from age 21 to age 50, so the expected value of a tax paid at age 50 is multiplied by 0.89. Likewise, since his chance of surviving from 21 to age 70 is about 67 percent, the expected value of the benefit received at age 70 is multiplied by 0.67.

Our model also performs the elaborate calculations necessary to determine the benefit that would be paid to a worker's survivors if the worker died in any year after age 21, and weights each possible benefit stream according to the probability of occurrence. This includes the value of benefits not only for retired widows but also for young surviving children and their widowed parents.[24] Thus, our calculations include the full actuarial value of all Old-Age and Survivors Insurance benefits. For our purposes here, Disability Insurance benefits and taxes, and the chance of disability, are excluded from the analysis.[25]

A unique set of survival probabilities is used for each sex and cohort, based on mortality tables published by the Social Security Administration.[26] These take into account the longer life expectancies of women, as well as improvements in life expectancy for each new generation. Unfortunately, mortality tables that differentiate among people with different lifetime income levels are not available. Since there is evidence that income level has a significant effect on life expectancy, we present a sensitivity analysis later to provide appropriate qualifications to our general conclusions.

We continue to focus here on hypothetical workers and families with "low," "average," and "high" earnings histories. Although these workers may be unrealistic in some respects (e.g., uninterrupted employment between age 21 and retirement), the simplifying assumptions will not significantly affect most of our conclusions.[27] Calculations are performed for cohorts born every five years between 1875 and 1985 (reaching age 65 between 1940 and 2050).

To see how the system treats people of different family types, we examine four types of households: single male and female workers, one-earner couples, and two-earner couples. Again, among two-earner couples, a high-wage man is assumed to be married to an average-wage woman, while average- and low-wage men are assumed to be married to low-wage women. Widowed spouses are assumed not to remarry, and divorce is not taken into account.[28] Couples are assumed to be the same age and to have two children, born when the parents are 25 and 30, who may be eligible for survivors benefits in the event that the worker dies at an early age.[29]

A number of results can be foreseen. Women will fare better than men with identical earnings histories,[30] since their life expectancies are considerably longer. The single worker naturally does worse than couples, since the survivors' and dependents' insurance portions of OASI will have zero value for such a worker. Although workers who remain single over their entire lives will tend to fare relatively badly under such a system, they represent a very small portion of the population. The one-earner couple category is a best-case scenario because the couple is eligible to receive full spousal and survivors benefits even though the wife in this example pays no Social Security taxes. This family type can be expected to become increasingly rare in the future. Falling between these two extremes is the two-earner couple, probably the most representative for cohorts of current workers. In this family type, survivor benefits have at least some value, since they typically supplement the benefits earned by a widow in her own right, and also provide benefits to surviving children.

All projections are based on currently scheduled law (assuming a 10.65 percent OASI tax rate after 1992) and the best-estimate economic assumptions in the 1993 Social Security trustees reports (Board of Trustees, OASDI 1993). OASI faces a 75-year imbalance of about 1.32 percent of taxable payroll under these assumptions. As a result, our projections represent what current law requires, not what it can produce. Eventually, there would have to be some change in tax rates, benefit levels, or both. These projections, nonetheless, accurately portray the baseline from which reform efforts will have to begin, and show the direction in which the current unamended program is heading.

Annuity Value of Benefits and Taxes: An Example

To illustrate the results of these actuarial calculations, we start with the cohort of individuals who turn 65 in 1995. As demonstrated in figure 1, the OASI benefit in the first year of retirement ranges from about $5,900 for a low-wage single person to $23,300 for a two-earner couple with high and average wages. In the top half of table 1, we add up the expected value of these payments over the remaining lives of the beneficiaries, assuming they have already survived to age 65. Because remaining life expectancy at age 65 is substantial, the annuity value of benefits—the amount that would have to be paid to an insurance company at age 65 to provide the same level of benefits—ranges from $78,100 for the low-wage single male to $357,300 for the high-income two-earner couple. The taxes these two types of households would have paid over their lifetimes would have been $49,500 and $300,200, respectively. As a result, they receive positive subsidies, or *net transfers*, of $28,500 and $57,100, respectively, beyond what they contributed.

Next, in the bottom half of table 1, we adjust for the chance of death in all years after age 21. This reduces the value of both benefits and taxes. After all, some members of this cohort simply will not survive long enough either to collect old-age benefits or to pay taxes in all years up to age 65. A male in this cohort has about a 74 percent chance of surviving from age 21 to age 65; thus, adjusting for the chance of death in all adult years reduces the value of benefits for a "typical" male member of this cohort to about three-quarters of what it would be if he were guaranteed to survive to age 65. Taxes are reduced by a smaller amount, since workers who die before age 65 are likely to have contributed to the system for many years, with the average age at death being closer to 65 than to 21. Therefore, the net transfer for a single worker decreases sig-

Table 1 Lifetime OASI Benefits and Taxes for Cohort Turning 65 in 1995 (in Thousands of Constant 1993 Dollars)

	Single Male			Single Female			One-earner Couple			Two-earner Couple		
	Low wage	Avg. wage	High wage	Low wage	Avg. wage	High wage	Low wage	Avg. wage	High wage	Low & Low	Avg. & Low	High & Avg.
Assuming survival to age 65												
(A) Total OASI benefits	78.1	128.8	179.8	95.1	157.0	219.1	143.6	237.1	330.9	173.2	244.3	357.3
Worker's benefit	78.1	128.8	179.8	95.1	157.0	219.1	78.1	128.8	179.8	173.2	224.0	336.8
Spousal and survivors benefits	0.0	0.0	0.0	0.0	0.0	0.0	65.6	108.2	151.1	0.0	20.4	20.5
(B) OASI taxes	49.5	110.0	190.2	49.5	110.0	190.2	49.5	110.0	190.2	99.0	159.6	300.2
(C) Net transfer (A – B)	28.5	18.8	–10.4	45.6	47.0	29.0	94.1	127.0	140.7	74.2	84.8	57.1
Adjusting for the chance of death in all years after age 21												
(D) Total OASI benefits	58.0	95.7	133.6	80.6	132.9	185.5	134.9	223.4	305.4	155.2	226.6	312.6
Worker's benefit	58.0	95.7	133.6	80.6	132.9	185.5	58.0	95.7	133.6	138.5	176.2	266.5
Spousal and survivors benefits	0.0	0.0	0.0	0.0	0.0	0.0	76.9	127.7	171.8	16.6	50.4	46.1
(E) OASI taxes	45.4	100.8	170.7	47.2	104.8	179.0	45.4	108.8	170.7	92.5	148.0	275.5
(F) Net Transfer (D – E)	12.6	–5.1	–37.1	33.4	28.1	6.5	89.5	122.5	134.7	62.6	78.6	37.1

Notes: All amounts are discounted to present value at age 65 using a 2 percent real interest rate. Includes actuarial value of all OASI workers, spousal, and survivors benefits payable over a lifetime. Includes both employer and employee portions of OASI payroll tax. Couples are assumed to be the same age and to have two children born when parents are aged 25 and 30. Assumes retirement at OASI Normal Retirement Age. Projections are based on intermediate assumptions from the 1993 OASDI Board of Trustees report. OASI tax rate is assumed to be set at 10.65 percent beginning after 1992.

nificantly under this adjustment. Among couples, however, the reduction in a worker's benefits is offset to some extent by benefits for surviving spouses and children. In the one-earner couple examples, the compensating survivors benefits are so large that there is almost no reduction in the net transfer when we move to a calculation accounting for the chance of death in all adult years.

Calculations similar to table 1 are made for 23 different cohorts who turn 65 between 1940 and 2050. . . . The subsections following demonstrate some significant trends and draw some important conclusions about the distributional impact of Social Security.

Growth in Lifetime Benefits

In the Social Security program to date, lifetime benefits have increased in value even more dramatically than have annual benefits. Table 2 provides a simple example to illustrate the nature of this growth. Consider one-earner couples where the worker earns average wages. For such a couple retiring in 1960, the annual benefit was about $9,400 at age 65. For a couple retiring in 1995, the annual benefit is approximately $14,600, an increase of about 56 percent. Now consider the value of these benefits over the entire retirement span, assuming survival to age 65. Total retirement benefits for the couple turning 65 in 1995 are worth $237,100, or about 65 percent more than the $143,700 annuity their counterparts received 35 years earlier. The faster rate of growth in the value of lifetime benefits mainly reflects improvements in life expectancy.

When one adjusts for the chance of death in all adult years (not just post-65), the historical growth in benefit payments is yet more dramatic. The annuity value of lifetime benefits for an average-wage one-earner couple grows from $98,900 in 1960 to $223,400 in 1995, a 126 percent increase. Because this calculation takes into account the fact that people are now far more likely to survive their adult years and to reach retirement, it reflects the full growth in the value of retirement insurance protection provided to a typical family. These numbers also reflect considerable growth in the value of survivors' insurance, partly because of longer periods of coverage as the system matured.[31] Both of these factors help explain how the cost of the Social Security system could rise so much in its early decades, even when annual benefit levels rose at a more moderate rate.

Between 1995 and 2030, the value of lifetime benefits is pro-

**Table 2 OASI Benefits for Average-Wage, One-Earner Couples
(in Thousands of Constant 1993 Dollars)**

		Lifetime benefits	
Year cohort turns 65	Benefit in first year of retirement	Assuming survival to age 65	Adjusting for the chance of death in all years after age 21
Amount			
1960	9.4	143.7	98.9
1995	14.6	237.1	223.4
2030	20.8	323.6	312.8
% Increase			
1960–1995	56%	65%	126%
1995–2030	42%	37%	40%

Notes All amounts are discounted to present value at age 65 using a 2 percent real interest rate Couples are assumed to be the same age and to have two children born when parents are aged 25 and 30 Assumes retirement at the OASI Normal Retirement Age Projections are based on the intermediate assumptions from the 1993 OASDI Board of Trustees report

jected to grow at a rate much closer to that of annual benefit levels. A statutory increase in the Normal Retirement Age tends to offset the effects of improving life expectancy. The expected growth in the lifetime value of OASI benefits is nonetheless still quite large. After adjusting for the chance of death in all adult years, OASI benefits are expected to be worth about $312,800 to an average-wage one-earner couple in the cohort turning 65 in 2030, which is 40 percent more than the value of benefits going to their counterparts born 35 years earlier (see table 2).

Growth in Lifetime Tax Contributions

Continuously increasing tax rates have been required throughout Social Security's history to pay for longer retirement spans, more retirees relative to workers, and higher benefit levels. Each successive cohort has contributed to Social Security at higher tax rates for longer time periods. Those who retired at the beginning of 1960, for example, paid Old-Age and Survivors Insurance (OASI) taxes for 23 years at most, and never paid at a combined employer-employee rate higher than 4.5 percent. Steady workers retiring in the recent past have typically been subject to the payroll tax for 40 years or more, but also paid at relatively low rates for most of

Table 3 Lifetime OASI Benefits, Taxes, and Transfers (in Thousands of Constant 1993 Dollars)

Year Cohort turns 65		Single Male			Single Female			One-earner Couple			Two-earner Couple		
		Low wage	Avg. wage	High wage	Low wage	Avg. wage	High wage	Low wage	Avg. wage	High wage	Low & Low	Avg. & Low	High & Avg.
1960	Benefits	30.1	45.5	50.6	45.7	69.0	76.7	66.3	98.9	111.0	76.8	102.0	122.1
	Taxes	4.0	9.0	13.8	4.3	9.6	14.6	4.0	9.0	13.8	8.4	13.3	23.4
	Net Transfer	26.1	36.5	36.8	41.4	59.4	62.1	62.3	89.9	97.2	68.4	88.7	98.7
1980	Benefits	54.3	90.2	114.6	80.8	134.3	170.5	129.3	209.9	264.3	146.9	208.4	273.2
	Taxes	22.9	51.0	71.9	24.2	53.9	76.1	22.9	51.0	71.9	47.2	75.2	125.7
	Net Transfer	31.4	39.3	42.7	56.6	80.5	94.4	106.4	158.9	192.4	99.7	133.3	147.5
1995	Benefits	58.0	95.7	133.6	80.6	132.9	185.5	134.9	223.4	305.4	155.2	226.6	312.6
	Taxes	45.4	100.8	170.7	47.2	104.8	179.0	45.4	100.8	170.7	92.5	148.0	275.5
	Net Transfer	12.6	-5.1	-37.1	33.4	28.1	6.5	89.5	122.5	134.7	62.6	78.6	37.1
2010	Benefits	69.0	115.2	175.9	93.6	156.1	238.4	154.6	258.8	388.6	178.9	261.7	394.2
	Taxes	68.2	151.5	310.8	70.4	156.5	322.4	68.2	151.5	310.8	138.6	221.9	467.3
	Net Transfer	0.9	-36.3	-135.0	23.2	-0.4	-84.1	86.5	107.3	77.7	40.3	39.8	-73.1
2030	Benefits	84.0	139.6	220.3	113.7	189.0	298.1	187.4	312.8	493.0	215.9	316.5	498.1
	Taxes	88.1	195.8	468.8	91.3	202.8	485.4	88.1	195.8	468.8	179.4	287.1	671.6
	Net Transfer	-4.1	-56.2	-248.5	22.5	-13.8	-187.3	99.3	117.0	24.2	36.5	29.4	-173.5

Notes: All amounts are discounted to present value at age 65 using a 2 percent real interest rate. Adjusts for chance of death in all years after age 21. Includes actuarial value of all OASI workers, spousal, and survivors benefits payable over a lifetime. Includes both employer and employee portions of OASI payroll tax. Couples are assumed to be the same age and to have two children born when parents are aged 25 and 30. Assumes retirement at the OASI Normal Retirement Age. Projections are based on the intermediate assumptions from the 1993 OASDI Board of Trustees report. OASI tax rate is assumed to be set at 10.65 percent after 1992.

those years. Those retiring after 2030, by contrast, will have paid OASI taxes at combined employer-employee rates exceeding 10 percent over their entire adult lives.

The magnitude of growth in lifetime Social Security tax contributions is apparent in table 3. For an average-wage male worker in the cohort turning 65 in 1960, the annuity value of lifetime OASI contributions was only about $9,000 (excluding those who died before age 65, the amount is still only $12,000). This figure increased more than elevenfold in constant dollars, to $100,800, for the cohort turning 65 in 1995. Even without any further increases in payroll tax rates after 1995, the actuarial value of taxes for average-wage males in the cohort turning 65 in 2030 is expected to nearly double in real terms, to $195,800.

Net Transfers

The *net transfer* provides perhaps the best summary measure of how the system redistributes income within and across generations. A positive net transfer—the difference between lifetime benefits and taxes—means that an individual or family receives a subsidy above and beyond the fair annuity value of contributions, whereas a negative net transfer indicates that benefits are worth less than contributions. Those with positive net transfers have lifetime income redistributed *toward* them, while those with negative net transfers have lifetime income redistributed *away* from them. Changes in net transfers over time, adjusting for the chance of death in all years after age 21, are illustrated in table 3 and figure 3. An examination of these transfers yields a number of interesting results, summarized in the paragraphs following.

> First, almost all individuals who have retired in any year between 1940 and today—no matter what their income level or family type—have received large positive transfers from Social Security beyond the sum of their contributions to the system and a reasonable rate of return on those contributions.

This phenomenon—large positive transfers to virtually all past and current retirees—is largely a function of the way in which Social Security has evolved over the years. For the first generations of retirees, almost no taxes were paid into the system. Benefit payments represented mainly transfers from the working generation.

Figure 3. Net Lifetime OASI Transfer (in Thousands of Constant 1993 Dollars)

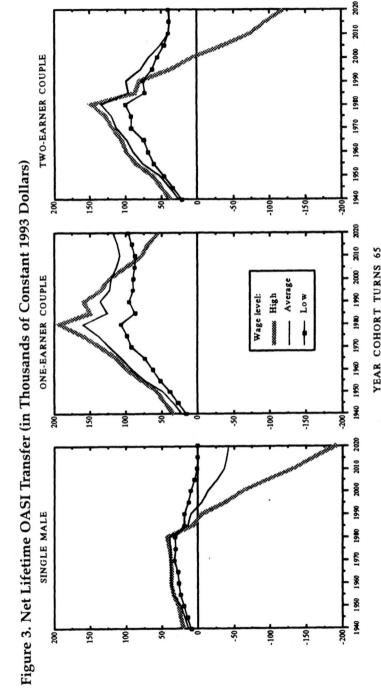

Notes: All amounts are discounted to present value at age 65 using a 2 percent real interest rate. Figure adjusts for chance of death in all years after age 21. Includes actuarial value of all OASI workers, spousal, and survivors benefits payable over a lifetime. Couples are assumed to be the same age and to have two children born when parents are aged 25 and 30. Assumes retirement at OASI Normal Retirement Age. Data cover cohorts born every five years beginning in 1875.

As Social Security matured, this early phenomenon continued. Although lifetime benefits and taxes were both growing rapidly for each successive cohort of retirees, benefits for new retirees over most of this period grew by a larger amount than the taxes they had paid during their working lives. As a result, the gap between benefits and taxes—the net transfer—actually increased. Even people who earned well above the maximum wage subject to Social Security taxation throughout their careers have historically received very large net transfers from the system.[32]

> Second, for most of Social Security's history, the system has been *regressive within generations.* That is, within a given cohort of retirees, net transfers have been inversely related to need: people with the highest lifetime incomes have tended to receive the largest absolute transfers above and beyond what they contributed.

This result may appear surprising given the "progressive" nature of the benefit formula. An example can illustrate how within-generation regressivity could occur even though the benefit formula is intended to provide a higher rate of return on the contributions of low-income workers. Consider one-earner couple families from the cohort that turned 65 in 1980. The annuity value of lifetime OASI contributions for a low-wage one-earner family was about $22,900 in constant 1993 dollars. This family's lifetime OASI benefits are worth more than 5.6 times as much, or $129,300, for a net transfer of $106,400 (see table 3). A high-wage one-earner family's contributions, in turn, amounted to about $71,900. Their benefits are worth about 3.7 times that amount, or $264,300, for a net transfer of $192,400. As one would expect from the way the benefit formula is structured, the lower-income family receives a much higher rate of return on its contributions. More importantly, however, the absolute amount of money transferred to the high-income family is nearly double the size of the transfer going to the low-income family.

This example shows why comparisons of rates of return or benefit-to-tax ratios are incomplete if one wants to know how different people fare under Social Security. Simply put, these measures do not show how to "weight" for differences in the amount of money contributed. If you receive a subsidized return of 25 percent on $100 worth of contributions and I receive a subsidized

return of 20 percent on $1,000, I am being treated much more gen-
erously than you, even though your "rate of return" is higher.
Moving beyond Social Security for the aged, imagine that the government created a welfare system for the population in which the
rich received back tens of thousands of dollars for paying a few
dollars of taxes, while the very poor received a grant of a few hundred dollars without paying any taxes. One could hardly claim this
to be a progressive or need-related system, even though the poor
had a rate of return (and a benefit-to-tax ratio and perhaps a
replacement rate) that was infinitely higher.[33]

> Third, for the first century of retirees in the system, the largest
> amount of net transfers go to high-income individuals who turn
> 65 around the year 1980.

Suppose we want to ask which group in the population
received the best treatment from the system. Given the small contributions made by those retiring early in the system's history, we
might be suspicious that they were the grand winners. Because of
the progressive benefit formula and the way benefits are scheduled to grow over time, on the other hand, we might also suspect
that those low-income individuals retiring many years hence
would fare the best. In actuality, however, for the first century of
retirees in the system, the largest amount of net transfers go to
high-income individuals who turned 65 around the year 1980.[34]
Net transfers going to high-income families in this cohort amount
to $147,500 for two-earner couples and $192,400 for one-earner
couples (see table 3). No low-income workers, past, present, or in
the foreseeable future, will ever receive treatment this generous.[35]
Within each income group, the historical peak in net transfers also
occurs around 1980. Thus, among average-income workers, those
retiring in 1980 receive much more favorable treatment than those
retiring in 1960 or those retiring in 2030.

> Fourth, net transfers will decline for most people among future
> generations of retirees, and the distribution of net transfers will
> become increasingly progressive within generations.

Although Old-Age and Survivor's Insurance has been essentially regressive within generations for most past and current
retirees, the system is becoming more progressive. This is not

because low- and moderate-income people will be faring better under the system, but mainly because high-income people will be faring worse. Using current law and best-estimate economic and demographic assumptions of the Social Security Administration, we find that net transfers will decline slightly for most low- and average-wage persons retiring in the next century, but will still generally remain positive. Meanwhile, net OASI subsidies will gradually be phased out for many high-income persons. Lifetime contributions begin to exceed lifetime benefits for high-wage single males retiring in the 1980s. Positive net transfers are eliminated for high-/average-wage two-earner couples retiring after the turn of the century. Figure 3 demonstrates that high-wage single workers and two-earner couples retiring in the 2020s and later will face very large negative transfers (or positive net lifetime taxes) from the system. For example, a high-/average-wage two-earner couple turning 65 in 2030 faces net taxes or negative transfers of approximately $173,500 (see table 3); their benefits will be worth about 74 percent of their contributions.

The changing income tax treatment of Social Security, which is not included in these calculations, can also be expected to increase the progressivity of the system over time. Employer OASI contributions (as well as accumulated "interest" on contributions) have always been excluded from income taxation. This represents preferential tax treatment relative to other forms of income and savings, and is most valuable to higher-income people. A growing proportion of this tax preference will be offset in the future, however, by income taxation of benefits, which will also have its largest impact on those with high incomes.[36]

The decline in net transfers during the next century occurs not because of any slowdown in benefit growth, but because lifetime contributions are growing faster than benefits. Since the system is set up mainly on a "pay-as-you-go" basis, benefit payments to retirees are dependent on the tax revenues raised from the working population. The growth in transfers going to those who have retired since 1940 could be financed only by rapidly accelerating payroll tax rates on the working population. In effect, the system has been able to keep tax rates rising fast enough to provide more than a generous quid pro quo for almost all workers who have reached retirement age up to now. Those retiring in the future, however, will have contributed vast amounts over their lifetimes to support the transfers going to those who retired before them.

Meanwhile, the ratio of retirees to workers will increase dramatically. As a result of these two factors, payroll tax rates would have to rise astronomically if they were to continue to finance net subsidies for all participants, including high-income persons.

So long as there is some transfer to low-income recipients remaining in the system—a natural consequence of a benefit schedule that pays higher rates on initial dollars of earnings—high-income recipients inevitably have to start paying more in present-value terms than they take out. The transition to this type of system, although only partial and incomplete, began only recently.

Fifth, under current law, many middle- and upper-income households will continue to receive generous positive transfers from Social Security far into the future.

Although the largest of positive transfers have been granted to those who retired in the past (particularly those who are now in their late seventies and early eighties), many current and future retirees will still receive significant subsidies from the OASI system despite being quite well-off economically.

The one-earner couple provides perhaps the major future exception to the increasing within-cohort progressivity of the system. Households of this type continue receiving positive net transfers well into the next century, regardless of income level. High-wage one-earner couples retiring in the near future receive very large transfers, often exceeding $100,000 (see table 3). Indeed, high-income one-earner couples retiring before the turn of the century continue to receive *larger* net transfers than anyone else. Under our projections, positive subsidies continue to flow to high-wage one-earner couples retiring as late as 2050. As we move into the next century, moreover, average-wage one-earner couples will continue to receive larger transfers than low-wage couples.[37] Of course, many fewer couples will fit the one-earner profile in the future. Nevertheless, it remains clear that even in the distant future, not all the subsidies provided by Social Security system will be targeted in a fair or efficient manner or one that follows a logical set of principles.

Net Transfers as Percentage of Lifetime Income

To put the amount of redistribution caused by Social Security in perspective, figure 4 shows net transfers as a percentage of lifetime earned income.[38] Lifetime earned income here excludes any income above the maximum wage subject to Social Security taxation, and includes wages earned before the system began. Transfers going to cohorts retiring in the recent past are quite large relative to lifetime earnings. As an extreme example, consider one-earner couples turning 65 in 1980. Net lifetime OASI transfers represented 21.2 percent of lifetime income for a low-wage worker with a non-wage-earning wife and two children. In other words, this worker not only receives insurance protection equal to the full value of his lifetime OASI contributions but also receives a redistribution of income from Social Security that is equivalent to a lifetime negative tax on earnings of 21.2 percent. The corresponding figures for average- and high-wage workers in this year are 14.2 percent and 11.3 percent, respectively. Not only do these middle- and high-income workers receive back their OASI tax contributions with interest; for many, the redistributions even offset much or all of lifetime federal income tax payments.

On the other hand, consider a high-/average-wage two-earner couple turning 65 in 2030. As stated earlier, this couple faces a lifetime actuarial loss from the OASI system of about $173,500 (table 3). While the amount may appear quite large, it represents only a small portion of this couple's lifetime income—approximately 2.77 percent. In other words, if this couple faces a statutory OASI tax rate of 10.65 percent over most of their careers, approximately 7.88 percentage points could be considered provision for their own retirement, while only 2.77 percentage points represent a transfer to the less fortunate. If the high-wage worker in this family were to earn more than the maximum wage subject to OASI taxation, moreover, the negative transfer would represent an even smaller portion of lifetime income.

Even in a worst case—a single male worker retiring many years hence—the net tax is significantly smaller than the gross rate of tax. For a high-wage single male worker retiring in 2030, the net tax equals about 5.67 percent of lifetime earnings subject to Social Security.

ADJUSTING FOR SURVIVAL DIFFERENCES AMONG INCOME GROUPS

One difficulty with the preceding calculations is that they assume identical mortality probabilities for all people of the same gender

Figure 4. Net OASI Transfer as Percentage of Lifetime Income

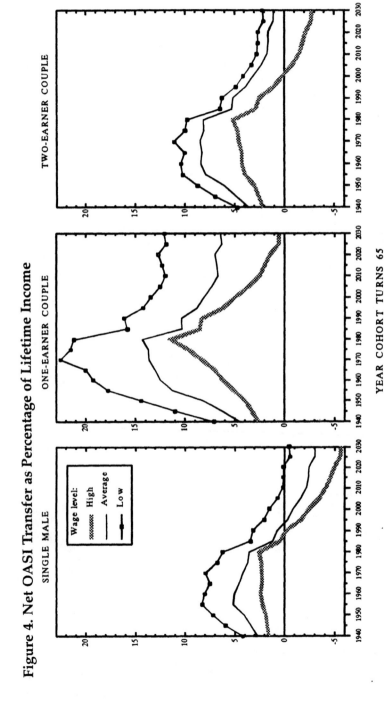

SINGLE MALE

ONE-EARNER COUPLE

TWO-EARNER COUPLE

YEAR COHORT TURNS 65

Wage level:
High
Average
Low

Notes: All amounts are converted to present value at age 65 assuming a 2 percent real interest rate. Figure adjusts for the chance of death and value of spousal and survivors benefits in all years after age 21. Couples are assumed to be the same age and to have two children born when parents are aged 25 and 30. Assumes retirement at OASI Normal Retirement Age. Data cover cohorts born every five years starting in 1875.

and birth cohort, regardless of income level or other characteristics. As indicated earlier, lower income and shorter life expectancies are related. Among the factors that may cause lower-income people to experience higher mortality rates are limited access to health care, poor diet, stress, dangerous jobs, and exposure to violent crime. As a result, their likelihood of receiving Social Security retirement benefits is probably lower than for high-income people. Many analysts have argued that Social Security's progressivity may be reduced significantly by differential mortality rates. Indeed, both Duggan, Gillingham, and Greenlees (1993a, b) and Henry Aaron (1977) have demonstrated that differential mortality rates may have a significant impact on the distributional nature of the Social Security system.

Substantial evidence has existed for some time that there is a strong correlation between race and longevity. In 1989, for example, white men and women had life expectancies at age 21 that were about 15 percent and 9 percent longer, respectively, than those of their black counterparts.[39] Much of this difference is probably attributable to the lower average incomes, educational levels, and living standards of blacks relative to whites. A number of recent studies have also found a strong relationship between income and mortality that is independent of race.[40] Rogot, Sorlie, and Johnson (1992) examined a U.S. Bureau of the Census sample of over 800,000 white persons between 1979 and 1985, and constructed estimated life expectancies by income level based on the observed mortality rates in the sample. As table 4 demonstrates, males and females in the highest category of family income were found to have life expectancies at age 25 that were 7.2 percent and 1.8 percent longer than average, respectively. Men and women in the lowest income category, by contrast, had life expectancies of 12.8 percent and 5.8 percent lower than average. Another study by Duggan and colleagues (1993b) analyzed a sample of 38,000 workers who were born between 1900 and 1923, and examined their subsequent mortality patterns between 1937 and 1988. They found a strong correlation between wages earned at ages 41 to 45 and remaining life expectancy after age 45. According to the relationship they estimated,[41] a male with twice-average income would live about 10.2 percent longer than average, while a male with only 45 percent of average income would face a life expectancy 5.6 percent shorter than average. The corresponding figures for women were plus 8.1 percent and minus 4.5 percent, respectively.

Table 4 Estimated Remaining Life Expectancy for
White Males and Females at Age 25, by Family Income

Family income in 1980 dollars	Remaining life expectancy at age 25, in years		Percentage difference from overall average life expectancy	
	Male	Female	Male	Female
Less than $5,000	43.6	53.7	−12.8%	−5.8%
$5,000–9,999	46.1	56.0	−7.8%	−1.8%
$10,000–14,999	48.7	56.6	−2.6%	−0.7%
$15,000–19,999	50.8	56.9	+1.6%	−0.2%
$20,000–24,999	51.5	57.9	+3.0%	+1.6%
$25,000–49,999	52 4	57.8	+4.8%	+1.4%
$50,000 or more	53.6	58.0	+7.2%	+1.8%
Overall average	50.0	57.0	0.0%	0.0%

Source: Rogot, Sorlie, and Johnson (1992). Note. Data are based on the National Longitudinal Mortality Study 1979–85 follow-up, which itself is based upon samples drawn from Current Population Surveys (CPS) of the U.S Bureau of the Census.

Adjusting our own results precisely for differential mortality rates by income is impossible, since the necessary information is not available in sufficient detail. We can, however, use these previous studies to make some reasonable assumptions about differential mortality rates and see what effect they have on our calculations. Let us assume that men and women in our low-income households have life expectancies at age 21 that are 7 percent and 4 percent shorter than average, respectively. Men and women in high-income households, by contrast, can be assumed to have life expectancies at age 21 that are 7 percent and 4 percent longer than average, respectively. We further assume that the impact of income on mortality rates at different ages shows a pattern similar to the impact of race on mortality at each age. The ratio of black-to-white mortality rates is fairly high at young ages, peaks during the forties, and then declines gradually; at very advanced ages, there is only a small difference in mortality rates between blacks and whites.[42] The upshot is that the income-mortality relationship probably causes many more low-income people to die *before* reaching retirement, but has only a modest effect after retirement.

Table 5 displays the estimated value of lifetime OASI benefits, taxes, and transfers for two selected cohorts, under the revised mortality assumptions just described. Although our differential mortality rate assumptions do cause a modest reduction in the apparent progressivity of the system, the impact is not large enough to change significantly any of the major conclusions we drew in the last section. The lifetime net transfer for low-income male workers retiring in 1995, for instance, is reduced only by about $7,500 under these assumptions, whereas the lifetime transfer going to high-wage male workers increases by $16,300.

Among couples, the impact of our revised mortality assumptions is even smaller, because changes in the value of a worker's benefits are offset partially by changes in survivors benefits. For one-earner couples retiring in 1995, the net transfer falls by about $3,500 for those with low wages and rises by about $9,900 for those with high wages. The impact is slightly larger for two-earner couples. In any case, the net change is only a small percentage of the total value of benefits and net transfers for these families.

When one examines the cohort turning 65 in 2030, the impact of differential mortality rates is larger than in 1995 only when the absolute value of transfers is compared. Relative to total benefits, differential mortality rates are even less important in the future. Although progressivity is again reduced slightly, the basic pattern of redistribution remains close to that in our earlier analysis. Single high-wage workers and high-/average-wage two-earner couples still face very large negative transfers, while others continue to receive positive subsidies.

These tables, of course, do not take into account some other possible differences between income classes. For example, the tendency of those with lower incomes to enter the labor force at an earlier age could reduce the progressivity of the Social Security system a bit further. Suppose that a high-wage male completes some graduate school and delays entry into the labor force until age 24, while a low-wage male begins working at age 18. Among past and current retirees, this differential working pattern would have little effect on net transfers. Tax rates were so low when they were young that paying a few more years didn't matter much. In the cohort turning 65 in 1995, for instance, entering the labor force three years later only improves a high-wage male's lifetime net transfer by about $1,700. Entering the labor force three years earlier reduces the transfer for a low-wage male in this cohort by less than $500. Among cohorts retiring in the future, however, the impact would be more substantial. In the cohort turning 65 in 2030,

Table 5. Lifetime OASI Benefits, Taxes, and Transfers, Assuming Income Has a Strong Effect on Mortality (in Thousands of Constant 1993 Dollars)

	Single Male			Single Female			One-earner Couple			Two-earner Couple		
Year Cohort turns 65	Low wage	Avg. wage	High wage	Low wage	Avg. wage	High wage	Low wage	Avg. wage	High wage	Low & Low	Avg. & Low	High & Avg.
1995 Benefits	48.4	95.7	158.0	73.3	132.9	203.2	129.3	223.4	323.5	142.6	226.6	338.9
Taxes	43.3	100.8	178.9	46.2	104.8	182.8	43.3	100.8	178.9	89.5	148.0	285.5
Net Transfer	5.1	−5.1	−20.8	27.0	28.1	20.4	86.0	122.5	144.6	**53.1**	**78.6**	**53.5**
Net effect of income-related mortality	−7.5	0.0	+16.3	−6.4	0.0	+13.9	−3.5	0.0	+9.9	**−9.5**	**0.0**	**+16.4**
2030 Benefits	70.9	139.6	259.4	102.9	189.0	328.3	178.9	312.8	520.0	204.6	316.5	534.1
Taxes	84.7	195.8	483.8	89.9	202.8	491.2	84.7	195.8	483.8	174.6	287.1	689.0
Net Transfer	−13.8	−56.2	−224.3	13.0	−13.8	−162.9	94.2	117.0	36.2	30.0	29.4	−154.9
Net effect of income-related mortality	−9.7	0.0	+24.2	−9.5	0.0	+24.4	−5.1	0.0	+12.0	−6.5	0.0	+18.6

Notes: Amounts are discounted to present value at age 65 using a 2 percent real interest rate. Table adjusts for the chance of death in all years after age 21. In high-income households, men and women are assumed to have life expectancies at age 21 that are 7 percent and 4 percent longer than average, respectively. In low-income households, men and women are assumed to have life expectancies at age 21 which are 7 percent and 4 percent shorter than average, respectively. Includes actuarial value of all OASI workers', spousal, and survivors benefits payable over a lifetime. Includes both employer and employee portions of the OASI payroll tax. Couples are assumed to be the same age and to have two children born when the parents are aged 25 and 30. Assumes retirement at the OASI Normal Retirement Age. Projections are based on the intermediate assumptions from the 1993 OASDI Board of Trustees report. OASI tax rate is assumed to be set at 10.65 percent after 1992.

delaying work until age 24 would improve a high-wage worker's net transfer by about $17,300. Entering the labor force at age 18 reduces the net transfer by about $3,000 for a low-wage male in this cohort. On the other hand, these changes may be offset to some extent by the greater likelihood that a low-wage worker will become unemployed or disabled. Indeed, if entry and exit from the work force is more probable among lower-income workers, then the system is even more progressive.

In sum, certain characteristics that are closely related to one's income level, such as mortality rates and age when one begins working, probably do weaken the progressivity of Social Security.[43] Even under strong assumptions, however, it appears that the impact is not very large. The basic story remains largely unchanged: within-generation redistribution in the Social Security system remains regressive for most past and current retirees, but turns strongly progressive for most people retiring in the distant future.

NOTES

1. For example, a recent article in the *New York Times* noted: "No one knows for sure whether the Social Security system, on balance, is progressive or regressive—whether, in other words, the taxes and benefits tilt in favor of the rich or the poor" (Rosenbaum 1991). This is not to argue that there is no research on the subject. On the contrary, a large number of studies have examined this issue in a variety of ways, although not all come to the same conclusions (see note 16 below). We merely mean to suggest that an issue that is complex even among experts may be considerably more murky to the public.

2. Perhaps the most notable recent exception to the smooth growth path came about with the retirement of the so-called notch babies, a group born between January 2, 1917, and January 1, 1922, who reached age 65 between 1982 and 1986. The 1977 overhaul of the Social Security benefit formula took away from these notch babies some of the unintended benefits accruing to those who were born just a few years beforehand. The 1972 amendments to the Social Security Act contained a technical error that resulted in an overindexing of benefits—that is, benefit levels for most retirees were rising at a much faster rate than Congress had intended (see figure 1 for an illustration of this growth). This rapid growth was seriously threatening the financial health of the Social Security system, and the overindexing could not be maintained. It took legislators until 1977, how-

ever, to correct for this overindexing. Notch babies were those who retired during the transition correction period when benefits were brought back down to the growth path that was originally intended. For a more detailed explanation, see U.S. General Accounting Office (1988) and National Academy of Social Insurance (1988). From numbers presented here, it can also be seen that notch babies were still among the big winners in the Social Security system in terms of net transfers received.

3. Benefits for future high-wage workers increase faster than those of low- and average-wage workers because the maximum wage subject to Social Security taxation was increased significantly in real value during the late 1970s and early 1980s.

4. Under the old 50 percent maximum, the SSA intermediate projections indicated a 4.3 percent average tax rate on benefits for 2030. Estimates by the Joint Committee on Taxation (1993) and the Office of Management and Budget (OMB 1993a: 12) on the near-term impact of the new law suggest an ultimate increase in revenues of between 60 percent and 80 percent relative to the old law.

5. The final rate of reduction of benefits depends upon the statutory rate at which the last dollars of tax are paid, as well as the Social Security benefit inclusion rate. If a top-bracket taxpayer were paying a tax rate of 40 percent on 85 percent of benefits, for instance, then net benefits would be reduced by 34 percent.

6. In the 15 percent tax bracket, for instance, taxation of 50 percent of benefits implies a marginal reduction of only 7.5 percent under current law. Taxation of 85 percent of benefits increases that rate to 12.9 percent. Most benefits, however, would not even fall in the 15 percent bracket. Although inflation will erode the base levels of income at which Social Security taxation begins to apply, personal exemptions, standard deductions, and other special provisions for the elderly are still likely to keep a significant amount of Social Security income nontaxable.

7. Authors' estimate based on the intermediate projections in the Board of Trustees, SMI (1993), adjusted for the estimated impact of 1993 enactments.

8. Assume a retired average-wage worker faces an average tax rate on benefits of 2 percent in 1995 and 8 percent in 2030, and the annual SMI premium rises from $493 in 1993 to $1,729 in 2030 in constant 1993 dollars. An average-wage worker's after-tax after-premium OASI benefit still rises from $9,056 to $11,088 in constant 1993 dollars, a 22 percent increase.

9. See, for example, Derthick (1979).

10. These figures differ slightly from those usually published by the

SSA, since their replacement rate calculations generally do not adjust for inflation in this last year.

11. For high-income individuals, the cycle in replacement rates (see figure 2) is due largely to fluctuations in the maximum wage subject to Social Security taxation. The maximum declined in real value relative to the average wage until the mid-1960s, then was increased again through later legislative enactments.

12. Replacement rates were so low at the beginning of Social Security because workers had only participated in the program for a few years before retiring. Barring changes in wage and price levels, longer spans of participation would have eventually caused the original formula to produce replacement rates similar to those we have today. See Robert Ball in *The Report of the Committee on Economic Security of 1935: 50th Anniversary Edition* (1985: 167) and Myers (1993a: 36165).

13. See Myers (1993a: 205–11) for estimates of net replacement rates after taxes and work expenses.

14. Replacement rate measures used here and by the SSA express benefits as a percentage of earnings in the last year or few years before retirement. Because these calculations are based on hypothetical workers whose wages grow in each year at the same rate as average wage growth in the economy, earnings in the last years before retirement are higher in real value than earnings in earlier years of work.

15. The logic of replacement rates derives from a notion that one will be happier if expenditures out of one's lifetime income are balanced over the life cycle. For instance, adequate food at all points in life is probably better than an abundance at one time and an absence at another. At best, then, the replacement rate can be a means of measuring whether or not a program is responding to one particular pattern of needs of individuals (for balanced spending). If the basic concern is need, however, then one must return to the more fundamental progressivity principle—which requires a comparison with other needs in society—in trying to determine whether replacing one person's income (say, that of a millionaire who has contributed little to the system) is more important than meeting some other need. As we will see, consideration of the replacement rate as a principle has historically led to large net transfers to high-income individuals even when there were many greater needs in society.

16. Meyer and Wolff (1987) offer a good survey of this literature. Some studies that have examined various aspects of this question include: Aaron (1977), Boskin, Arvin, and Cone (1983), Boskin et al. (1987), Bulkhauser and Warlick (1981), Cohen and Male (1992), Feldstein and Pellechio (1979), Goss and Nichols (1993), Hurd and Shoven (1985),

Kollman (1992), Myers and Schobel (1983, 1993), Nichols and Schreit-mueller (1978), Pellechio and Goodfellow (1983), and U.S. Congress, House Committee on Ways and Means (1992: 1258–69). Most of these studies, however, show only selective or limited results (such as benefit to contribution ratios only for a selected cohort), so that comparisons with our results are limited.

The technique employed by Boskin et al. (1987) is one of the closest to ours. They show distributional patterns that are generally similar to those shown here. Our study, however, shows somewhat higher internal rates of return and better net transfers. A number of factors may account for these differences. They use a 3 percent real interest rate to calculate present values, whereas we assume 2 percent (this only affects the net transfer calculations, not the internal rates of return). Our calculations are on a before-income-tax basis, whereas they make a rough estimate of the impact of income taxation of benefits. We also assume that the OASI tax rate is reduced to 10.65 percent after 1992, in accordance with currently pending legislation. Our calculations include the value of survivors benefits for young children and widow(er)s of deceased workers, whereas theirs do not. Their calculations are based on the assumptions in the 1983 Trustees reports, while ours are based on the 1993 reports (Board of Trustees, OASI 1983, 1993) (except for mortality rates, which we base on 1992 assumptions). Our more recent mortality rate assumptions result in significantly longer life expectancies than theirs, although this is offset to some extent by our lower real wage growth assumptions. Finally, the earnings levels of their "low-" and "middle"income workers are consid-erably higher than ours, and they use different assumptions for wage growth over the life cycle.

Myers and Schobel (1993) perform calculations of benefit-to-tax ratios for single workers that are also comparable to ours, using similar assumptions for wage growth, mortality, and interest rates. After adjusting for the fact that they consider only the employee portion of the OASI tax, and assume survival to retirement, we found that our results are consistent with theirs. Goss and Nichols, of the SSA Office of the Actuary (1993), also perform actuarial calculations of OASDI benefit-to-tax ratios for hypothetical workers, using approaches and assumptions that are not far from ours. Our results also appear roughly consistent with those in this latter study, after adjusting for differing assumptions.

17. Calculations in this chapter assume that the combined employer-employee OASI tax rate is set at 10.65 percent in all years after 1992, in accordance with currently pending bills that would reallocate tax rates between OASI and DI. Under this tax rate and the SSA's 1993 interme-

diate assumptions, OASI suffers a 75-year actuarial imbalance of approximately 1.32 percent of taxable payroll. . . . Net transfers are a bit worse for future retirees under this assumption, but the basic pattern is the same.

18. The consumer price index for all urban consumers (CPI-U) is used here. As with all other economic variables, we use the SSA's 1993 intermediate assumptions to project future growth in the CPI. A number of different inflation indices are sometimes used by economists, but the CPI-U is the most common. Cost-of-living adjustments in Social Security, by contrast, are based on the CPI for urban wage and clerical workers (CPI-W). The CPI-U is regarded as superior to the CPI-W for most purposes, since it covers a wider spectrum of consumers. The difference between the two indices is negligible; average annual inflation between 1968 and 1988 was 6.3 percent when measured by CPI-U and 6.2 percent under the CPI-W.

19. In precise terms, the present value of a benefit or tax in any given year is determined by multiplying its real value by $(1 + r)^x$, where r is the real interest rate and x is 65 minus the worker's age during the year in question. This, of course, means that any taxes or benefits paid before age 65 are *increased* by conversion to present value, while taxes or benefits after age 65 are *reduced*. Present value calculations thus adjust for the *time value of money*: a dollar today is worth more than a dollar, say, 10 years from now, since a dollar today could be invested and accumulate a large amount of interest over those 10 years.

20. The nominal interest rate in any given year is 1.02 times the inflation rate; that is, if inflation were 4 percent, the nominal interest rate would be 6.08 percent ($1.04 \times 1.02 = 1.0608$). We believe that a constant real interest rate over time is the fairest way to make comparisons among different generations. This prevents our results from being affected by arbitrary fluctuations in rates over time, and provides a uniform standard of individual equity for all generations.

21. It might be argued that higher-income individuals should be granted a higher rate of return because they make "better" investments. As a matter of policy, of course, it would be highly questionable to argue that the rich should get better treatment for each tax dollar contributed. In addition, high-income investors can still offset Social Security contributions by borrowing at the prevailing interest rate, and then make high-yield investments with the borrowed money. The appropriate discount rate, therefore, would be the interest rate on the borrowing, which is lower than the average yield on their investments.

22. Technically, an annuity calculation that assumes survival to age 65 slightly overstates the return one receives on lifetime contributions.

Like any other insurance scheme, a private annuity system pools risks. The contributions of those who do not survive to retirement, therefore, can be used to supplement the benefits of those who do. In an actuarially fair annuity system where workers contribute over their entire careers, the expected value of benefits for someone who survives to age 65 would exceed the value of his or her contributions plus interest. This effect may be offset to some extent by survivors benefits for the families of workers who die before retirement. Our calculations, which adjust for the chance of death in all years after age 21, fully account for both of these effects, and thus provide a comparison of the value of contributions and benefits in a broader annuity framework.,

23. We adjust for the chance of death in all years after age 21 for all cohorts, even those who turned 21 before the system was established. This effectively provides a comparison of how the system treated typical members of different cohorts.

24. Once again, we adjust for the probability of death each year for each of these beneficiaries. Children's chance of death is taken into account at all ages after birth. The SSA's 1992 intermediate cohort- and gender-specific mortality rates are used for all children born in 1990 or earlier, assuming the elder child is male and the younger child is female. For children born later than 1990, we had to use the 1990-cohort gender-specific mortality tables, since they are the last cohort for which the SSA produced such tables. This has an insignificant impact on the total value of benefits.

Surviving children are assumed to be eligible for survivors benefits until the maximum possible age for a nondisabled child; for instance, the calculations include benefits for surviving full-time students aged 18-21 during the years when that provision was in effect. Our calculations include the value of benefits for surviving mothers and fathers with eligible children, adjusted according to the earnings test when appropriate.

Widowed members of two-earner couples may adopt a "switching" strategy that will unambiguously increase the lifetime value of their benefits. They can begin to receive either their own benefit or a survivors benefit before the Normal Retirement Age (NRA), and then switch to the other kind of benefit upon attainment of the NRA, without suffering any actuarial reduction on the second benefits. Our calculations assume that they take advantage of this provision, but continue to work until the NRA. All earnings test reductions, actuarial adjustments, and historical rule changes are accounted for when appropriate. A widowed member of a low-wage two-earner couple is assumed to begin receiving survivors benefits as early as age 60, and then to switch to his or her own benefits at the NRA. A low-wage widow of an average-wage husband is assumed to begin collecting her own benefits as early as age 62, and then to switch to survivors benefits at the NRA. An average-wage widow of a high-wage husband is assumed to begin collecting her benefits a year before the NRA, and then to switch to survivors benefits at the NRA (the earnings test makes this her optimal strategy). Average- and high-wage men in our examples cannot take advantage of the switching provision because the earnings test wipes out their survivors benefits. In our tables in the text . . . , we count all extra benefits arising from the switching provision as survivors benefits, regardless of their official designation.

25. These factors are omitted because of the scarcity of data on these topics and the vast uncertainty surrounding future projections. Adding in DI benefits and accounting for the chance of disability would probably improve net transfers from the Social Security system slightly for most workers. In a separate study (Bakija and Steuerle 1993), we estimate the impact of Disability Insurance on the value of Social Security for hypothetical workers born in 1965. The distributional impact of DI in this cohort is similar to that of OASI, but on a much smaller scale.

A related issue is the interaction between DI and OASI programs. A so-called disability freeze provision improves net transfers for workers at all income levels. The disability freeze allows years spent receiving DI payments to be excluded from the AIME calculation. As a result, the chance of disability reduces the actuarial value of lifetime tax contributions without affecting benefit levels significantly. The net result of adjusting for DI taxes and benefits and the disability freeze adjustment would be a small improvement in net transfers for most workers. For the purposes of this book, the value of the disability freeze provision—mainly the lower taxes required to support later old-age benefits—is treated as a disability benefit even though there is no technical or formal reimbursement from the DI to the OASI trust funds for this purpose.

26. These mortality tables published by the SSA are the same as those used to construct the intermediate or "best-estimate" projections in the 1992 Social Security Trustees reports (SSA, Office of the Actuary 1992a). Data for a few additional cohorts not covered in this publication were furnished to the authors by the SSA. Mortality assumptions in the 1992 Trustees report are virtually identical to those used in 1993.

27. The assumption of continuous work between age 21 and the Normal Retirement Age is somewhat unrealistic, particularly in the case of working women. Because of drop-out years in the average indexed monthly earnings (AIME) calculation, a few years spent out of the labor force would tend to reduce lifetime tax contributions somewhat without significantly reducing benefits.

For simplicity's sake, low- and average-wage workers' earnings are assumed to grow at the same rate as the average national wage in each year. A worker's income, however, typically starts lower and rises faster over the life cycle. If we were to examine workers with the same level of aggregate lifetime earnings, but with more realistic life-cycle earnings patterns, we would also find that their benefit payments were slightly higher relative to taxes paid. This occurs because most years of lower earnings would be dropped out of the benefit calculation, while years that are included in the calculation would be somewhat higher. There would, however, be some offset for many cohorts whose higher-earning years were at the higher tax rates later in life. For high-wage workers, fluctuations in income above the base limit do not affect the calculations but few probably began to earn such high wages immediately at age 21. This probably causes us to overstate their tax payments slightly, without affecting benefit levels.

28. The assumption that widows remain single has only a small impact on our analysis. Survivors benefits going to those who are widowed at an early age, when remarriage is at least somewhat likely, represent an extremely small portion of the total value of benefits in our analysis.

29. We also assume a larger number of children would have little impact on the results, since annual benefits for a surviving parent and two children are already above the maximum family benefit level. Additional children, however, would likely add to the number of years that the maximum benefit was made available.

30. No adjustment is made here for the fact that women have lower earnings than men on average. This does not, however, affect the validity of our results for the benefits and taxes for women at the hypothetical earnings levels. One simply needs to remember that women have been more likely than men to fall into the "low-" and "average-", rather than "high-", wage categories.

31. The cohort retiring in 1995 was covered by survivors insurance for a much longer time than was a cohort retiring in 1960, since the system only started up in 1937. For the earlier cohort there were no Social Security benefits for survivors of workers who died before age 44.

32. OASI benefits may alternatively be viewed as replacing transfers that workers would have made otherwise to their retired parents. Workers retiring during the first few decades of the system often had parents who had not been covered by Social Security. Some of these workers may have made significant private transfers to help support their retired parents. When these workers retired, however, Social Security made private transfers from their children less necessary. The smaller lifetime private transfers

these workers receive from their children might be viewed as an offset to large public transfers given to them (Goss and Nichols 1993).

Trying to trace the net transfers under such a scenario would not be easy, and there would still be many large winners and losers, both within and between generations. Among the issues raised are the following. First, it is impossible to measure private transfers; later generations may be just as generous to their parents as previous ones, since they have greater economic resources. Second, earlier generations of workers were far less likely to have parents survive to retirement than today's workers. Third, those who retired during the 1970s and 1980s received the largest public transfers of all, yet had parents who were usually covered by Social Security themselves. Finally, treating OASI contributions as gifts to one's parents weakens the whole individual equity argument for tying benefits to past contributions. Although contributions to a pension plan clearly entitle one to commensurate retirement benefits, the fact that someone makes a generous gift to his parents does not necessarily entitle him to an equally generous gift from his children.

33. Internal rates of return, of course, do serve other purposes. They can provide a way to check on the sensitivity of present-value calculations to interest rate assumptions. They also permit a comparison of Social Security and market rates of return. For comparisons of the redistribution achieved among people with different amounts of contributions, however, they are inadequate.

34. These results are only moderately sensitive to discount rate and similar assumptions, given the low tax rates and increasing benefits in the first few decades of the program.

35. If one performed calculations going out into the 22nd century, low-income couples retiring then might be found to receive the same level of real transfers as high-income individuals in the late 1970s and early 1980s, although even this appears unlikely under our projections.

36. Since OASI benefits were completely exempt from taxation for many years, but employer contributions and accumulated interest received favorable tax treatment, taking these factors into account would improve the value of OASI slightly for most past retirees. The introduction of taxation of benefits, and its recent expansion, will offset some or all of the value of the tax exclusion for employer contributions for most future retirees. The exact portion that is offset depends on a variety of factors, and the calculations would be quite complicated. Recent calculations by the SSA Office of the Actuary (Goss 1993) suggest that taxation of 85 percent of OASI benefits is consistent with the current practice of taxing pension benefits, even for most future retirees. This implies that

OASI, on a lifetime basis, receives income tax treatment at least as favorable as tax-preferred private pensions, and more favorable than most other private savings.

37. Note that these results are affected to some extent by our assumption that the wife never works for wages; if the wife worked for at least a few years, the family's net transfer would be reduced. Many couples will fall somewhere between our one-earner and two-earner couple examples. In general, the less a wife works for wages, the better will be the family's net transfer from the system.

38. Lifetime earned income, like benefits and taxes, is discounted to age 65 using a 2 percent real interest rate and adjusting for the chance of death in all years after age 21. All lifetime wages since age 21 are used in these calculations even if those wages were earned before the inception of the Social Security program. Wage histories before 1935 are constructed by assuming that all workers experienced real wage growth every year equal to the real growth in average wages for all U.S. employees, based on an estimated historical series published by the U.S. Bureau of the Census (1975: ser. D 722-727 and D 735-738).

39. The average life expectancy at age 21 was 53.0 years for white males, but only 46.2 years for black males. Among females, the figures were 59.2 years for whites and 54.4 years for blacks (U.S. Bureau of the Census 1992a: 76). Note that this is a "period" life expectancy, which is typically lower than the cohort-specific life expectancies used throughout the text. A period life expectancy is constructed based on mortality rates at each age in a given year, while a cohort life expectancy is constructed using mortality rates at each age for a given cohort.

40. Aside from the studies cited in the text, Hadley (1982), Kitagawa and Hauser (1973), Menchik (1993), Rosen and Taubman (1979), and Taubman and Rosen (1982) also provide evidence that there is a significant correlation between mortality and such factors as education and income level in the United States. In addition, numerous studies in the United Kingdom have found that people in lower-paying occupations have significantly higher mortality rates. See Wilkinson (1986), Townsend and Davidson (1988), and Whitehead (1988).

41. Duggan et al. (1993a: 11) found that for every additional $1,000 of average income (in constant 1988 dollars) between ages 41 and 45, men experienced a 0.97 percent increase in life expectancy, while women experienced a 0.78 percent increase.

42. To adjust for the impact of income on mortality, we constructed new mortality tables that will result in desired level of life expectancy at age 21 for people at each income level, using the SSA's cohort- and

gender-specific mortality tables (SSA, Office of the Actuary 1992) as a base. We constructed each table according to the formula:

$$Q^1 = Q_x R_x B_1 \qquad (5.1)$$

where Q_x^1 is the constructed mortality rate at each age x for a given cohort and gender after adjusting for the effects of income; Q_x is the SSA's standard mortality rate for that age, cohort, and gender; R_x is the ratio of black to white mortality rates at that age and gender in 1989; and B is a parameter, found by iteration, that results in the desired life expectancy. For low-income persons, B is between 0 and 1, whereas for high-income persons, B falls between 0 and –1. The black-to-white mortality ratio at each age is thus used as a rough proxy to simulate the strength of income's influence on mortality at each age. Mortality rates after age 85 are assumed to be unaffected by income.

43. In the case of years of work, horizontal equity is also an important issue. That is, two individuals with the same annual income levels may work a very different number of years, contribute very different amounts to the system, and yet still receive the same value of benefits.

19

The Sky's *Not* Falling,
The Sky's *Not* Falling!

Newsday Editorial

I t's an exercise that never fails to intrigue Daniel Patrick Moynihan. When New York's senior senator asks audiences of young adults how many of them believe Social Security will be there for their retirement, no hands go up.

Months of public admonition that Social Security faces a back-breaking fiscal imbalance when the huge baby boom generation retires have convinced much of the nation that the situation is nothing short of calamitous. In one poll, commissioned by the Generation X political group Third Millennium, more young adults said they believed in UFOs than in the idea that Social Security would be there for them when they retire.

The public panic has spawned a cottage industry to develop theories and schemes not only to fix Social Security but to fundamentally alter it—to change it from a government-run social-insurance program to a private investment plan for future retirees. But before anything that radical is tried, it's worth stepping back, taking a breath—and recognizing that the sky is not falling.

Yes, Social Security faces an enormous fiscal imbalance partway into the next century. That's a function of two demographic trends: The baby boom generation, people now in their 30s, 40s,

From Newsday *Currents*, December 15, 1996, pp. A41–A42. Reprinted with permission, © Newsday, Inc., 1996.

and early 50s, is much larger than the generation of workers expected to support it through payroll taxes. And people are living longer, so retirement—once a short phase of life—is stretching. From an actuary's perspective, it's becoming more costly.

But the situation is not so dire that it cannot be solved by using fixes that have been employed time and again to keep Social Security afloat during its 61 successful years. And it is certainly not time to junk a system that has worked astonishingly well and replace it with a riskier, personal investment plan that wouldn't have the same protections for most average and low-income workers—and wouldn't provide predictable benefits to *any* retiree.

Switching to a personal investment plan would end Social Security as a social-insurance system, where virtually all American workers and their employers share a mutual burden—and reap a mutual benefit—from paying into a collective system. It would break the enduring bonds between current workers and the older generation of retirees; between high-wage earners and those who work but earn very little; between workers who stay healthy and work continuously right up to retirement—and those who become unable to support their families because of disability or death.

THREE MYTHS ABOUT SOCIAL SECURITY

To understand why Social Security should be saved, not slain, it is necessary to debunk the myths that have grown up around it.

• **The first myth** is that the coming crisis is so dire that the system will fail completely unless it is fundamentally changed. That is simply untrue. Without any changes at all, the Social Security trust fund has a surplus sufficient to last until 2029, nearly two decades after the first baby boomers begin retiring. After that, Social Security could still pay benefits at about 75 percent of current levels. That's unacceptable, to be sure. But it is far from the extinction predicted by the doomsday prophets.

• **The second myth** is that a gargantuan tax increase would be needed to keep the system as is. This argument is advanced by those who want to privatize the system, replacing most of Social Security with individual retirement accounts managed by workers themselves and invested in stocks and other financial instruments. In fact, the Social Security trustees estimate that the entire fiscal imbalance could be eliminated with a payroll-tax hike of 2.2 percent—not so different from the increase imposed when the system was last restructured in 1983. And, a little-known aspect of most privatization plans, including the two put forward by members of the official advisory council on Social Security's future, involve a tax hike of similar size. That is because to switch to a new system, current workers would have to pay twice: first to support retirees who've earned benefits under the existing system, and then to put money into their own personal savings accounts.

• **The third myth** is that workers cannot expect to "get back" from Social Security all they put in and, as a group, would do better with a privatized system that allowed for individual investment decisions. In fact, today's retirees get back all the tax money they paid out in just 18 months to 3 years, depending on how high their wages were. With interest, the employee's contribution is paid back over 6 to 11 years—not so bad, considering that life expectancy after retirement is now 15 years.

It's true that the payback period is longer for future generations. But even for those born in 1968—today's Generation X—an average worker would recover all Social Security taxes plus interest in 11 years. Life expectancy after retirement for this group is estimated at 16 years.

Certainly, high-income workers whose payroll contributions would be large, and who would probably make informed investment choices, might do better under a privatized system. But what about workers in cyclical industries who endure long layoffs and wouldn't have contributions made into the accounts while they're out of work? What about women who move in and out of the workforce? And what about Social Security's other, vital function: providing a safety net for workers who, through no fault of their own, can't work anymore.

Of the 44 million current Social Security recipients, only 27 million are retirees. The remaining 17 million are disabled workers and the survivors of those who've died before retirement. The prospects of one's death or disability mustn't be discounted: 30 percent of today's 20-year-olds will become disabled, and 20 percent of workers in this age group will die before retirement, actuaries say.

All the privatizers say they will provide for these people. But politically, the viability of a system that would essentially separate the healthiest and wealthiest from those whose luck isn't as good would be shaky. There would doubtless be calls to impose an income test on disability and survivors' benefits. And even for middle-income people who work their whole lives, there are pitfalls: What if the market turns bearish in the five or six years before retirement, and the annuity to be purchased with the investment account provides a lot less than anticipated?

In short, an idea that sounds good in broad strokes—especially given Wall Street's recent performance—looks far less attractive in detail.

HOW TO SAVE THE SYSTEM

Luckily, there are alternatives, which, if put in place now, would cure Social Security's long-term ills. There is broad agreement on the advisory council on a series of benefit cuts and tax changes that should be applied. These include requiring newly hired state and local employees to pay taxes and be covered by Social Security; assuming a small downward adjustment in the Consumer Price Index to reflect biases in the inflation index that pushes benefits upward annually; changing the number of working years on which benefits are calculated, and taxing Social Security benefits in the same way the government now taxes private pensions.

Then there is the idea put forward by a group on the advisory council headed by Robert Ball, a former Social Security commissioner, for investing a portion of the trust fund in the stock market. This is attractive because it would increase returns and provide new revenue for the trust fund. But it, too, raises serious questions. Foremost among them is how to keep such a fund insulated from political pressure, such as demands for divesting of tobacco stocks or securities of other unpopular businesses. And there are serious issues to be explored about the impact of having so much government-controlled money invested in private markets at all.

At the moment, the debate should be less about specific revisions and more about the broader question of maintaining a social-insurance system that has been the most successful experiment ever tried in this country. Taking a universal, mutually beneficial system and changing it to one based on individualism wouldn't fix the program. It would end Social Security as we know it.

20

The Myth of the 2.2 Percent Solution

Neil Howe and Richard Jackson

Each year, the Trustees calculate a measure of Social Security's long-term fiscal health called its "actuarial balance." In 1996, this balance was determined to be minus 2.2 percent of taxable payroll. In theory, this is the total amount by which we would have to raise taxes or cut benefits, starting today, to keep the Social Security trust funds solvent over the next seventy-five years.

Those who would minimize Social Security's troubles regularly trot out this measure (and this figure) as evidence of how small the problem is. How can anyone seriously talk about a crisis, they say, when that crisis could be solved by a "mere" 2.2 percent of payroll tax hike? The press, assuming that because this number is official it must be meaningful, routinely repeats it.

There's just one catch: Actuarial balance greatly understates Social Security's true burden on our future. Unfortunately, the recent report of the Social Security Advisory Council gives new ammunition to defenders of the status quo. While the council was divided about reform options, all members lined up behind actuarial balance as the basic measure of Social Security's long-term health. Such unanimity is puzzling. This indicator not only misleads the public about the magnitude of the future fiscal burden

---

From *Facing Facts* 3, no. 1 (January 10, 1997): 1–2. Copyright © 1997 The Concord Coalition.

posed by Social Security, it says nothing about the program's impact on national savings and generational equity, the concerns that led five of the council's thirteen members to advocate that we transition to a funded system of personally owned accounts.

THE CENTRAL FALLACY

In the framework of actuarial balance, Social Security will be solvent until the year 2029—meaning that, until then, its trust funds are projected to possess sufficient assets to cover current-law benefit promises. If we were to enact the 2.2 percent solution, the trust funds would be solvent for the next seventy-five years.

The problem is that this solvency is an accounting fiction. Actuarial balance assumes that trust-fund surpluses accumulated in prior years constitute genuine economic savings that can be drawn down to cover trust-fund deficits incurred in future years. They don't. Since the assets held by Social Security consist of nothing but Treasury IOUs, when it's time for the trust funds to redeem them Congress must raise taxes, cut other spending, or borrow more from the public to raise the cash.

What really matters is Social Security's operating balance— that is, the annual difference between its outlays and its earmarked tax revenues. Under current law, this balance is due to turn negative in 2012 and widen to an *annual* deficit of $650 billion, or 3.8 percent of payroll, by 2029, the last year the trust funds are technically "solvent." Even if the 2.2 percent solution were enacted, Social Security would still face large and steadily growing operating deficits starting in 2021.

Status quoists will counter that trust-fund assets do indeed constitute genuine savings because, if Social Security had not run surpluses, the federal government would have run larger deficits. This is an interesting argument—but there's little evidence to support it.

Behaviorally, the argument implies that our political system tracks and targets some desired balance in the rest-of-government, rather than in the unified budget. This isn't so. Over the past dozen years (the era in which we built up today's trust-fund assets), there have been many plans and processes aimed at balancing the unified budget, but none aimed at balancing the budget excluding Social Security. Remarking on Washington's failure even to attempt this, Senator Moynihan notes that Social Security's surpluses have simply allowed Congress to tax less and spend more than it otherwise would, and so denounces them as a "fraud." As for the future, no one, least of all the status quoists, is insisting that we run a $104 billion unified budget surplus in 2002—which is what will then be required to balance the budget excluding Social Security.

This budget reality explains an apparent paradox that the status quoists often pose: If individuals and private pension funds are engaged in genuine savings when they invest in Treasury bonds (and they are), why then is such investment by the trust funds fundamentally different? The reason is that when a private citizen decides to buy a Treasury bond, it doesn't induce Congress to incur a larger debt than it otherwise would.

Admittedly, the whole question of how Social Security surpluses do or do not change the overall budget balance (and national savings) will strike many Americans as quite abstract. A more vital question is whether what the status quoists are advocating for future fiscal policy makes any sense given where our economy and society find themselves today. The logic of actuarial balance rests on a fantastic proposition—namely, that America's lofty savings rate in the 1990s, due to the thriftiness of government, is paying in advance for a sumptuous deficit banquet twenty years from now. In other words, it's OK to save less than we ought tomorrow because we're saving *more* than we ought today.

In the end, there's only one possible defense of trust-fund accounting, and that is to insist that Social Security is an entirely separate realm of government—not just another federal agency, but a kind of independent republic exempt from the sovereignty of Congress. Thus, if we didn't save enough publicly in the 1980s and 1990s, it's the fault of the rest of government. And if we will need to undertake some draconian belt-tightening in the 2020s and 2030s, that too is the fault of the rest of government. But why should we think of Social Security this way? Not because the contributions are owned or managed by the workers who make them and not because the benefits are economically funded or legally guaranteed. None of this is true. As it turns out, the most often-cited reason for why Social Security should be considered a self-contained deal is that it's a trust fund. Thus does the logic become a perfect and empty circle.

OTHER MISCONCEPTIONS

Entirely apart from the savings fallacy, there are several other misconceptions about actuarial balance, and in particular the 2.2 percent solution, that need correcting.

- The 2.2 percent solution is hardly trivial. If enacted as a tax hike, it would mean a tax increase of $69 billion this fiscal year. From now to 2002 it would mean an increase of $467 billion—a larger tax hike than Dole's proposed income tax cut. A tax hike of this size is inconceivable in today's political climate. Certainly, no one would dream of calling it "small" or "bearable" if it were actually (and not just rhetorically) proposed.
- It's already too late to enact the 2.2 percent solution, since this figure presupposes that the reform was implemented starting in 1996. Yet each year that we delay, the level share of payroll required to bring the trust funds into balance rises. Let's assume that the earliest we could enact a savings package is 2002. This delay would raise the required savings by roughly 0.4 percentage points—to 2.6 percent of payroll.
- The forgoing calculation assumes that 2070 will forever remain the horizon for trust-fund solvency. In other words, it assumes that while we today would require the trust funds to be in balance over seventy-five years, our children will be satisfied with forty years and our grandchildren will drive over the cliff with their eyes closed. But Social Security has always (and sensibly) been required by law to calculate its balance over a full seventy-five years. Assuming this remains true, each passing year will add a new higher-cost year and subtract a new lower-cost year, raising the savings needed to balance the trust funds by roughly 0.06 percentage points per year in every future year. By 2002, the required savings will be about 0.4 percentage points higher—that is, it will be 3.0 percent of payroll, not 2.6 percent. And even if this savings were enacted, the total will keep climbing in later years—to 3.5 percent by 2010, 4.1 percent by 2020, and 4.7 percent by 2030.
- Even these figures may understate the magnitude of the required savings. If we accept the Trustees' "high-cost" scenario, whose key economic and demographic assumptions

more closely reflect the actual experience of the past two decades, the number the status quoists cite (2.2 percent) would instantly rise to 5.7 percent.

THE REAL ISSUE

In the end, trust-fund accounting sidesteps the real issue, which is not how to meet some official solvency test, but how to ensure Social Security's economic sustainability and generational equity. It is these concerns that have led a growing number of voices, including the five Advisory Council members, to advocate transitioning to a funded system of personally owned accounts. By linking benefits to genuine economic savings, such a reform not only addresses the fiscal challenge. It would generate much higher returns on contributions for future retirees, and hence would redress the cascading pattern of generational inequity that now destines each new birth cohort of Social Security participants to receive a worse deal than the last. It deserves a serious hearing.

As for the 2.2 percent apologists, one gets the impression that they don't much care about these broader questions, and that their only real purpose is to minimize changes for current and soon-to-retire beneficiaries by making Social Security look solvent on paper. Let's not be fooled by the trust-fund shell game.

21

Don't Worry, Generation X: Why the Demographic Nightmare of the Twentysomethings Isn't Likely to Come True

Richard C. Leone

History records that, as the last turning of a millennium approached, much of Christendom expected nothing less than the end of the world. Maybe this explains the fantasy that currently fixates many young Americans, so-called Generation X. They imagine a starkly different future America: Slow growth and the aging of the population will reshape the nation. The extremely large, older baby-boom generation will hold the whip hand politically. As a result, those young enough to work will be near wage slaves to the needs of the elderly.

These images are the stuff of nightmares, but fortunately, they are not a reasonable picture of the future. In fact, it would be smart for Generation X to put aside fears of tomorrow and to take a close look at yesterday. Its members might start by asking the most obvious question: How did the Boomers' parents cope with their own extraordinary fertility? It wasn't easy.

By the time the soaring postwar baby boom birthrate started down in the mid-1960s, children under the age of twenty accounted for over 40 percent of the population. Currently 29 percent, Boomers will be displaced as the largest group early in the next century by members of the "Baby Boomlet" generation. As kids, the Boomers overloaded local school systems, irritated their elders with a burst of teenage culture, and even added to law enforcement costs. During their unprecedented college years, America lived through the wrenching roller coaster called the '60s. Later, the labor market was jolted by a vast expansion of the work force, creating issues that are still with us.

In the early days the Boomers' parents turned to the public sector for help; the political response was generous, particularly when it came to education. The government initiated vast programs to build schools, train teachers and, later, to provide college loans and grants. Between 1952 and 1970, elementary-secondary school expenditures increased more than 275 percent in inflation-adjusted dollars. Between 1964 and 1980, the number of college and university students increased more than 125 percent, and the number of college instructors more than doubled. America also housed and fed the nearly 30 percent of boomers who lived some part of their childhood in poverty.

The cost of raising the Boomers was high, but of course much of the price was "paid" within families—child support is an accepted moral obligation and a legal requirement. (Should we "solve" the aging problem by treating parental support the same way?) Still, there was no free lunch, even within families; growing up, the Boomers consumed goods and services from the real economy—the actual production of those at work at the time.

This concept is important: When people sound the alarm about the aging of the Boomers, they always refer to the growing "burden" on those still in the work force. In fact, the best way to measure this "burden" on workers is to compare the size of the entire dependent population and the resources available per person. One key ratio is that of young and old dependents to workers. In 1993, it was about 70 to 100. It will rise to 83 per 100 in 2030, the peak. But in 1964 it was 96 per 100.

Odd, isn't it, that no one—including the Boomers' parents—recalls the 1960s as an era of economic deprivation?

Moreover, in 1964 the real economic pie that got sliced up between workers and non-workers was considerably smaller. The Boomers' parents shared a gross domestic product that, per capita, was $12,195 (inflation adjusted). We now produce $20,469 per capita, and in 2030 we'll have an estimated $35,659 per capita—at the height of the Boomer retirement years.

Strangely, almost every discussion of the aging crisis ignores the critical importance of this reality of greater resources per person. But, the truth is that it is the size of the real economy, not demography, that matters most. Of course, Boomers and the Xers can and should help the economy grow by saving and investing more. But in the end, there is no trick way to wish away the need for any group, including the elderly, to eat, to have shelter, and to obtain health care.

Thus, the sheer number of Boomers means that they always have required a substantial chunk of the real goods and services being produced in the economy. What they got depended on many factors. In the United States, for an individual, your share of the economic pie is determined by the outcomes of capitalism and democracy (and, of course, the accident of your birth—you get more with wealthy parents or supportive children). For a generation growing old, the size of its collective slice depends on the wealth its members have accumulated, their pension claims, public policies and, importantly, how much the economy grew during their working years. A bigger pie, other things being equal, means more to go around. And, while Boomers came into the world with nothing, on their way out, they'll have a few trillion in pension funds and real estate to help pay the freight.

By then, America will be grayer, but not poorer. And perhaps only then, will Xers learn the ultimate lesson from today's elderly, the parents of the baby boom generation: "Stop worrying, we've been there and done that—and did it when we had even less to go around."

Oh yes, and one other thing: "If you're worried about who will support you when you're old, the best advice is: go forth and multiply and be sure to raise enough of your kids to be liberals who believe in healthy entitlements for the elderly."

22

Listen Up, Generation X

Neil Howe and Richard Jackson

According to Richard Leone's "Don't Worry, Generation X" [see chapter 21 in this book], the aging of America is a non-problem. Leone, president of the Twentieth Century Fund, repeats two old canards that have recently cropped up in a number of op-eds. The first is that future workers will face little extra "dependency" burden because the growth in the number of seniors will be mostly offset by a relative decline in the number of children. The second is that rising incomes will in any case make the extra dollar burden easily affordable. Leone concludes by declaring that an older America will be "grayer, but not poorer"—and by tut-tutting the young for whining about nothing.

There's a problem with this argument: It's wrong.

THE DEPENDENCY FALLACY

Let's start with the first point. A stable ratio of dependents to workers does not mean that America's aging will impose only a minor extra burden on tomorrow's workers. Leone's demographic numbers alone say nothing about the vastly greater cost of sup-

From *Facing Facts* 2, no. 5 (May 2, 1996): 1. Copyright © 1996 The Concord Coalition.

porting each senior. At the federal level, the ratio of per capita spending on the elderly to spending on children is eleven-to-one. Even including state and local spending and hence the nation's entire education budget, the ratio is at least three-to-one and maybe as high as five-to-one in favor of the elderly. (There are no up-to-date numbers on state and local spending by age group.)

Yes, families spend a lot of their own money on their kids, and if we took this into account it would narrow (but not eliminate) the gap in dependency costs. But why should we? In our economy, there's an obvious difference between personal spending and public spending (for one thing, only the latter runs up the national debt). And in our political system, there's an obvious difference between compulsory transfers and voluntary giving. Some might argue that personal spending on a dependent is not really voluntary. But this doesn't wash. Perhaps some people may regard helping out grandma as an other-than-voluntary burden. But this is not ordinarily the case with children, since the decision to raise a family is usually a matter of choice.

A premise that seems to underlie Leone's argument is that family transfers adjust dollar for dollar in response to public transfers. Thus, increasing a public benefit leaves no one better or worse off. But this flies in the face of the presumed purpose of public benefits which is to take from workers and give to dependents in precisely those cases where workers don't give the money themselves. Otherwise, why have the programs?

Then there is the most profound issue of all. To the dependency theorists, any worker income spent on someone other than oneself is a worker-burden—regardless of whether the transfer (or gift) represents saving for the future or paying off the past. Leone is perplexed that Americans look forward to the senior boom with anxiety but didn't consider the 1960s an era of "deprivation," even though the total demographic dependency ratio was higher in 1960 than it will be in 2030. The different is that thirty-five years ago adults were sacrificing to *build the future* while thirty-five years hence they will be sacrificing to *reward the past*.

THE INCOME FALLACY

As for the other point, it's simply not true that a growing economic pie will allow future workers to enjoy a rising living standard while honoring today's entitlement promises. . . . The rising cost of just three programs—Social Security, Medicare, and Medicaid for seniors—will, under the Social Security Administration's official intermediate scenario, erase *all* growth in real after-tax worker incomes between now and 2040. And this is an optimistic scenario that assumes a *one-third* improvement in productivity over the record of the past twenty-five years. Under SAA's high-cost scenario, real after-tax incomes would suffer a catastrophic decline of 59 percent.

Listen up, Generation X. You've got good reason to worry about your economic future, and you'd better start doing something about it. Perhaps the place to start is to set up a Twenty-First Century Fund.

23

Turning Workers into Investors

Carolyn Weaver

S ocial Security is in trouble again. An infusion of $3.1 trillion, we are told, is required to keep benefit checks going out in the long range—assuming we don't experience any more "adverse" economic or demographic shocks, like living longer than expected. This cash infusion could be met by a payroll tax increase of about one percentage point, on average, every decade over the next 70 years. Alternatively, benefits for middle- and high-wage workers who retire after the turn of the century could be reduced by 25 percent to 30 percent.

If cash-flow deficits were all that ailed the system, the situation would be difficult enough. But it is actually more serious. Since Social Security basically operates on a pay-as-you-go basis—with income roughly equal to outgo—it holds few assets against accruing liabilities.

This has two important implications. First, Social Security can now offer younger workers an average real rate of return on their taxes of no more than 1 percent to 2 percent, the real rate of growth of wages. That is substantially below the real return of private capital investment. Cuts in benefits and increases in taxes can only aggravate these poor returns and undermine political support among young workers.

Second, even if the deficits were closed, Social Security would have an enormous unfunded liability. The current $550 billion reserve fund is a mere 5 percent of the estimated $9 trillion to $11 trillion in net benefits that Social Security has promised to current workers and retirees. This "off the books" liability, or implicit debt, is fully double the Government's explicit debt of about $5 trillion.

The fundamental economic problem with financing Social Security in this way—through income transfers from younger to older generations—is that it depresses savings and investment, resulting in a lower capital stock, lower real wages and less national income than there would otherwise be. Workers—and society, more generally—have forgone the opportunity to invest in real private capital and to earn the higher return it affords.

While it is too late to recover the income lost as a result of the Government's past decisions, it is not too late to halt the losses caused by the continued growth of these promises. The Personal Security Accounts Plan that I support would sharply curtail the growth of future unfunded liabilities, while transforming Social Security into a straightforward retirement savings program backed by a Government safety net. The benefits to American workers, and to their children and grandchildren, would be very large.

The P.S.A. plan would gradually replace one-half of our pay-as-you-go retirement program with a system or personal accounts that would be owned and invested by workers and managed by the financial institutions of their choice. Workers would receive a rebate of part of their taxes for investment in their P.S.A.'s, allowing workers at all earning levels to begin accumulating real wealth. The balance of the retirement program would gradually be converted to a flat benefit, set at a level that would ensure all full-career workers—those who work all or most of their adult lives, low- and high-wage alike—a base level of retirement income at or above the poverty level.

Under this plan, digging out from Social Security's debt while continuing to provide basically full benefits for current retirees and older workers would involve significant transition costs. It would require a supplemental payroll tax of 1.5 percent (or equivalent spending reductions) over a 70-year-period, substantial reductions in long-range spending, and new—explicit—Federal borrowing. Despite these transition costs, this plan, when compared with the alternatives, holds the greatest promise for increasing national saving and expanding economic outputs over the long haul.

The benefits of the P.S.A. plan are not limited to increasing national saving. Under reasonable assumptions, single workers and two-earner couples are expected to fare better than they would under either of the other plans or a shored-up, pay-as-you-go system. Younger workers stand to gain the most. In addition, workers and families would be directly involved in the financial decisions that will affect their own future well-being. While workers would take on financial risks, they would gain ownership of their P.S.A.'s and shed some of the political risks attached to Government benefit promises 20, 30, or 40 years down the road.

Critics decry the idea of workers managing their own accounts—somewhat surprising in a nation with extensive experience with 401(k) plans and various mutual funds, not to mention the most sophisticated financial markets in the world. But what is the alternative? With literally trillions of dollars at stake, it is essential that our investment policy be structured so that workers' taxes are actually saved and invested for the future, rather than spent on current consumption, and that the allocation of capital in the economy is shielded from political manipulation.

Those of us who support the P.S.A. plan believe that securing Social Security in the decades ahead will take more than the traditional "nip and tuck" changes. Creating a system of real value to younger workers requires reforms that create real wealth, bolster expected returns, and lessen the political risks attached to the Government's long-term promises.

24

First, the System Is Hardly in Crisis

Robert M. Ball

The difficulty of balancing Social Security over the next 75 years is being greatly exaggerated. There is no need to make major cuts in promised benefits or to make major increases in contribution rates. And certainly there is no need to substitute uncertain returns from individual savings accounts for part of the basic Social Security system. There is, in short, no need to panic.

Here are the facts:

- It is estimated that without chancing present law, full benefits can be paid on time until 2029.
- After 2029, without changing present law, 77 percent of benefits could still be paid—and even after the end of the 75-year projection, 70 percent of benefits could be paid.
- Common-sense adjustments—several of which are desirable in any event—would make full benefits payable on time through 2050 and reduce the 75-year deficit from the present estimated 2.17 percent of payroll to 0.80 percent of payroll.
- This remaining deficit can be eliminated in several ways, and there is ample time to evaluate the options calmly. A system in balance until 2050 is hardly in crisis.

From the *New York Times,* January 19, 1997. Copyright © 1997 by The New York Times Co. Reprinted by permission.

The common-sense changes we support should be made promptly. They include improving the accuracy of the cost-of-living adjustments; taxing the Social Security benefits that exceed what the worker paid in, just as other private and public contributory defined-benefit pension plans are taxed today, and making Social Security universal by covering new hires in some 2.7 million full-time state and local government jobs not now under Social Security.

It would also be necessary to either cut the benefits of future recipients modestly, by an average of 3 percent, or increase the contribution rate by three-tenths of a percentage point on employers and employees combined. And we need to correct an anomaly in the allocation of Social Security taxes to the Medicare program.

As stated above, these modest steps would bring the 75-year deficit down to eight-tenths of 1 percent of payroll. In considering how to bring Social Security into complete balance and how to improve the return people get on what they pay in, there is no reason to put a part of Social Security's promised benefits at risk by substituting private individual investment accounts for basic benefits. If we want to improve the return on Social Security contributions by investing in stocks—rather than putting all the accumulated funds in long-term Government bonds as is now the case—the Social Security Administration could do this directly. That would be a much safer and more prudent approach.

The idea of Social Security investing, say, as much as 40 percent of its accumulating funds in passively managed stocks indexed to the broad market is certainly worth considering. Through the higher returns expected on the investments in the stock market, the program could come fully into balance and would not compromise any of the principles that have been so successful over the last 60 years in greatly reducing poverty among the elderly and forming the foundation on which just about all Americans build protection for their retirement years.

We recommend for immediate action the common-sense changes advocated by the six Advisory Council members backing the Maintenance of Benefits Plan. And we recommend for further study the proposal to directly invest a portion of Social Security funds in stocks. Such actions protect Social Security and avoid the major uncertainties of the individual investment accounts advocated by some council members.

With our approach, there would be no need for an increase in the payroll tax of more than one-and-a-half percentage points beginning in 1998. (To finance the system beyond 75 years, we do recommend such an increase, but not until 2045.)

There would be no need to cut Social Security's defined benefit plan by 30 percent, as in the Individual Accounts Plan, a proposal that is based on the hope that the return from individual investments would *on average* make up for the cut. There would be no need to borrow $2 trillion from the Federal Government and greatly increase the Federal deficit and debt, as called for in the Personal Security Accounts Plan. Over time that approach would abolish Social Security as we know it and substitute a flat benefit of $410 a month (increased in line with average wages), supplemented by whatever the individual might earn from a compulsory savings plan.

We do not believe that the Advisory Council has produced three acceptable choices. It has produced just one; the other two plans would be high-risk, high-cost gambles.

25

Benefit Cuts, Kind and Gentle

Edward M. Gramlich

In trying to reform Social Security, I am guided by three goals. The first is to retain the important social protections of this program that has worked so well for 60 years. The second is to make these social protections affordable by bringing Social Security back into long-term financial balance. It is not in balance now. The third is to add new national savings for retirement—both to help individuals maintain their own standards of living in retirement and to build up the nation's capital stock in advance of the baby boom retirement crunch.

In the recently released report of the Advisory Council, I have introduced a compromise proposal, the Individual Accounts Plan, that tries to achieve all three goals. I would preserve the important social protections of Social Security and still achieve long-term financial balance through what might be called kind and gentle benefit cuts. Most of the cuts would be felt by high-wage workers, with disabled and low-wage workers being largely protected from the cuts. Similarly to the other two proposals offered by Advisory Council members, the I.A.P. would involve some technical changes, like including all new hires of state and local government.

Then, beginning in the 21st century, there would be a slight increase in the normal retirement age for all workers and a slight reduction in the growth of Social Security benefits for high-wage workers. Both changes would be phased in very gradually to avoid actual benefit cuts for present retirees and "notches" in the benefit schedule—instances in which younger workers get lower real benefits than older workers with the same earnings records.

These adjustments would result in a modest reduction in the overall growth of real Social Security benefits. When combined with the rising number of retirees, the share of the economy's annual output devoted to Social Security spending would be approximately the same as at present, eliminating this part of the impending explosion in future entitlement spending.

These benefit cuts alone would mean that high-wage workers would not experience rising real benefits as their real wages grew. So I would supplement these changes with another measure to raise overall retirement (and national) savings. All workers would be required to contribute an extra 1.6 percent of their pay to new individual accounts.

These accounts would be owned by workers but centrally managed. Workers would be able to allocate their funds among 5 to 10 broad mutual funds covering stocks and bonds. Central management of the funds would cut down the risk that funds would be invested unwisely, would cut administrative costs and would mean that Wall Street firms would not reap a financial bonanza. The funds would be converted to real annuities on retirement, to protect against inflation and the chance that retirees would overspend in their early retirement years.

Together, these changes would mean that approximately the presently scheduled level of benefits would be paid to all wage classes of workers, of all ages. The difference is that this plan would mean that these benefits would be affordable; under present law, they are not.

The changes would eliminate the system's long-term financial deficit while holding together the important retirement safety net that Social Security provides. But the changes do move beyond the present pay-as-you-go financing plan by building up the nation's capital stock in advance of the baby boom retirement crunch.

Contributors

RUSSELL BAKER is a columnist for the *New York Times*.

JON M. BAKIJA is a graduate student at the University of Michigan.

ROBERT M. BALL is former Commissioner of the Social Security Administration.

JOHN C. DANFORTH is a former Republican U.S. Senator from Missouri.

ROBERT A. GEORGE is Assistant to the Speaker of the U.S. House of Representatives.

EDWARD M. GRAMLICH is dean of the University of Michigan School of Public Policy.

NEIL HOWE is the co-author of *The Fourth Turning, Generations: The History of America's Future* and *13th Gen*. He is a historian and economist, and is a senior adviser to the Concord Coalition.

RICHARD JACKSON is an economist with the Concord Coalition.

J. ROBERT KERREY is a Democratic U.S. Senator from Nebraska.

MICHAEL KINSLEY is currently editor of *Slate,* an online magazine.

HEATHER LAMM is the chairperson of Third Millennium and former staff member of the Bipartisan Commission on Entitlement and Tax Reform.

RICHARD C. LEONE is president of the Twentieth Century Fund, a nonprofit public-policy research organization in New York.

MAYA MACGUINEAS is a graduate student at the Kennedy School of Government at Harvard University.

SUSAN A. MACMANUS, author of *Young v. Old*, is professor of public administration and political science at the University of South Florida-Tampa.

STUART MILLER is a contributor to *Swing* and other publications.

PETER G. PETERSON is chairman of the Blackstone Group, a private investment bank. He served as U.S. Secretary of Commerce under President Nixon.

JEFF SHESOL draws the syndicated comic strip *Thatch* and is the author of *Mutual Contempt: Lyndon Johnson, Robert Kennedy, and the Feud That Shaped a Decade*.

ALAN K. SIMPSON is a former Republican U.S. Senator from Wyoming.

C. EUGENE STEUERLE is a senior fellow at the Urban Institute.

WILLIAM STRAUSS is the co-author of *The Fourth Turning, Generations: The History of America's Future* and *13th Gen*. He is the co-founder and director of the Capitol Steps, a political cabaret.

LESTER C. THUROW is professor of management and economics at the Massachusetts Institute of Technology.

RICHARD L. TRUMKA is secretary/treasurer of the AFL-CIO.

CAROLYN WEAVER is director of Social Security and pension studies at the American Enterprise Institute.